The Reality Game

The Reality Game is an introduction to the skills used in individual and group therapy. For those training, practising or lecturing in humanistic and integrative psychotherapy and counselling it is an essential guide to good practice.

Always keeping in mind the needs of students, this extensively revised new edition responds to the questions most often asked by trainees in these disciplines and includes a new chapter on the highly topical issues of professional ethics. The book guides the reader through the theoretical and practical aspects of establishing and developing the relationship between counsellor and client, and covers assessment; the initial interview; the opening sessions; aims; transference; resistance and supervision. In giving a humanistic account of each element it complements texts on psychoanalytic and cognitive-behavioural therapy, and shows that the humanistic approach is broader than generally imagined.

The author also looks at the social and political aspects of psychotherapy and on research and supervision in this field. He shows how pressure from funding bodies for cheaper and quicker forms of therapy should be resisted in the interests of a therapy which aims at liberation rather than adjustment.

John Rowan is a counselling psychologist in private practice and teaches and supervises at the Minster Centre in London. Other books by John Rowan include *Healing the Male Psyche* and *Ordinary Ecstasy*.

The Reality Game

A Guide to Humanistic Counselling and Psychotherapy

Second edition

John Rowan

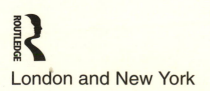

London and New York

First edition published 1983
Routledge & Kegan Paul plc

Second edition published
by Routledge
11 New Fetter Lane, London EC4P 4EE

Simultaneously published in the USA and Canada
by Routledge
29 West 35th Street, New York, NY 10001

© 1983 John Rowan

This edition © 1998 John Rowan

Typeset in Times by Keystroke, Jacaranda Lodge, Wolverhampton
Printed and bound in Great Britain by TJ International Ltd, Padstow, Cornwall

British Library Cataloguing in Publication Data
A catalogue record for this book is available from the British Library

Library of Congress Cataloguing in Publication Data
Rowan, John.
    The reality game : a guide to humanistic counselling and psychotherapy /
John Rowan. – 2nd ed.
    Includes bibliographical references and index.
    1. Humanistic counselling. 2. Humanistic psychotherapy.
I. Title.
BF637.C6R68   1998
158′.3–dc21   97–46440

ISBN 0–415–16433–8 (hbk)
ISBN 0–415–16434–6 (pbk)

This book is dedicated to the memory of Bill Swartley,
from whom I learned so much and from whom
I would like to have learned more.

Contents

Preface

This is a handbook for people who are, or who want to be, counsellors or psychotherapists. It tries to cover both theory and practice, and will be particularly useful to those who are in training to be humanistic or integrative psychotherapists or counsellors. What are the differences between this and the first edition? Every chapter has been thoroughly revised, and there is one new chapter, on ethics. In the first edition, page numbers for references were usually not given, as was quite normal in those days. I have tried to add page numbers where I still had the books, but some of them were too hard to track down, so there is some inconsistency there. I have not tried to seek out the latest editions of books quoted earlier, because there seemed no point. So in general I have tried to bring the book up to date, but it is still the same book, and I have not had to change it in any radical way.

It takes a humanistic stance. There are plenty of books for psycho-analysts and plenty of books for behaviourists and their cognitive friends - and there are plenty of highly-specialised books on specific approaches in the humanistic field – but there is hardly anything for the general humanistic practitioner, working on a one-to-one basis. In fact, when I started to write this book, I thought there was nothing at all; but I discovered later the book by Brammer, Shostrom and Abrego (1989) which is very big and very American and very thorough (except that it says very little about regression and very little about the transpersonal) and makes an excellent complement to this present work.

Another and very important complement is that excellent book on group work by Ernst and Goodison (1981), which makes it unnecessary to have a chapter on groups in this present volume as was the original intention. It covers all the approaches which I mention, and although it claims to be addressed specifically to women, it is in fact equally applicable to mixed groups - which is not surprising, because a great deal of the experience which went into it was obtained in a mixed group, in which I also participated. It is also suitable for men's groups or any other groups I can think of.

In writing this book I have been very conscious of the needs of students, and the kinds of questions which they raise. In this I have been helped considerably by the students in my supervision groups at the Institute of Psychotherapy and Social Studies, at the Serpent Institute and at the Minster Centre, who have raised all the awkward issues and tricky problems that I have tried to tackle here. I would very much value any feedback from readers, too, indicating which chapters are lacking or improvable in any way.

I hope this book will be found useful in the training of counsellors and psychotherapists, because the issue of training is going to become more and more important in the years to come. I have been involved with three major efforts to look at standards of practice in this field: the AHP Practitioners group, which is for people who want to defend and raise standards of practice in the humanistic field; the BAC Accreditation Subcommittee, which is for counsellors who want to defend and raise standards in their area of work; and the UK Council for Psychotherapy, which has sections covering all or most of the therapeutic schools in its area. All three of these have made it abundantly clear that good training is crucial to good practice. I hope that this book will be a useful tool in helping the development of the training which is so much needed. Working in this way, I have become aware of the importance of the issue of the possible integration of therapeutic approaches and methods, and this will be referred to many times in the chapters that follow.

For those few readers who object to the words 'counsellor' or 'psychotherapist' as exemplifying the dubious professionalisation of what should be a simple human function – listening in a helpful way to other people's troubles – let me say that for me the basic model is that of personal growth. In other words, one person can help another person to grow – and this doesn't depend on the other person having a problem. This task, of helping another person to grow and become more integrated, more whole, is not an easy one; it is not just a matter of listening to another person's troubles. It is a kind of compassionate skill, a kind of love work. And the main obstacle to doing it is one's own reluctance to work on oneself, to face one's own pain, one's own buried potentials rising to the surface; it is our reluctance to give up parts of ourselves which we are not yet ready to let go. Any humanistic practitioner must go through their own process first, before taking anyone else through it.

That is a clear value for me and for all those I have worked with in the organisations mentioned above.

One other thing: the word 'humanistic' is often misunderstood. Some people misunderstand it by thinking it means that we are humanists, in the sense of members of the British Humanist Association; this is far from the truth, because we value spirituality and feeling and intuition in a way which would offend the average humanist very much. Others misunderstand it by thinking it means that we are soft and mushy and want to spread peace and love all the time; but we are not in the peace and love business, we are in the reality business. Or better still, since there is always some element of play in good therapy, the reality game.

Chapter 1

Humanistic psychotherapy, counselling and personal growth

This is a book intended for the practitioner in psychotherapy, counselling or personal growth who wants to adopt a humanistic approach. It is also intended for courses which train people in humanistic methods. While mainly devoted to one-to-one work, nearly everything in this book also applies to group work, because this is a central interest for the humanistic practitioner.

Humanistic psychology was first named when Abraham Maslow, Anthony Sutich and a few others were trying to find a name for a new journal. The Journal of Humanistic Psychology started to come out in 1961. It defined itself as differing from psychoanalysis on the one side and the cognitive-behavioural approach on the other. Humanistic psychology is particularly concerned with self-actualisation and with body–mind unity, and has a great deal to say about that, as we shall be seeing later. People in this orientation are very concerned about human diminution, and the way in which social roles can diminish people. It has a good deal to say about liberation from the shackles of compulsion, whether they be internal or external.

It is quite diverse within itself, and includes some people, like Abraham Maslow and Carl Rogers, who are very optimistic about human nature, and other people, like Rollo May, Jim Bugental and Alvin Mahrer, who are not particularly optimistic at all. One of the standard misunderstandings about humanistic psychology is to think that it is all about Maslow and Rogers, and even a good critic like Spinelli (1994) makes this mistake.

In the process of change and development, a number of different names and titles have been used for humanistic psychology. Sometimes it has been called 'third force psychology' (the other two being psycho-analysis and the orthodox academic behavioural-cognitive approach); sometimes the 'self-awareness movement' (because awareness seemed to be quite a key word); sometimes the 'human potential movement' (because of its insistence that the average and the normal are actually less than the possible average and less than the possible normal); and sometimes just 'personal growth', because of its belief that people could continue to grow beyond their usual limits, if they were allowed. However, this phrase 'personal growth' has been used now by many people outside the humanistic camp, apparently not realising that it is a humanistic concept. Today humanistic psychology is less of a movement and more of a tendency or approach within the whole field of the human sciences.

In today's world, with its fierce challenges and fast changes and hard lessons, we have to know ourselves much better, and how to relate to others much better, if we are to survive at all. But we can do much more than survive – we can realise our potential. We can be all that we have it in us to be. The humanistic practitioner is particularly concerned with this aspect of therapy, and because of this tends to use the word 'therapy' to mean psychotherapy and those deep forms of counselling which are therapeutic in much the same way. In relation to the ongoing controversy as to whether counselling and psychotherapy are the same thing or two different things, Carl Rogers had this to say:

> There has been a tendency to use the term counselling for more casual and superficial interviews, and to reserve the term psychotherapy for more intensive and long-continued contacts directed toward deeper reorganization of the personality. While there may be some reason for this distinction, it is also plain that the most intensive and success-ful counselling is indistinguishable from intensive and successful psychotherapy.
>
> (Rogers 1942)

Fifty-five years later, it is hard to see any better statement being made than this.

Because all the pioneers of humanistic psychology were very individual people, there is no one single accepted theory which we can lay out and say – this is it. But there are some very consistent themes running through all the material put forward by these people.

The first is that, deep down underneath it all where it really counts, you are OK. This goes against many other and much older theories which say that people are fundamentally bad, selfish, narrow and nasty. By saying that people are fundamentally OK, we do not at all mean that people are not sometimes destructive, or that there is no evil in the world (see for example Goldberg 1995). What we mean is that if someone will agree to work with us on his or her destructive actions or evil wishes, in an atmosphere of trust and acceptance, that person will discover that the evil and destructiveness are just as phoney and just as forgettable as the false niceness of other people, which apparently causes no problems.

In other words, we believe that personal nastiness and personal niceness are most often, in both cases, masks and illusions, put on for reasons which seemed good at the time, but which have now become stuck and rigid, and out of our control. In that sense, if you want to use labels, we are all neurotic. By working on ourselves to unstick the rigidities and loosen the mask, we can eventually learn how to live without needing masks at all – though it may still be useful to put one on occasionally, as we might do with a dress suit or an evening gown.

So when we talk about self-actualisation, about getting in touch with what is the deepest truth within us, and allowing that to come out, we are not talking about something fearful or dangerous. People often say 'How do I know I won't hate my deepest self when I come across it?' But this is an unrealistic fear, and we may sometimes suspect that it is really designed to enable the person to avoid the necessary effort. We shall be examining this point in detail in Chapter 5.

The second thread which runs all through humanistic psychology is an emphasis on the whole person. If we say that human beings exist on at least five levels – body, feelings, intellect, soul and spirit – then we have to do justice to all five of those levels in all our efforts at realising human potential. If I want to be that self which I truly am, then I have to be it on all five of those levels – I must not leave any of them out. Any theory, any therapy that leaves out one or more of these must be inadequate to deal with the full human being who has to be met and responded to.

Now today there is much more interest in the body – diet, exercise and so on – but much of that interest seems to us very external. It is as if we were supposed to be somewhere outside our bodies, disciplining them and making them do things, sometimes under protest. But the humanistic approach is to say that I *am* my body. If you touch my hand, you are touching *me*. So I am just as responsible for my body as I am for my thoughts, feelings, mental pictures or whatever – it is me doing it. This total responsibility for our own bodies, feelings, ideas and intuitions is very characteristic of humanistic psychology, and theoreticians like Mahrer (1989) and Schutz (1979) have made it clear exactly how this works.

This means that we are interested in integration. By integration we mean that the splits in the person can be healed, and that the holes in the personality can be filled. The various parts of the person can get to know each other better, accept each other more, and change in that process. This is not a process of subordinating all the various tendencies in the person to one overall control, like some kind of totalitarian ego – it is more like a harmony of contrasts. We shall have more to say on this later.

The third thread we can follow all through the humanistic approach is the emphasis on change and development. Human beings are seen not as static victims or villains, but as people in a natural process of growth. This process can continue, if we let it, in adulthood too. We have all seen people we recognise as being further ahead than us, more complete, more evolved, more themselves. What humanistic psychology says is that we could all continue to grow if we did not limit ourselves and sell ourselves short.

Most of us normally think that if we have enough worldly goods, then we can do what we want to do, and then we can be happy. The sequence is HAVE–DO–BE. But what we say in humanistic psychology is that it is exactly the other way round. If we can be who we really are, we will find ourselves doing things which genuinely satisfy us and give us enjoyment, and then we shall have all we really want. The sequence for us is BE–DO–HAVE.

ORIGINS

This begins to sound almost religious, and it is one of the characteristics of humanistic psychology which distinguishes it very sharply from secular humanism that it has a place for the spiritual. This is because its origins are complex. Let us now look at some of the history, some of the sources, of the humanistic approach. There are nine different origins of humanistic psychology as it exists today.

The phenomenological tradition

Coming from Edmund Husserl (1859–1938) originally, this approach says that it is possible to cleanse our perceptions and see things as they are. But we can only do this by a rigorous examination of our assumptions, first of all becoming aware of them and then learning how to set them aside or bracket them (Jennings 1992). This requires a degree of self-knowledge which can only be obtained through psychotherapy, because otherwise our unconscious assumptions (unaware beliefs, if you do not like the word 'unconscious') can trip us up all the time. This lays great stress on our responsibility for not taking for granted anything about the ground on which we stand when we make any general statement. We have to put everything in doubt, and assume that nothing is absolutely true. This idea has been taken over by feminism and constructivism and also by humanistic psychology.

Husserl took from Franz Brentano (1838–1917) the notion of intentionality. This says that consciousness is always directed towards the real world in order to interpret it in a meaningful manner. Consciousness is always consciousness of some thing. So in humanistic psychology we do not talk about behaviour, we talk about action. The difference is that action is always intentional. Simon du Plock tells us that Husserl used the word 'intentionality' to refer to the creativity in our acts, not a static directedness (du Plock 1996: 42).

Gestalt therapy in particular, which is one of the central humanistic disciplines, lays great stress on its phenomenological roots. 'Phenomenology . . . is the philosophical approach which is at the very heart of Gestalt' (Clarkson 1989: 13).

The person-centred approach also leans heavily on phenomenology. We only have to look at the use Carl Rogers makes of the phenomenological notions of noema and noesis as 'the primary means with which to maintain unconditional positive regard' (Spinelli 1990, p.19). Du Plock again makes the point that Rogers found this set of concepts a very useful one (du Plock 1996: 44).

Ronald Laing (1965) pointed to the close connection between phenomenology and existentialism, and so did Merleau-Ponty (1908–61), who said 'The world is not what I think, but that which I live.' This is one of the most characteristic beliefs of humanistic psychology.

Phenomenology is one of the most important influences in the new study of consciousness which is arousing so much interest in philosophical circles. People like Shaun Gallagher (1997) and Francisco Varela (1997) argue that we cannot understand the nature of consciousness until we fully bring phenomenology into the argument.

The existential tradition

Coming from Sören Kierkegaard (1813–55), this tradition lays stress on the inescapable dilemmas of the human condition – death, the inner struggle over anxiety, the need for authentic living. Rollo May (1909–94) is one of those within humanistic psychology who has written a great deal about existentialism, and has claimed that William James

(1842–1910) was an existential thinker who in fact influenced Husserl. May wrote one of the best books (1983) on the existentialist approach to psychology and psychotherapy. Existentialism lays great stress on choice, and Jean-Paul Sartre (1905–80) actually said that we are our choices. He made autonomy and authenticity central, and regarded the individual as 'free and alone, without assistance and without excuse' (Sartre 1964: 139). We are condemned to be free. This is a bare and bleak doctrine, which gives little comfort or reassurance.

From Martin Heidegger (1889–1976) comes the central idea of authenticity. He says that we are thrown into the world, and that our existence in the world is simply a matter of being-there (*Dasein*). If we deny this, and try to erect fantastic stories about our existence, we become inauthentic and cannot take responsibility for our own lives. One of the main things we have to accept about our existence is that it will end. Our being-there is a being-toward-death. To accept this is to enter into a relation of care with oneself and the world. And to do this is to be authentic. So authenticity is a combination of self-respect (we are not just part of an undifferentiated world) and self-enactment – we express our care in the world in a visible way. Jim Bugental puts it well when he says:

By authenticity I mean a central genuineness and awareness of being. Authenticity is that presence of an individual in his living in which he is fully aware in the present moment, in the present situation. Authenticity is difficult to convey in words, but experientially it is readily perceived in ourselves or in others.

(Bugental 1981: 102)

Again, it is Gestalt therapy which has stayed most strictly close to this existentialist position. Fritz Perls claimed that Gestalt therapy was one of three existential therapies, the other two being Frankl's logotherapy and Binswanger's *Dasein* therapy (Perls 1969a).

But Moreno too (who we shall return to in a moment) thought of himself as an existentialist, and David Brazier says 'Psychodrama evolved from the existential approach to psychotherapy of Jacob Levi Moreno. Although it is possible to graft psychodramatic methods on to other philosophical approaches, the method is primarily attuned to an existential outlook' (Brazier 1991: 1).

Martin Buber (1878–1965) is another representative of the existential position who has had much influence upon humanistic psychology. He says 'There is genuine relation only between genuine persons . . . Men need, and it is granted to them, to confirm one another in their individual being by means of genuine meetings.' The encounter group, one of the innovations of humanistic psychology, is founded on this idea of genuine meetings (Rowan 1992).

Another humanistic psychotherapist strongly influenced by existentialism is James Bugental (first president of the Association for Humanistic Psychology), who actually calls his approach 'Existential-Humanistic Psychotherapy'. He has written a number of books, including *The Search for Existential Identity* (all about patient–therapist dialogue), *Psychotherapy and Process* (his main theoretical book), *The Search for Authenticity* and *The Art of the Psychotherapist*. In the latter book he lists his own set of 'givens': Embodiedness (implying change), Finitude (implying contingency), Ability to act or not act (implying responsibility), Choicefulness (implying relinquishment) and Separate-but-related-ness (implying being at once a part of and apart from another person). Bugental says this:

> For me, the truest existentialism is humanistic and the soundest humanism is existential. The two are not the same, but their overlap is rich in potential for greater understanding of human experience and for greater effectiveness in the effort to enrich that experience.
>
> (Bugental 1981: 10)

Bugental is one of the most important voices in the humanistic field, and we shall refer to him often.

Much influenced by existentialism is Alvin Mahrer, another theorist we shall be referring to many times in this book. He has reworked the whole humanistic-existential connection in a very exciting way. He continually quotes Binswanger, and to a lesser extent Boss, and also Laing and May. But he is not a slavish follower: he disagrees with the standard existential position, for example, that one person can never really know another. He shows that it is indeed possible for one person to get inside another person's skin, to know from the inside what it is like to be that other person (Mahrer 1996).

Self-actualisation

This refers to the theory of Abraham Maslow (1908–70) that there is a hierarchy of needs, ranging from lower needs like food and security up to higher needs like self-esteem and self-actualisation. Ernesto Spinelli (1989) has said that 'The notion of authenticity bears striking similarity to Maslow's ideas concerning self-actualization.' Self-actualisation is all about being that self which I truly am, and the notion of the real self is central to humanistic psychology (DeCarvalho 1991). We shall return to the question of what exactly this self is, which is to be actualised, in Chapter 5.

Abundance motivation

Most orthodox psychology is based on a homeostatic model (coping model), which is deficiency-oriented. Action is thought of as initiated by a need or want. Most organisms, however, seek tension-creating and tension-maintaining situations, as well as tension reduction (Fiske and Maddi 1961). Achievement motivation, need for varied experience, curiosity and so forth can be comprehended under the concept of abundance motivation. We do not just cope: at our best we can actively seek experience for its own sake. Maslow called this Being motivation, and wrote about it a good deal, particularly in his book *Toward a Psychology of Being*.

The person-centred approach

Carl Rogers (1902–87) believed that people were capable of growing and developing into what he called 'the fully-functioning person', and used counselling, psychotherapy and group work to achieve this. His ideas are highly compatible with those of Maslow. In his work he laid great stress on empathy, nonpossessive warmth and genuineness. This emphasis on genuineness reminds us of Buber, and Rogers and Buber had a famous dialogue which helps us to see the similarities and differences between them rather clearly (Kirschenbaum and Henderson 1990). The person-centred approach is one of the central disciplines within humanistic psychology, and is still being developed today (Merry 1995), even after the death of its founder.

Importance of the body

Humanistic psychology owes to Wilhelm Reich (1897–1957) a strong emphasis on the importance of the body. Alexander Lowen was one of Reich's students, and introduced an approach to psychotherapy which he called Bioenergetics (Lowen and Lowen 1977). Later on, David Boadella (1988) in Britain developed a further extension of this which he called Biosynthesis. Other important contributors to this strand are Stanley Keleman (1985), Ron Kurtz (Kurtz and Prestera 1976) and Jack Painter (1986).

In contrast to this approach is the body work developed by a few

German women, including Elsa Gindler, Magda Proskauer, Marion Rosen, Ilse Middendorf, and Doris Breyer (Moss 1981). Their work promotes mind–body awareness and integration using such techniques as movement, touch, natural breathing, sensory awareness and voice work. These are much more nonstressful and nonpainful practices. We shall see more about this in Chapter 6.

Group dynamics

Coming from the early T-groups of Kurt Lewin (1890–1947), the idea developed that authenticity could be cultivated by having a kind of group where the leader forced the group to lead itself. This kind of paradoxical approach was largely superseded by the encounter group, as developed by Will Schutz (1989). But another huge input to this tradition was the work of Jacob Moreno (1889–1974) who invented all the techniques of psychodrama, and laid great stress on creativity and spontaneity. This again is a discipline which is still being developed further (Holmes *et al.* 1994). Moreno (1974) points out that his existential concept of 'encounter' (genuine I–Thou meeting) was later taken up by Carl Rogers and Will Schutz and never lost its existentialist character. Schutz (1989a) stole many ideas from Moreno, and others too, and created an integrative type of group, which could do justice to the regressive, the existential and the transpersonal – the open encounter group (Rowan 1992).

Peak experiences

Actual experience of mystical states of consciousness, usually spontaneous and unplanned, were labelled by Maslow (1970) 'peak experiences'. He advocated that they should be studied and cultivated. He was a bit appalled, however, when in the 1960s people started having such experiences as a result of taking hallucinogenic drugs, or by deliberately setting up group experiences for the purpose. Still, the evidence does seem to be that it is possible to have a peak experience by using LSD, and many thousands of people have done just that. Some scientific evidence for the efficacy of psychedelic drugs in inducing genuinely mystical experiences is given by Doblin (1991). Maslow said that self-actualisation could be done without any transcendental experiences, but that the higher type of self-actualisation always did include peak experiences. In my view peak experiences represent the foothills of mysticism proper, and make humanistic psychology inhabit a fascinating borderline area, representing the end of the personal and the beginning of the transpersonal. We shall be discussing this more later.

Eastern philosophy

The four Eastern philosophies (which always include some psychology as well) which have had the most influence on humanistic psychology have been: Zen Buddhism, with its emphasis on letting go; Taoism, particularly in its ideas of centring and the yin-yang polar unity of opposites; Sufism, particularly with its emphasis on regaining one's naturalness and acquiring creative vision; and Tantra, particularly in its emphasis on the importance of the body as a spiritual energy system. (See Fadiman and Frager (1994) for a full discussion of Yoga, Zen and Sufism. The chapter on Yoga also has an excellent flow chart showing how to do meditation.)

THE HUMANISTIC APPROACH

Let us start by placing the humanistic approach in the context of the older and better-known approaches of psychoanalysis and behaviourism. Humanistic psychology originally started as a 'third force' in relation to these two, and has remained distinct ever since, so this will be quite an appropriate way of proceeding.

If we now look at Chart 1.1, the first thing we can see is that the humanistic approach is similar to psychoanalysis in looking behind behaviour to what is producing it. This may sound odd to people familiar with Rogerian therapy, Gestalt therapy or personal construct therapy, which explicitly dissociate themselves from this view. But in practice all three of these do in fact have a psychodynamic approach, inviting people to explore those deep inner areas where early conflicts and early traumas are to be found. All they do is to name things rather differently: psychoanalytic 'repressed material' becomes Gestalt 'unfinished business', and so on (see Chapter 5). The theory of Alvin Mahrer, which we shall meet later, can be regarded as a fully-formed humanistic psychodynamics. It is interesting to note that the word 'psychodynamic' was first used in the nineteenth century, and that there was a professor of psychodynamics in 1899.

The second point on the chart is that we are similar to the behaviourists in laying a lot of stress on action, both in the therapy session and out of it. In the group situation in particular, we invite people to try out new forms of behaviour right there in the group. We are often much more interested in what people do than in what they say (Kepner and Brien 1972). We encourage people to practise what they have learned (see Chapter 6). In this we are also similar to the cognitive therapists, though we do not usually hand out homework as they do.

Chart 1.1 Comparisons of therapy characteristics

Characteristic	Psychoanalytic	Behaviourist	Cognitive	Humanistic
1 Psychodynamic approach – looking for what is behind surface behaviour	Yes	No	Yes	Yes
2 Action approach – looking at actual conduct of client, trying new things	No	Yes	Yes	Yes
3 Acknowledgement of the importance of interpretation, transference, resistance, etc	Yes	No	Yes	Yes
4 Use of guided fantasy and imagery techniques	No	Yes	Yes	Yes
5 Emphasis on need of therapist for similar therapy	Yes	No	No	Yes
6 Emphasis on the body as source of problems, and touching body by therapist	No	Yes	No	Yes
7 Emphasis on the body as expressing problems, and variety of touching	No	No	No	Yes
8 Emphasis on liberation, joy and ecstasy	No	No	No	Yes
9 Adoption of medical model of mental illness	Yes	Yes	Yes	No
10 Encouragement of transference relation	Yes	No	No	No
11 Emphasis on theory guiding action	Yes	Yes	Yes	Yes
12 Interest in a spiritual aspect of psychotherapy	No	No	No	Yes
13 Favourable to old paradigm research methodology	Yes	Yes	Yes	No

Third, we are similar to the psychoanalysts in acknowledging the importance of the actual moment-to-moment relationship between the therapist and the client. For many years a great many humanistic practitioners denied this whole area, particularly if they worked mainly in groups, but the more they started to get into long-term one-to-one relationships with their clients, the more they were forced to recognise it, and today probably few humanistic practitioners would maintain the old view (see Chapters 7 and 8). Similar things have happened with the cognitive therapists, and we now see some combinations such as Cognitive-Analytic Therapy (CAT) which has developed in recent years. There is a good discussion of these matters in Petruska Clarkson's (1995) book on the therapeutic relationship.

Fourth, we are similar to the behaviourists and the cognitive therapists in using guided imagery a great deal (Singer 1974). On the whole we use a much less structured form of imagery, but the broad overlap is still there (see Chapter 6). Jungians (Samuels 1985) of course also use imagery a great deal, but they do not form a large enough group to consider here; similarly with transpersonal therapists (Gordon-Brown and Somers 1988) and process therapists (Mindell 1985).

Fifth, we are also like the psychoanalysts in saying that the therapist should have been through the same kind of therapy that he or she is trying to practise with other people. Otherwise there is going to be a lack of awareness which is going to hold the client back (see Chapters 7 and 12). We do not really understand the reluctance of the behaviourists and the cognitive people in resisting this truth. The argument is simply that we can only help clients up to the limit of our own resistances and blocks and hangups, most of which we are probably unaware of. Becoming aware of our own limitations, our own compulsions, is one of the aims of therapy for the therapist.

The sixth point opens up an area where again we are similar to the behaviourists (as in points one and two). We believe in working very directly with the body and with behaviour: in fact, one of the classic papers in Gestalt therapy is entitled 'Gestalt therapy: A behaviouristic phenomenology' (Kepner and Brien 1972). We often ask the question – after a particular breakthrough or illumination – 'how will that make a difference on Monday morning?' Mahrer says 'It is almost a rule that if the patient carries out the new way of being and behaving in the real world, actual changes will continue to occur' (Mahrer 1996: 341).

In point seven however, we differ from all three of the other schools. We see the body as expressing a great deal about what the client has been doing, and what the client is up to now, and we try to tune in to body language a great deal (Dreyfuss and Feinstein 1977). Many humanistic practitioners touch the bodies of their clients, whether out of ordinary human sympathy, encouragement to regress, provocative massage designed to bring out feelings, re-enactment of birth, etc. So humanistic practitioners have to be much more aware of their own bodies, and must have worked through a great deal of such material themselves before working with other people in this way (see Chapter 6).

Eighth, we are also different both from the other three schools in our emphasis on good feelings. Most clients are just as incapable of feeling deep joy as they are of contacting their deep pain. And so we look for ecstasy as evidence of real change in the personality. Such an experience is evidence that the person has started to emerge from the constraints of their previous personal and social position. If the client has a peak experience this is welcomed as being just the sort of thing we are aiming at in the long run. For most clients, such experiences do not last long, but as Anthony and his associates (1987) point out, they are *glimpses* of what lies ahead in the process of psychospiritual development. This is nothing to do with support or reassurance – it has to do with radical change of the whole personality structure (see Chapter 5).

Now we come to some of the things we don't do. Our ninth point is that, unlike the other three schools, we do not adopt a medical model. This idea of a medical model is all-pervasive in our Western culture, and hard to get away from. It is a mechanistic view, holding that the client is a kind of machine, which only has to be treated in the right way to get invariable results. We think the client has choices, and that the object of therapy is to increase the range of choices, and encourage and enable the client to handle successfully this increased range of choices. And we think the medical approach tends to reduce choice, even though this is not what the medical practitioner intends. Wheelis (1972) has the basic argument on this – that if you treat a person like a machine they lose freedom (see Chapter 5). But even in medicine itself, there is nowadays much more interest in holistic medicine – forms of medical practice where the patient is seen as a whole human being who is responsible for their own process. Perhaps the best discussion of this whole question is to be found in the book by Ken Wilber and his wife, entitled *Grace and Grit* (1991). This is much more so in psychotherapy and counselling, which have always taken the view that the responsibility for change lies with the client. We do not believe that there is a disease or illness, which with suitable treatment will be cured (see Chapter 2). We believe rather that the client needs to own up to what they are doing: that awareness in itself, together with its empathic reception by a therapist, is productive of change.

Tenth, unlike psychoanalysis, we do not try to build up a transference neurosis between therapist and client. There is a good discussion of this from a humanistic point of view in Clarkson (1995). We do not use transference very much in therapy, though we do recognise its existence and its very real importance (see Chapter 7).

Eleventh, most psychotherapy and counselling argues, or tries to assume in some way, that theory should guide action. The humanistic view is that theory is important and worth pursuing, both in preparing for work as a therapist, and in talking to a supervisor or other professionals. But it should be left outside the consulting room. It should not intrude into the relationship between therapist and client. Hence the humanistic objection to manualisation – that is, the belief that therapy should be conducted strictly in accordance with a manual, thus enabling scoring and assessment to be carried out more easily. There are some indications in recent writings that some body therapists and some Gestalt therapists are departing from this view, so it is not something which should be taken completely for granted. But the main humanistic tradition is clear about this.

Twelfth, we differ from the other schools in having a place for spirituality. We shall consider this more fully in the next section. All we need to say here is that this is a most important aspect of the work, which I have described in full detail elsewhere (Rowan 1993).

And finally, the other schools, because of their external orientation, go in for styles of research which do not permit any of the important things that happen in therapy to be expressed. This *old paradigm* research, as it is now called, measures variables instead of finding out what is going on inside people. Humanistic psychotherapy is more in favour of *new paradigm* research (Reason and Rowan 1981) which sees people from the inside – see Chapter 11 for much more detail and argument on this.

THE TRANSPERSONAL APPROACH

So far we have been distinguishing humanistic psychotherapy from its predecessors, two of which (behaviourism and psychoanalysis) are mainly concerned with adjustment to existing society and the over-coming of hangups. But there is also a quite different frontier, as it were, which we need to consider.

Transpersonal therapy is a successor rather than a predecessor of humanistic therapy. Transpersonal psychology has been called the 'fourth force', and it clearly comes after the 'third force': in fact, the same man – Anthony Sutich – who edited the *Journal of Humanistic Psychology* later became the first editor of the *Journal of Transpersonal Psychology*. It is not easy to produce a definition of transpersonal psychology, but the most succinct version I have seen is that of Stan Grof where he says it is concerned essentially with 'experiences involving an expansion or extension of consciousness beyond the usual ego boundaries and beyond the limitation of time and/or space' (1975: 155). In more recent years we have found in Ken Wilber (1979, 1980) an excellent guide to this area, and we shall follow his general approach here. He says that there are three broad areas of human development – the physical, the mental and the spiritual. And if we put them on a developmental line, they sit like this:

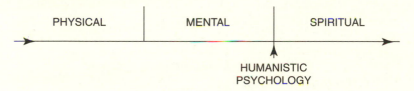

It can be seen that, in his estimation, humanistic psychotherapy comes just at the point where the mental turns into the spiritual. In other words, it is neither concerned very much with the mental (psychoanalysis does that quite well, though other cognitive therapies do it as well and quicker) nor with the spiritual (Jungian analysis does that quite well, though other transpersonal therapies do it as well and quicker), but with the space in between the two. What is this space? Wilber expands the relevant bit of the diagram as follows:

In order to get from the mental-ego level of development to the centaur area we have to pass through the biosocial bands – a difficult, confusing and often traumatic transition – involving the radical questioning of our social roles and our self-image, as explained in Chapter 5.

In order to get from the centaur level of development into the spiritual area, we have to pass through the transpersonal bands, again a difficult

Chart 1.2 A comparison of methods of personal change

	Psychotherapy	Personal growth	Transformation
(Wilber level)	(Mental ego)	(Centaur)	(Transpersonal)
(Rowan level)	(Ego/persona)	(Real self)	(Higher self)
Self	I am defined by others	I define who I am	I am defined by the Other
Motivation	Need	Choice	Surrender
Personal goal	Adjustment	Self-actualisation	Union
Social goal	Socialisation	Liberation	Salvation
Process	Healing – Ego-building	Development – Ego-enhancement	Enlightenment – Ego-reduction
Traditional role of helper	Physician (Analyst)	Teacher (Facilitator)	Priest(ess) (Guide)
Representative method	Hospitalisation Chemotherapy Psychoanalysis Directive therapies Transactional analysis (Cognitive therapy) (Rational-emotive therapy)	T-group Gestalt therapy Encounter Sensory awareness (Body therapies) (Psychodrama) (Co-counselling) (Regression)	Zen Yoga Arica Altered states Mysticism Monasticism (Psychosynthesis) (Jungian therapy)
Focus	Individual (Group)	Group (Individual)	Supportive community

Source: A.G. Banet (ed.) Creative psychotherapy: A Sourcebook (1976)

and somewhat traumatic crossing in many cases, and this involves a radical questioning of the centaur. The following chart (Chart 1.2) shows the difference quite well.

It can be seen from this chart that humanistic psychotherapy, if it focuses as I am suggesting on the centaur stage, is quite different from transpersonal psychotherapy – just as different on that side as it is from psychoanalysis and behaviourism on the other side. It should be said, however, that psychosynthesis prefers to work back and forth between the humanistic and the transpersonal (Ferrucci 1982) and would be unhappy about making too big a division between the two. We shall return to these concerns again in Chapters 5 and 9, but again it seems important to locate and situate our position from the word go, so as not to get confused about our aims and what we can actually do effectually and consistently. If Wilber is right, as I believe he is, we can see exactly how we fit in with the whole field of therapy, counselling and growth which we are trying to look at in this book.

THE FIELD

This area is a very confusing one, and it seems worthwhile to spend a little time on getting clear about it as a whole, before getting into detail about any one part of it.

The first term which is often bandied about is *psychiatry*. This is a medical specialism, where doctors of medicine (actually usually bachelors of medicine, but let that pass) have taken further qualifications in the field of mental illness. The vast majority of psychiatrists in Britain prescribe drugs, shock treatments and (to a much lesser extent) psychotherapy, but they have no training in psychotherapy of any kind. Confusion has arisen over this term, because in America the psychoanalysts were almost always doctors, and therefore called themselves psychiatrists. American films, therefore, show characters saying 'I've just been to see my psychiatrist', when they have been to see a psychoanalyst in private practice (in Britain most psychiatrists work for the National Health Service). Hence the many references to 'the psychiatrist's couch', which should really be 'the psychoanalyst's couch'. But in Britain and many other countries, many psychoanalysts are psychologists, or have other forms of basic training, and so do not call themselves psychiatrists at all.

So the second term we should look at is *psychoanalysis*. This is of course the approach developed by Sigmund Freud. There are some disagreements as to whether certain followers of Freud are orthodox enough to be called psychoanalysts, so the borderline is not altogether easy to draw. There is also a distinction made between psychoanalysis proper (lying down on the couch, five days a week) and psychoanalytically-oriented psychotherapy (sitting on a chair, three, two or even one day a week). This is sometimes called psychodynamic psychotherapy. This is a fair distinction, but at the same time all of these things are usually included under the general heading of psychotherapy.

Psychotherapy is any approach to mental distress which involves encouraging the distressed person to uncover and face their problems, and work through them in constructive ways. Usually this involves mainly talking, but it may involve body work as well. Psychotherapy may be of just one school, in which case it makes sense to say that the therapist is 'a Gestaltist' or 'a bioenergeticist', etc.; or it may be eclectic or synthetic, integrative or syncretic, combining more than one approach. The tendency in recent years has been for therapists to become more eclectic or integrative, because of the large number of effective methods which have been developed during the years since 1960. Psychoanalysts sometimes make a false distinction between supportive therapy and uncovering therapy, maintaining that analysis is the only real uncovering therapy. We deny that distinction, believing that there is no such thing as supportive therapy (if it is supporting the neurosis, it is not therapy at all) and that all therapy is uncovering therapy.

Clinical psychology is practised by people who have a degree in psychology, and who have taken further qualifications in the field of mental hospital work. They used to be mainly involved in doing routine tests for psychiatrists, but nowadays many of them get involved in treatment, particularly those kinds of treatment which are most acceptable to the medical establishment, such as behaviour therapy, behaviour modification and cognitive therapy. In recent years some new hybrids have been found acceptable within the NHS, such as cognitive-analytic therapy (Ryle 1990).

Behaviour therapy is based on the work of Pavlov and Watson and was developed particularly by a South African doctor, Joseph Wolpe. Its best-known exponents in Britain are Eysenck (1969) and Rachman and Philips (1978). It has been particularly successful in the treatment of phobias and obsessions, where there is a clear behaviour problem, and a clear result when the problem is solved. Similar remarks could be made about behaviour modification, which is based on the work of B.F. Skinner in America. Again, this works best where it is possible to get clear behavioural objectives. Much more popular today is cognitive-behaviour therapy (Dryden and Golden 1986), which tries to rescue behaviourism from its rather mechanistic image, but really replaces it with a different form of mechanism. Again, it fits in with the medical model, relying as it does on concepts of cure and correct treatment.

Counselling covers an enormously wide range of activities, including testing and guidance, and so on, as well as the more therapeutic work. Many of the actual techniques of counselling are exactly the same as the techniques for psychotherapy, and indeed Rogerian counselling is exactly the same as Rogerian psychotherapy. Carl Rogers (1951) is the great pioneer in bringing these two fields together more. All the schools of psychotherapy are also represented within counselling. But really both the counsellor and the psychotherapist are limited by what they are ready to handle, based on their experience, their training and their talent.

Personal growth is what happens when a healthy person with no very obvious problems decides on a process of self-exploration for self-understanding, simply in order to be more able. Because such people have generally what is called 'a strong ego', or 'Sufficient Available Functioning Adult Autonomy' (Mowbray 1995), it is possible to use a very wide range of techniques with them – hence the development of the open encounter group and the growth centre. In personal growth all the methods of psychotherapy and of counselling can be used, and they have exactly the same effect. In other words, problems are uncovered and dealt with, barriers are taken down, blocks are removed, insights are obtained and so forth. This has the effect, just as it does in therapy and counselling, of releasing energies which had been locked up in internal conflicts and self-defeating patterns of action. Or in other words, there are no (or very few) normal people, in the sense of being healthy and free from mental hangups. And indeed, as we shall see later on, supposedly normal people are often less well off than supposedly neurotic or psychotic people, because they are blocking off awareness of their very real problems. Hence it becomes evident that someone who goes in for a personal growth experience may sometimes encounter deep problems or disturbances for which they are unready. So a practitioner of personal growth methods needs just as deep a training as a psychotherapist or counsellor.

Having covered this much ground very briefly, we can now say that the humanistic practitioner is concerned with psychotherapy, with counselling and with personal growth; not, however, with psychiatry, psychoanalysis, behaviour therapy or behaviour modification. The humanistic practitioner does not use drugs or shock therapy, does not make more than incidental use of transference (the main mechanism of psychoanalytic therapy), and does not make more than incidental use of the principles of reciprocal inhibition or systematic desensitisation (behaviour therapy) or of the principle of reinforcement (behaviour modification). The humanistic practitioner seldom uses tests, but can be a clinical psychologist so long as a reasonably free hand is allowed.

Further, we can say that the humanistic practitioner sees psychotherapy, counselling and personal growth as all using the same methods and the same approach. For the rest of this book, then, we will refer only to therapy (mainly because it is the shortest, as well as the most general, of the three words) on the understanding that everything we say will be applicable to counselling and personal growth too. Of course there are differences of practice, with psychotherapists generally having the most reserved attitude to therapy. Counselling is much more likely to be a front-line activity, and personal growth is available to all, though a preliminary interview may be required for new people embarking upon certain particularly demanding types of work.

The reader who is familiar with the standard literature in this field (most of it written by psychoanalysts) may be horrified at this seemingly cavalier treatment. What about the important distinction between the normal and the neurotic, between the neurotic and the borderline case, between the borderline and the psychotic? What about the importance of selecting the right patient for the right treatment? This brings us to the whole question of diagnosis, or assessment as it is now more often called, and it is to this that we must now turn.

Chapter 2

Assessment

The question of assessment is one of the most striking areas in which humanistic practitioners differ from the older orthodoxies. It seems at first sight, and certainly it must be so if one adopts a medical model, that there is no way out of some responsibility for assessment. Surely we must find out what problem a person has before we can put it right? A doctor has to find out the disease before he knows what drug to prescribe; a motor mechanic has to find out what is wrong before fitting a spare part; a plumber has to find out the cause of the trouble before he can put it right. Isn't mental illness like this?

THE PROBLEM

Certainly the vast majority of people working in the field of psychotherapy would argue in this way. And yet, after a hundred years or more of research in this area, we still find the authors of an encyclopaedic handbook of research (Garfield and Bergin 1978) saying this:

> Ideally, one would like to be able to say that, given Problem X, the optimal approach is Technique Y. In practice, as the reader will discover, things are rarely so simple or straightforward; on the contrary, since human problems are extraordinarily complex, so are the issues facing the therapist who attempts to deal with these difficulties in therapeutic ways. For the same reason it is unlikely that there will ever be a single optimal approach to the solution of a psychological problem.
>
> (1978: 4)

In other words, they don't have the answer. It seems that assessment is more problematic than we might have thought. This is worrying, because more and more courses nowadays are teaching people about the

American Diagnostic and Statistical Manual (DSM-IV), the fourth edition of which came out in 1994. Many agencies in the United States, though not very many in Britain as yet, ask for formal diagnostic classification of a client before they will pay insurance or other costs. But just as more and more people are taking it on, more and more criticisms are appearing too. For example, Mary Boyle (1990) has urged that there are real conceptual complications about accepting schizophrenia as a disease entity in medical terms. And in a more recent article, she has made a most important point. She says that the assessment of mental illness often states or implies that the labels used are the names of diseases. 'The problem with this language is that it confers on these concepts a permanence and solidity which is quite unwarranted, and suggests that they are entities possessed by people' (Boyle 1996: 7). This is very dangerous, because the human mind is fluid rather than solid. It flows, rather than being broken up into chunks. If assessment suggests that things are fixed, it lies. And it suggests that once someone has been classified, they have been identified in a fixed way. 'Calling individuals phobic, obsessive-compulsive, histrionic or dependent personalities holds at least the suggestion that they are in a class by themselves, that is, that they are a different kind of human being' (Costello *et al.* 1995: 71). Another objection is that assessment hides everything it takes for granted. The famous DSM-IV diagnostic manual hides the fact that it was designed by psychiatrists, with their particular base of experience and knowledge coming from mental hospitals. This is very different from the experience and knowledge established in the counselling field. As Peter Ross says:

> It is difficult to draw up a list of diagnostic categories. The most glaring difficulty is that different theoretical orientations can persuade one to see problems in a very different light. A second problem is that a typical young person's counselling service sees large numbers of developmental problems rather than clinical ones. There is even less agreement among experts on how to categorise developmental problems than there is on how to categorise clinical ones. A third problem is that a counselling service of any size will have to face the necessity of getting all its counsellors to agree definitions so that when counsellor A records a client as 'mild reactive depression' and counsellor B records the same for a different client a month later, they mean the same thing. If they do not, the computer will be producing very hollow information.
>
> (Ross 1996: 478)

In this particular case, Ross and his co-workers went on for six years trying to make a system work, but up to the moment of writing there is no successful result. Well, if assessment is no good for classifying people, perhaps it is good for predicting their treatment and its outcome? For example, we might well feel that at least assessment could tell us one important thing – which patients were going to go crazy if they start into psychotherapy. This is sometimes referred to as 'precipitating a psychotic episode', sometimes as 'provoking a breakdown' and sometimes as 'inducing decompensation', but it's all the same problem, and a fairly obvious one, at that. Surely assessment can at least get us this far? Well, apparently not. In a book (Malan 1979) on the science of psychodynamics by one of the best-established therapists at one of the most reputable clinics, the author has this to say:

> During many years at the Tavistock Clinic, I have accumulated a long list of patients in whom this question arises [relief vs increased disturbance]; and, even being wise after the event, I have found myself quite unable to distinguish between these two possibilities. I am constantly being surprised by patients whom I would not expect to break down, who do break down, and those whom I would expect to break down, who don't. This remains an area where systematic research is badly needed.
>
> (1979: 223)

But the humanistic practitioner doesn't want to do this systematic research, because of severe doubts not only about the efficacy, but also about the morality, of this process of assessment. Because to diagnose someone is to label them. And labelling does harm to people, even when the labels are correct. As Irvin Yalom says: 'The standard diagnostic formulation tells the therapist nothing about the unique person he or she is encountering; and there is substantial evidence that diagnostic labels impede or distort listening' (Yalom 1980: 410).

Human beings do have problems, but when it comes to psychotherapy, they are not isolable separate problems which can be treated like a disease or a faulty component or a blocked pipe. They are problems connected with being that person. This is why one label can never be enough to tell us what to do about a person. One of the main characteristics of the humanistic approach is a refusal to label people in any firm or final way. Of course we have tentative ideas as to what is basically wrong with any client, but as George Kelly once said, 'The client does not ordinarily sit cooped up in a nosological pigeonhole, he proceeds along his way' (Kelly 1955: 773). Accordingly, he advocated making a 'transitive assessment' which gives us a lead for action, but which is open to change as the interaction goes on.

Possibly the best discussion to be found of this whole area is that to be found in the book by Walkenstein (1975). She tells of giving patients labels – 'Your assessment is Excessive Politeness . . . the only cure for you is to practise some excessive rudeness.' 'You're a Zombie.' 'You're a marshmallow.' These are all temporary labels: they don't have the certainty or the permanence of science, they just represent a moment of insight, a moment of seeing the obvious in a flash of clarity. They have implications for something to do about changing them.

To someone like Walkenstein, the symptoms represent a shield; they don't represent the personality. The assessment then becomes not a life sentence but rather something to be put aside when the person is ready to do so. She looks on the symptoms as a message, a plea for attention, and the assessment as a method of giving that attention, in a temporary and nonhurtful manner. And by the way, Jung agrees with this: 'Jung pointed out, somewhat ironically, that the really correct diagnosis is to be made only at the end of treatment' (McCurdy 1985: 48).

LABELLING

Much of what we have been saying comes under the heading of what is often called 'social constructivism'. Social constructivism says that social situations tend to be ordered in accordance with social meanings and intentions of various kinds. That is, a whole series of expectations are created just by the way the set-up is arranged. Whatever then happens within the boundaries of that set-up will be in terms of those specific expectations, and no others. That behaviour which fits in with the expectations will be seen as normal, and any behaviour which does not fit in will be seen as deviant. And this opens up the whole question of assessment. How is it constructed, and who has the contract for the construction process?

In the field of 'mental illness', just as in the field of criminality (see Rowan 1978) there is a great deal of leeway and a great deal of negotiation involved. If we want to have a good look at how diagnostic decisions are made in practice today, we can make a good start by considering the classic paper by Daniels (1970) on military applications of assessment. One of the main points she makes is that the assessment of mental illness is dependent not only on the symptoms of the patient, but also on the doctor's awareness of the consequences that a specific diagnostic label may have for the career of the patient. In her actual words:

In situations where diagnostic procedures carry clear consequences for disposition of cases, the principle seems to be: Tell me what is feasible or reasonable to do with this person and I will give you a diagnosis which can explain, justify, or in some cases, modify that disposition. These principles are by no means limited to the military setting . . . they also suggest that the construction of psychiatric reality may be almost entirely social.

Social, that is to say, as opposed to medical. This last assertion may seem to be on the strong side but, as we shall now see, it can be supported from several different angles.

It seems to be little known that diagnostic examinations are often very short. Scheff (1966a) reports studies of commitment hearings which show that the average assessment takes five minutes. This examination is peremptory and ritualistic, and determines sanity or insanity. The key to understanding this is that according to Scheff their actual goal is not to determine *whether* the patient is mentally ill, but only to decide *which* mental illness s/he has. He followed up his original study with further studies in England and Italy (Scheff 1966b) which showed exactly the same state of affairs to exist in these places.

It is not surprising to find, then, that assessment is very much open to influence, as Temerlin's experiment (1975) showed. He played a tape of an interview between a 'patient' (actually an actor who had been given a script indicating a person who was about as normal and average as possible) and a psychiatrist to various groups of psychiatrists. For one group the remark was dropped that this was a very interesting man because he looked neurotic but was actually perfectly normal. For another group the remark was dropped that this was a very interesting man because he looked neurotic but was actually quite psychotic. The first group voted 100 per cent that the person was healthy and normal. In the second group, 60 per cent voted him psychotic, and 40 per cent neurotic. Control groups who were told nothing about the person *never* said he was psychotic, and only a minority thought him neurotic at all. These are striking results. It seems clear that a one-sentence suggestion from someone who is thought to be important and relevant is regarded more highly than the evidence of one's own ears. The unfortunate patient is likely to be put away even if everything s/he says is perfectly normal, so long as someone has pronounced him or her a problem.

Similar doubts arise out of a much more realistic experiment discussed by Rosenhan (1975) which was widely reported at the time. Eight researchers gained admission to mental hospitals by posing as patients; some went to more than one hospital, so that twelve hospitals were sampled in all. They behaved perfectly normally and told the truth about their lives except for three points: they changed their names; those who were in mental health professions changed their jobs to something unconnected with medicine; and they gave as their symptoms that they had been hearing voices which were often unclear, but seemed to be saying 'empty', 'hollow' and 'thud'. They were all diagnosed as schizophrenic – except one in one hospital (the most expensive) who was diagnosed manic-depressive – and admitted immediately. Once in, they applied to get out again, but found it very hard to do so. The length of their stay varied from seven to fifty-two days, with an average of nineteen days. When they went up to a doctor to ask to be let out, the doctor in most cases kept moving on with his head averted and did not reply; the same thing happened with nurses and attendants.

The accuracy of the diagnostic process is again questioned in a follow-up to the original investigation, where a research and a teaching hospital had heard of the study and doubted whether such things could happen in their hospital. All the staff at this hospital were therefore alerted to the possibility of pseudopatients applying for admission. In a period of three months while this was operating, 193 patients were seen. Of these, forty-one were reckoned to be pseudopatients by at least one person; twenty-three were considered suspect by at least one psychiatrist; and nineteen were suspected by one psychiatrist and one other staff member. Actually, however, no pseudopatients attended at all. So what can we say about these nineteen cases where applicants were judged sane? One thing is certain: any assessment process that lends itself so readily to massive errors of this sort cannot be a very reliable one.

So it seems that psychiatric assessment is fallible and open to influence – but what is interesting is what influences it most in practice. This was put under the microscope by Greenley (1975) in a study of 125 consecutive admissions to a psychiatric unit in New England. He interviewed the psychiatrist and asked how bad the patient was, both absolutely and in relation to other patients; he interviewed the patient and asked whether he or she wanted to stay in the hospital or return home; and he interviewed one other family member, and asked whether the family wanted the patient to stay in the hospital or return home. He then related the answers to the eventual length of the hospital stay of the patient. It turned out that the strongest influence was the attitudes and wishes of the other family members. How does this work? One quote:

Sometimes when a family calls and says they don't want to see someone again, I know my [neurotic] assessment is wrong and that they are probably schizophrenic. If the family doesn't want them, they are usually more sick than I think, so I change and call them schizophrenic.

It could hardly be clearer that a psychiatric label is one of the best ways of getting rid of somebody. Just as the vast majority of 'crimes' are never 'brought to book' (Belson 1975), so the vast majority of mental distress is never brought to book, in the sense of labelling someone as neurotic or psychotic.

Who, then, are the people who are most likely to be labelled? They are the most powerless. Just as those criminals that are most likely to be caught are those who go most against the norms of a top-down society, so those other deviants that are most likely to be put inside are those who go most against the norms of such a society. As Brown (1974) reports, most prisoners in state psychiatric hospitals (sorry, most patients in state psychiatric hospitals) are working class, most are women, and third world people make up a disproportionate percentage of the patient population in relation to the general population. As he says: 'The social context of present-day America is of class, sex and race oppression, and those oppressed by these social relations are the prime candidates for the brain police.' This is no less true of Britain or any other country. It appears, then, that psychiatric assessment offers an acceptable 'scientific' story to justify taking a person out of his or her home and putting them in an institution.

It seems from this that social constructivism offers an account of 'mental illness' which makes social-psychological sense in a class patriarchy. For more evidence and an examination of the counter-case see the article by Scheff (1975) which examines the alternatives rather thoroughly, and Gove's book (1975) which deals rather less well with these matters.

But having seen some examples of how the theory works, it seems in order to examine the theory itself: what does it actually say? One application of social constructivism is labelling theory. Labelling theory starts with a simple distinction – that between explicit norms (rules whose breaking can be punished) and residual rules. The residual rules are not stated anywhere, and it may not be legitimate to punish infringements of them, yet they may on occasion be important to specific people. These much more vague and variable infringements tend, in each age, to drift into a catch-all category. Once it was witchcraft (and still is in a number of countries), once it was possession by spirits, sometimes it was possession by the Devil, and so on: today, in our culture, it is 'mental illness'.

When someone in our family is doing something unacceptable and inconvenient, which cannot be condemned under any existing law, but which makes us nervous or excited, we are liable to see that person as a candidate for the mental hospital. The case histories by Laing and Esterson (1970) give a rather clear picture of this process in action. So labelling theory says that the symptoms of 'mental illness' can be seen as the violation of residual rules. Scheff (1975) states nine formal hypotheses as follows:

1 Residual rule breaking arises from fundamentally diverse sources (that is, organic, psychological, situations of stress, volitional acts of innovation or defiance).
2 Relative to the rate of treated mental illness, the rate of unrecorded residual rule breaking is extremely high.
3 Most residual rule breaking is 'denied' and is of transitory significance.
4 Stereotyped imagery of mental disorder is learned in early childhood.
5 The stereotypes of insanity are continually re-affirmed, inadvertently, in ordinary social interaction.
6 Labelled deviants may be rewarded for playing the stereotyped deviant role.
7 Labelled deviants are punished when they attempt to return to conventional roles.
8 In the crisis occurring when a residual rule breaker is publicly labelled, the deviant is highly suggestible and may accept the label.
9 Among residual rule breakers, labelling is the single most important cause of careers of residual deviance.

This is to put more concisely what we have been seeing evidenced all through this chapter. It is rather like the old wives' tale about 'if your eyes are crossed when the wind changes, you'll get stuck like it'. You can cross and uncross your eyes many, many times and be none the worse for it, but if you get caught at the wrong moment, that's it – there is no going back.

The implication of this is that if we refused to label people, they would drift into and out of mental states often regarded as 'neurotic' or 'psychotic' without ever losing their status as citizen, friend, child, human being or whatever. And this is precisely it. A good example is given by Seymour Krim (1960) when he talks about his own psychotic episode:

> When I was considered out of my mind during my original upward thrust into the sheer ecstasy of 100 per cent uninhibitedness, I was aware of the 'daringness' of my every move; it represented at heart an existential choice rather than a mindless discharge; it could not be tolerated by society, and I was punished for it, but my 'cure' was ultimately chastisement, *not a medical healing process*.

Krim became a well-known author, and, according to him, benefited from the experience; but much of it was horror, because of the way he was treated. He had enough power and influence to fight back, but most patients don't. More examples are given in Berke's chilling little book (1979). Most patients get labelled and they stay labelled. They 'get stuck like it'.

ALTERNATIVE MODELS

It is clear that we must reject the medical model. In doing so we are on common ground with most psychologists, and the overwhelming majority of social psychologists. The *Handbook of Social Psychology* has an article by Freeman and Giovannoni (1969) describing the medical model of mental distress as 'entirely irrelevant and handicapping' and as 'unreliable or meaningless'. We have seen above how true this is.

Equally objectionable, from quite a different standpoint, is a social-determinist view, which says that mental illness can best be understood as caused by material conditions. The many environmental studies which have been carried out by such people as Faris and Dunham (1939) and Hollingshead and Redlich (1958) come under this heading: such studies show that people living in the run-down areas of the inner city have a far higher incidence of schizophrenia and other mental disorders than those living in the suburbs; the expectancy of a psychiatric disorder, the types of disorder found and the types of treatment likely to be offered or imposed are all significantly related to the person's position in the class structure. The moral often drawn is that living conditions can drive people crazy. Again such an argument is too one-sided, though this time from another direction. It seems at first to be very enlightened and politically challenging to get rid of the slums and improve the lot of the poor – but in fact it is just as mechanical as the medical model, in its own way. The person still gets labelled, only now it is the fault of society, or living conditions, or the class system or whatever. From the point of view of the individual involved, this doesn't make much difference; next year's political manifesto won't get this person out of hospital now.

Our view as humanistic practitioners is different from both of these. What we say is that people have problems. Where they attribute these problems to outside forces or other people, we can't help them much; we probably can't do a lot to change the people around them or the world in which they find themselves. (There are important exceptions to this, which we shall look at in Chapter 10, 'Listening with the fourth ear'.) But where they attribute their problems to themselves, or to what is going on inside them, then we have an opportunity to work with them on solving those problems.

From this point of view the standard psychiatric diagnoses are of no use. If you work in an organisation such as a counselling agency there may be rules which have to be followed about assessment. But it is not an ethical requirement and if there is any possibility of changing such rules this would be highly desirable. There is only one distinction which does seem to be useful and to be of practical import to a humanistic practitioner: can the person benefit from a 'session' (the usual one-hour session or an extended session) or do they need some form of residential care?

The question here is 'Can this person uncover their problems during the course of a session, and then cover them up again sufficiently to carry on their life (work, relationships, and so on) until the next session?' Or is this person all too easily able to uncover their problems, but unable to leave them on one side at the end of the session? If the person can 'go down' and 'come up' in the same session, then they are suitable for the usual once-a-week (or twice-a-week or more frequent) session, leading their ordinary life as housewife, clerk, lorry-driver, teacher, carpet-fitter or whatever at the same time. But if the person can 'go down' but can't 'come up' again in less than a week, a month or a year or more, then they need some kind of residential facility. Or to put it from a slightly different angle, a person going through therapy needs a good support network. Without this, it is unwise to proceed. I have developed a hand-out, using the work of Brammer, Shostrom and Abrego (1989) as a basis, giving some general hints on taking on clients or not (see Chart 2.1).

This may be very close to the conventional distinction between neurotic and psychotic states, but it is much more pragmatic. It doesn't rely on assessment, it relies on actual practice. It's highly checkable. It means that, as long as you have residential facilities on hand as a backup, you can take anyone on as a client in psychotherapy, counselling or

Chart 2.1 Should I take on this client?

A practitioner should not expect to be able to take on everyone who applies. Very often in training there is a preliminary interview by a staff member before a client is referred, but even at this stage there may be some people who are taken on in other ways. Some considerations:

1 *The nature and severity of the client's symptoms* For example, prolonged delusional thinking may be a sign of psychosis, and people suffering in this way usually need residential facilities, rather than once- or twice-a-week therapy. Or outbursts of uncontrolled anxiety or hostility again require quite secure environmental situations before a practitioner should be asked to deal with them.

2 *Length and persistence of symptoms* The longer something has been going on the longer it is going to take to deal with it. 'Am I ready to take on a client who may require constant attention for five years?' There is a responsibility not to bite off more than one can chew. One of the terrible things about some institutional setups is that personnel are transferred without any consideration of the possible effects on clients.

3 *The nature of the predisposing and precipitating experiences* If a client has had a series of severe traumas over a short period, there may be a need for sessions much more frequently than you can in practice offer. It may be better to refer the client to someone who can offer this. Do not be panicked into fire-fighting if you have not been trained as a fire-fighter.

4 *Past stability and defensive functioning* Has the person shown the ability to handle deep feelings in the past, or is there a history of breakdown, self-mutilation, attempted suicide or the like? You are going to be asking the person to explore their inner life, and you want to be reasonably sure that this is not simply asking for trouble. Again, residential facilities may be required.

5 *Resistance to therapy* If in the first interview there is a lot of blocking of your attempts to open up significant areas, this may because they are generally resistant to therapy, or it may be that they are resistant to you and your approach. Either way, it is not a good bet. It may also be that they are not ready to do therapy at the moment, but would be later. However, men are under a good deal of pressure to resist therapy, due to their conditioning, and a certain amount of this is to be expected.

6 *The person's network* Does the person have friends, relatives, colleagues and so on around and available? It is more acceptable to take on a difficult client who has such things than one who does not.

7 *Extent and adequacy of the practitioner's training* Generally speaking, although there can be exceptions to this, it is unwise to take on someone who has had more experience of therapy than you. There are games which can be played in therapy; if the client knows more of them than you do, the therapy may go off the rails. You can refer such a client to someone more experienced.

Chart 2.1 continued

---

8 *The problems of the practitioner* Often the practitioner is unable to handle feelings because the client's feelings touch upon sore spots of his or her own. If this is so, it may be better to refer the client on. Empathy can turn into sympathy, and sympathy into collusion to avoid what needs to be faced.

9 *The amount of time available* It is better not to take on long-term clients if you know you will be leaving the country or the neighbourhood, retiring or suchlike, within a relatively short period of time. (See also 2 above.)

10 *Institutional policy* If you are working for an agency or other organisation, they may have rules as to which clients you may take on, or how deep you are to go with them. These have to be observed, and you should think about whether you are willing to abide by such rules when you take on such a job.

---

personal growth. And in the end this may not be such an unusual conclusion. As Malan (1979) says at the end of his book, 'Perhaps the final lesson is certainly that one should undertake psychotherapy with one's eyes open, but that on the whole one should take the risks rather than avoid them.'

The humanistic practitioner is always prepared to go to the existential edge with a client, to go with the client to that point where the most difficult choices of life are to be faced and made. It is no part of our work to push the client over the edge, but until that sharp point is reached, no real change can take place. And this process must start from the very first meeting; it is not something to be kept in reserve for another time. This makes the initial interview a particularly testing arena for the worker who wants to adopt a humanistic approach, and it is this question that we shall examine next.

Chapter 3

The initial interview

The previous chapters have been of a more objective character, where it seemed important to give chapter and verse for each of the points made, and to justify each of the arguments put forward. In most of this chapter, however, I think it is more appropriate to adopt a more subjective posture, where I talk about what I do rather than what 'the humanistic practitioner' does, or should do. The reason for this is that no one has done a research study to establish what the general practice of humanistic therapists is, nor is there enough evidence to lay down ideals of practice. By talking about what I do, I am therefore putting myself forward as one humanistic practitioner who has thought a good deal about what he is doing, and has had to observe students making a great many mistakes and asking many awkward questions.

FIRST PHONE CALL

Very often the first contact between therapist and client is through a telephone call. The client rings up, often in an unhappy state from having made this key step. To admit that one needs the services of a psycho-therapist is often very difficult. The reception one gets from the selected practitioner is keenly observed and deeply felt. 'Am I acceptable?' is the unspoken question. There is a lot of research now to show that *inclusion* is the first issue to arise in any group situation (Schutz 1983), and this group of two people is no exception.

If this is so, then with the first phone call the therapy has started. The therapist may be busy or tired, may have no free places for new clients, but nevertheless the therapy has already started, and anything the therapist does is going to be therapeutic, nontherapeutic or anti-therapeutic. It is therapeutic to show concern and be of some help, so as to achieve rapport with the client. This concept of rapport is so important that we may as well spend some moments with it.

Rapport means being connected to the other person, relating well to the other person, being on the same wavelength, being able to communicate well and so on. Where rapport exists, the client feels accepted, welcomed and included. The client may soon begin to feel 'Here is someone who understands me' and this makes the whole task of therapy very much easier. The essential basic trust has been set up. So how do we achieve rapport? Bandler and Grinder (1979) have given this point a lot of thought and conclude that the best way to achieve rapport is to take your cue from the other person: not by responding to them in your own way, but by copying them in *their* own way. So if the person speaks slowly, I speak slowly; if they use visual images, I use visual images; if they talk quietly, I talk quietly. At this stage I feel that rapport is virtually the only thing I can achieve, so I may as well achieve it well. And I do it by mirroring the client.

Now all that refers not to what the client says, but to how the client says it. We must now consider what is said. It is important that the client should see somebody fast. They may or may not have an emergency, but they are at a point where they are ready for action, and I like to give them some. It may be that I have no appointments vacant for some days, but even so I like to see the person, if only for a short time, rather than to let them wait around. But I always make it clear as to what I am offering. If there is no prospect of my taking this person on at all, I refer him or her on to a colleague with available time.

I feel that a client is entitled to at least good will and sympathy from any therapist, and that it is important that someone who rings a therapist for the first time should feel these qualities coming across. If I can't feel reasonably warm and concerned about someone who rings me up with a problem, I wonder whether I should be a therapist at all.

If I listen well to what the client has to say during the first phone call, I can begin to collect impressions, information and data from the first moment. These can be useful in later work, so I make notes either during the phone call or after it; this in itself reminds me that the therapy has already started.

There is one issue which may arise on this first contact which I think is worth mentioning. If the person says that he or she is phoning about someone else, I always insist on seeing the telephoner first. A phrase like 'I need to get the full information about the background before I can come to any proper conclusions about the best course of action to recommend' is all that is required. The reason for this is that I can only work with a person who has a felt problem. It often turns out that the 'someone else' does not have a felt problem at all, and therefore is not a candidate for my kind of therapy. My general rule is that the complainer is the client.

If the person taking the call is not a therapist but simply a receptionist, secretary, assistant or colleague, the same considerations apply. This person is giving a certain impression, and it should be a therapeutic one, if that is humanly possible. This is not an ideal set-up, however, and it is much better if the therapist is the first person that the caller talks to. I personally would be reluctant to work in a situation where the person who does the initial interview is different from the person who continues to work with the client. This sometimes has to happen in training situations where the trainee is seen as not capable of assessing a prospective client in a professionally adequate way. And really much the same considerations apply to the first phone call. I would hate anyone else to take this call.

The reason is that any process which separates the entry to therapy from the therapy itself entails the medical model which we have just abandoned. If, as we have seen in Chapter 2, there is no such thing as legitimate diagnosis, there is no place for someone who does diagnosis and nothing else. The therapeutic process is inevitably begun during any initial interview which is going to be useful, and to pretend that this is not going to happen is to close one's eyes to reality. If we want to treat people as persons rather than as things – and all psychotherapy depends on this assumption – we should not hand their intimate openness on from one expert to another as if it were a car on an assembly line. It does harm both to the client and to the practitioner; the therapist who is faced with a client who has been handed on from someone else really has to start from scratch, for there is no way of taking a set of notes at face value and simply accepting what they say, and no way of going back to pretend that they do not exist. It seems illogical and self-contradictory to start a process designed specifically to restore someone to personhood by reducing them to nothing more than a machine with faults to be corrected. Jim Bugental says:

> I am aware that many settings call for the client to be seen by an intake worker who makes the assignment to the therapist. This may be administratively efficient, but I believe very strongly that the assignment should only be a recommendation, subject to the outcome of the first encounter of client and therapist and thus to their deeper reading of how they come together.
>
> (1978: 28)

Wilson (1996) suggests that there are three types of client: those in crisis, those who are 'visiting' and those who are willing to engage in a serious attempt at working on themselves. The 'visiting' category is an interesting one: here the person is just not ready for therapy, but thinks for some reason that they should be doing it. This is sometimes difficult to discern, but one clue is that such a person very often views their problems as caused and owned by another person or organisation. This seems to me a useful thought.

THE INITIAL INTERVIEW

Let us now assume that the contact has been made, by whatever means, and that the client now turns up for the first appointment. The first thing to be considered is the room in which the interview is to take place. My room has two mattresses, and a number of cushions of different shapes and sizes and colours, including some very large ones. It has a clock which I make sure is always correct. I have several boxes of tissues, a supply of paper to draw on and many felt pens and crayons of different colours. The light has a dimmer on it, and the curtains are heavy, so that the room can be made dim even on a sunny day. I have facilities for recording sessions on tape, and for playing music. I have a tennis racquet and a baby's feeding bottle. There is a bowl available for being sick into, and a towel for strangling, using as a poisonous snake and so on. If I were more body-oriented than I am, I would probably have a massage table, and I might well have a bioenergetic stool or a minitrampoline. The first sight of this room is not usually strange for my clients, because many of them hear of me through groups where these things are regularly used. If I get a client who has never been to a group, I sometimes explain that in therapy we often find it a good idea to change the actual body position, and this sort of arrangement makes it easier to do that.

When the client arrives, I go to the door and greet him or her warmly. Psychoanalysts worry a great deal about whether to shake hands or not, but with the humanistic practitioner handshakes, hugs, kisses or other marks of affection are not particularly unusual and do not give cause for concern, although of course they are noted as much as any other piece of body language. Whatever is thoroughly genuine and personally felt is probably going to be all right. In the initial stage, of course, the greeting is likely to be more tentative than it will be later, since both parties are sizing up the other and sounding them out.

I always like to leave it to the client where to sit. I used to use chairs, and there are good arguments in favour of that, but nowadays I don't use them any more. Emmy van Deurzen says very wisely:

> I personally favour an arrangement where clients have several choices of position, for different clients prefer different arrangements. Some like the closeness of facing confrontation, some like the armchair-to-armchair fireside talk, while others like to be able to stretch out in different directions by taking a position on the couch. Fixed positions are unhelpful; one-sided recommendations need to be viewed with suspicion. The client needs room to explore what comes naturally to them, whilst reflecting on the significance of such a preference.
>
> (1997: 193)

This whole question of the furniture and layout of the consulting room is of course an enormous one, and I have written elsewhere of the complex ins and outs of the appearance of the room where the client is seen (Rowan 1996).

Once the client is sitting down, I get him or her to talk. This is usually easy, because that is exactly what the client has come for. It just needs starting off, with one of those meaningless phrases like 'What seems to be the trouble?', 'What brings you here?', 'Why have you come to see me?' or 'How can I help you?'

There are some exceptions, however. It may be that this client has been sent by someone else – her husband, his mother, her superior, his doctor or whoever – and that there is no real commitment of a personal kind. Or it may be that this client has had to wait a long time, due to some mistake having been made somewhere along the line, and therefore comes in angry or resigned or with a problem which has changed considerably. Or it may be that the client has a secret motive for coming which is not obvious – to get up the courage for a divorce, to get help with an insurance claim, to gain support in changing jobs or moving house, or something like this. In such cases, I may have to work much harder to find out whether work with this client is going to be mutually satisfying.

For this is the task of the initial interview – to establish whether there is or is not a basis for working together. And this is a very ticklish task, because it essentially involves foreseeing the future, which is impossible. Experience shows that it is best to solve this impossible problem by treating the initial interview as therapy, rather than as history-taking, or as a diagnostic test, or as a questionnaire interview. The objection to this is that we may stir up sensitive material and then decide not to take this client on. The client is then left high and dry, it is said, feeling worse than at the beginning. This objection applies even more to the idea sometimes suggested, and which in fact I used to adopt, of a trial period with the therapist, of five or six sessions, before deciding whether it is good to work together on a more long-term basis. I gave this up on the grounds that it was unrealistic: the relationship is quite often formed in the first five minutes (Hobson 1985). The fifth or sixth session is very rarely a suitable point to consider the continuation of the relationship, and if the therapist insists on raising the point, many clients experience this as a rejection. What I do nowadays is to say that we should continue for at least a year before starting to worry about whether the therapy is working or not. That gets over the 'How long is a piece of string?' question, and gives a realistic sense of the work involved.

The answer to this objection (about stirring up sensitive material) is that there is nothing particularly fatal about someone having sensitive material stirred up. People have immense numbers of defences, and if they don't want stuff stirred up, not all the efforts of the most skilled therapist can persuade them to stir it up. If, on the other hand, they are good and ready to face that material at the moment, it may only take a word from any therapist to open the floodgates. It is not so much the therapist stirring as the client opening. It is the client doing it and not the therapist doing it, and this applies to everything in therapy. There is a good example in Malan's (1979) book – he is a psychoanalyst but it could have happened to anyone – where he picked up a clue from something a client said in an initial interview, and asked her whether she had ever been seriously depressed. She then came up with a very depressing story about how she had had a very bad experience with another therapist, as a result of which she had almost committed suicide and had been committed to a mental hospital. He then decided, for various reasons, not to take her on as a client. As he says, this was 'traumatic enough' for the client; but in spite of this, a good relationship continued afterwards between him and her, keeping in touch over quite a period of time, while she went to another therapist.

What we are saying here, then, runs very much in line with the recommendations of the classic book by Gill et al. (1954) where they come out in favour of a spontaneous unfolding of the client's problems in the initial interview. This makes it much easier to maintain rapport and hence to encourage the client to come back for more, so that information which does not come out in the initial interview has a chance to come out later instead. This is also in line with the views of William

Console (Console *et al.* 1978) as exemplified in the five initial interviews which he gives in full with a running commentary. So, we are to conduct the initial interview like a therapy session (which indeed it is). But how do we do this?

RAPPORT

Rapport again comes in here. We have already mentioned it in connection with the first phone call. But now, in this face-to-face situation, we have far more to go on, and far more possible responses. Bandler and Grinder (1979) point out that we can mirror the client in a three-dimensional way, always taking care not to mimic or ape the client in a way that is noticed and is interpreted as mocking. We can also now do cross-over mirroring. Instead of, for example, just breathing in the same way as the client, the therapist can use hand movements to copy the chest movements of the client. Or you can match the tempo of your voice to the rate of the client's breathing. This makes for great flexibility in the means of gaining rapport. The effect of all this is to put me in tune with the client, so as to make communication that much easier. I can feel the weight, as it were, of the client, by feeling my own responses. And this puts me in touch with the client in a very special way, because this is something which the client can experience at a body level, quite independently of what may be going on mentally.

One time I saw a film of Ronnie Laing doing a first interview with a client. He did exactly what I have been talking about, echoing the movements and positions of the client. I asked him afterwards whether it had been just intuitive or whether he had done it deliberately as a matter of policy. He said the latter, adding that he always did this nowadays. It felt strange and artificial when I did this for the first time, but it had such good results that I persevered with it, and now it comes naturally. All the way through this first interview, we are trying to gain rapport, because this is first base, so to speak. Unless this is achieved, the client will not come back for more. There are many cases of clients who come for one interview and are never seen again, and this is wasteful all round. Inexperienced therapists often think they can gain rapport by smiling a lot and being nice to the client, but this is not it at all.

The second thing we are trying to do in the initial interview is to get information. At the end of the interview we are going to have to say something to the client about coming back for more meetings. So the decision has to be made: do I take this client on for regular therapy, do I refer this person on to someone else, do I lay down certain conditions before I agree to take the person on, do I tell the person that what they need is not therapy but something else, or what?

Since we have already established that the humanistic practitioner is not interested in diagnosis, what is to stop us taking on every client who comes? As we said in the last chapter, the key issue is whether the person needs residential treatment or not. And there are certain key things which would point to this: if the person is very out of touch with reality, so that they do not respond to my suggestions or questions, but seem to spend a good deal of the time in a world of their own; if the person very easily gets into suicidal states as soon as certain subjects are mentioned; if the person gets very physically aggressive as soon as certain issues are raised – these and other obvious indications of deep disturbance show the need for residential treatment. So we certainly need information on such subjects as: Has the person ever been in a mental hospital? Is the person on a course of psychiatric drugs at the moment? Does the person have hallucinations? Does the person have violent and long-lasting mood swings? Has the person tried to commit suicide (and when, and how)? All these things are highly relevant to our most basic decisions about this person as a potential client. (See again Chart 2.1 in the last chapter on 'Should I take on this client?')

The question is, then, how do we get this information without doing or saying things to the client which could be antitherapeutic? We do it simply by making the initial interview the first therapy session. In therapy, we are all the time inviting the client to open up to what is really important and central for them: we are continually asking in some way the question 'Where does it hurt most?' And if we keep on probing in the normal way during the initial interview, all these points will come up spontaneously and of their own accord.

GOING WRONG

So what is this 'normal way' we have just referred to? It is slightly different for each therapist, but it essentially consists in paying attention to what the client is saying and doing, and responding in such a way that the client becomes more aware of what he or she is saying and doing. We shall be going into this in detail in the next chapter. What we can look at now are some of the typical ways in which the inexperienced therapist may get off on the wrong foot, and be unable to get back on to the right track again very easily. These are the main things which can get in the way of good communication in the therapy session.

Getting angry with the client: it is surprising how often the unskilled therapist will try to put the client down, score points off the client, punish the client and so on. It is easy to feel that the client is getting it wrong, not really trying, covering up, running away, avoiding the real issue, acting dumb or suchlike, and to express this in some form implying blame. But this is what is known as blaming the victim, and it doesn't help. Later on in therapy, when trust has been built up, the client can be confronted on things of this kind, but even then it is better if the client sees it spontaneously rather than having it pointed out by the therapist. The basic question is 'Who is going to benefit from this confrontation?' Is it for the client's benefit, or is it just to relieve the therapist's feelings?

Being scared of the client: some clients come out with statements which frighten the therapist – they may be about violence, craziness, sex, death or whatever – and from that point on the therapist keeps a noticeable distance from the client. Rather than block off communication, end the session or likewise, it is better for the therapist to admit to being scared, and to take it from there. Fromm-Reichmann (1950) has some good remarks on this, in telling of some experiences of her own. Ultimately it is about the therapist doing enough personal work to have dealt with any irrational fears.

Competing with the client: sometimes the therapist can have such a sense of wanting to hold on to all the power and control in the session that it turns into little more than a struggle about this issue, with the therapist almost certainly winning, but at the cost of losing the client. Again it is better to raise the issue explicitly, rather than keeping it under the surface. This may most easily happen where there is a male therapist and a male client, as I have explained at length elsewhere (Rowan 1997b).

Seducing the client: it is also possible for the therapist to be so keen on getting rapport going, being nice and approachable, achieving good contact and so forth, that he or she can quite overwhelm the client with warmth and smiles. This can be smothering and confusing for the client, who can be so sucked in as to lose all track of their inner processes. This again is usually due to nervousness on the part of the therapist. More about this in Chapter 4.

Getting confused by the client: sometimes the client is so vague or scattered that it is hard to pin down the real problem. A good basic question to ask yourself is 'Who is doing what to whom, and how is this a problem?' And a helpful background question is 'How do you think I could help you with your problem?' If these questions cannot be answered, I feel like digging further, perhaps asking 'How did you get to contact me at the particular time you did, rather than some other time?' Another question which can help in several different ways is 'What can you think of that would be a good sign that something was beginning to change?' This is sometimes called 'The Miracle Question', phrased in the form 'If you woke up next morning and your problem had disappeared by some miracle, what is the first thing you would notice that would tell you that had happened?' All the time we are encouraging the client to be more concrete. In some cases visualisation can be used, in this kind of way, asking 'Supposing somebody made a movie of your problem, and one scene in the movie really summed it up perfectly, what would this scene show?' Or I may just confess to the confusion and say something like 'I can't seem to cope with so much information at once; I'm getting muddled and confused. Out of all the things you've mentioned, which is the one that stands out most clearly, that seems to have most life in it for you?' Depending on the client, I may use phrases like 'has the most energy', 'speaks loudest', 'feels most painful', 'has the strongest colours' or whatever.

Getting intimidated by the client: oftentimes, when a therapist is still in training, clients will come along who have more experience of therapy than the therapist has. Suppose, for example, that the client says 'You had better have Dr N's notes before seeing me, because I've been seeing him for four years in the town I've just come from.' My answer to this is to say 'I'm sure that would be very useful, but I prefer to get my own sense of who you are and what is going on right now, before looking at what anyone else says.' Similarly, if the client asks questions like 'How old are you?', 'What are your qualifications?', 'How can you understand my problems when you're so different?', 'How come you work in a dump like this?' and so on, it is important not to be put on the defensive. It usually makes sense to say 'Can you make the statement behind that question?' In other words, without avoiding the question, probe for its meaning, what lies behind it. This is not an ordinary conversation, and the client does not really expect the normal rules of polite conversation to apply. Much more likely is that the client is testing the therapist in some way. So it is important for me not to get caught in obvious traps like letting the conversation turn on to me and my experience, rather than the client's experience.

After this digression, let us get back to the question of what information we are trying to get in the initial interview. One key issue is the question of relationships – past, present and future. Relationships in the early home environment up to school age, and then relationships at school, are certainly worth getting. How many siblings, and where in the sequence the client was born, can often be significant. How the client left home, and first job and marriage details, can be of value, and also relationships with the client's own children, if any.

Why this is important is that there may be some very obvious indications there of what problems there are, and what the answers to them may be. It helps us to see which of the client's reactions to events are exaggerated, neurotic, inappropriate, and so forth, and which are thoroughly justified and healthy and appropriate. It is often helpful to the client, too, in clarifying issues and making connections.

There are even some more basic reasons for getting this information. Supposing that we see a client, and have what we think is a very good meeting, where everything went well, and then we meet someone who says 'I hear you're seeing Charlie. Did he mention that all his three brothers committed suicide?' It seems that one would feel a little foolish if this had not come out. It is something we ought to know about, because how our client feels concerning this may be one of the things we should tackle first, just to check that he is not going to do the same thing. And of course in doing this, it is very important to listen properly. And this issue of listening is so important that we need to examine it in detail.

LISTENING

Why listening is so difficult for the new therapist is because there is a lot of unlearning to be done. In most conversations, we are formulating a reply when the other person is talking, so as to be ready when he or she finishes; we are going back and forth between what is being said and our reply, so that we never really hear properly all that is said. The therapeutic meeting is very different from that:

Ordinary listening	Therapeutic listening
Interest in the content of the statement – what it is intended to convey.	Interest in the statement itself as a symptom of things the client did not intend to say.
Trying to relate the other person's experience to your own.	Not paying attention to your own previous experiences.
Thinking of interesting replies to carry on the conversation and keep one's end up.	Not being concerned with replies or conversations, only with the client's efforts at self-exploration.

It would be tedious to enumerate all the ways in which therapeutic listening differs from ordinary listening; all that is intended here is to underline the point that there is a good deal of unlearning to be done. But the other important thing to realise about listening is that there are a number of different levels involved.

Content: what is being said. The thing here is continually to push the client into being more specific. If the statement is 'People don't like me', the next question is 'Which people? Name one.' If the statement is 'I know you have to make allowances', the client might be asked to change it to 'I know I have to make allowances', or asked the question 'Who exactly says you have to make allowances?' This gentle urging in the direction of being more specific and more personal is one of the most basic moves of the therapist, as Bandler and Grinder (1975) have pointed out. It always has the effect of moving the client into deeper levels of experience.

Feelings: the feelings behind what is being said. These come out most prominently in the way things are said. If the whole tone of voice is flat and depressed, for example, that may be more important than anything the client is saying. Sometimes you can hear a kind of suppressed panic in the voice which is very characteristic once you can spot it; in such a case I would want to get the person to relax more before doing anything else. Feelings of anger (resentment, irritation, antagonism, rage, etc.) and feelings of hurt (pain, suffering, injury, etc.) can be very important, because either one can cover up for the other: in men I have noticed that it is more common for anger to cover up for hurt, while in women it is more common for hurt to cover up for anger, but it can happen either way in either sex.

It is impossible really to listen for feelings without having feelings yourself. Hence this kind of listening (sometimes called empathy) can be hard on the therapist unless the therapist has fully worked through the same level of feelings in themselves. This is one of the main reasons why humanistic therapists need to go through the whole process of psychotherapy themselves. Another reason is that therapists tend to stop clients from going into a level of feelings deeper than those which they have experienced and worked through themselves. Thus clients can be cheated of part of their own experience, if the therapist has blocks still remaining.

The body: it is possible to listen also to body language. The way that a person is sitting may be all screwed up even when what they are saying sounds perfectly reasonable. Persistent gestures can be very revealing. Expressions of the face may tell you something, but the hands and feet are much harder to keep under control: the actual movement may be disguised, but the moment when it starts can say a lot. The breathing can be very important: often by breathing at the same rate and the same depth or shallowness as the client, you can pick up something worthwhile. How the person moves may be revealing – do they talk bold and act timid, or vice versa? Many clients have a stiffness or rigidity somewhere in their body. Where is it exactly, and how do they keep it stiff or rigid, and how come it is so important not to let go of it? How does the client sit – are they tense or relaxed, or tense at some times and relaxed at others; what do they do when they are tense, what do they do when they are relaxed? And what are the moments at which they switch? The body is a rich storehouse of memories and experiences, and it can tell us a lot if we can only pay attention to it.

Sexuality: a lot can be going on at a sexual level between therapist and client. Freud pointed out many years ago that the client can virtually fall in love with the therapist, and experience this as falling in love with a parental figure, hence feelings about incest and castration can arise, which can go back to the family situation at about five years old. In this area it is important to realise that in fact the therapist can appear to be a mother or a father, irrespective of what actual sex the therapist may be. But of course other and much more directly sexual feelings may arise. The therapist may seduce the client, the client may seduce the therapist, and spontaneous mutual falling in love cannot be ruled out. All these things are harder to sort out if the therapist is not clear in this area, so again it is important for the therapist to have worked through his or her own sexual material first. A therapist who is still engaged in a personal 'search for the beloved' can be a menace to all and sundry (Russell 1993). This is made doubly difficult by the fact that the humanistic therapist often touches the client in some way, and may ask the client to take off some or all of their clothes at certain times. For these reasons it is even more important for the humanistic therapist to have gone through the full process of psychotherapy than it is for the psycho-analyst. Otherwise there is likely to be a trail of broken hearts rather than a trail of real meetings.

Spirituality: a client is a spiritual being on a spiritual path (even though they may not be aware of it yet) and some of the material they bring up may be at that level (Boorstein 1996). Jung showed long ago how dreams might reveal spiritual directions and spiritual longings which could be quite surprising to the person at a conscious level, and in recent years James Hillman (1989) has been following up this insight. Unless we are listening for these things, we are quite likely to miss them.

We can in fact help the client to get into this area by using symbols. It is often possible to ask the person to put forth their problems in the form of a drawing, or by the use of a sand-box, or through a guided fantasy, or by just asking for an image or symbol of their problem. This deliberate use of symbols does not necessarily lead in a spiritual direction, but it is very compatible with spiritual exploration, and if the person is needing to go into that sort of direction, this is likely then to show up and become workable.

Again it cannot be overemphasised that the therapist who has not worked through this material in the course of their own development is likely to stop the client going through it. As always, the therapist needs to be at least a few steps ahead of the client in order to work effectively (Rowan 1993). And this spiritual area is likely to be particularly important for creative people, or those who want to be creative or more creative. It can open a whole new way of being creative, which the person did not have access to before.

The great clarifier in this area has been Ken Wilber, who has written with enormous clarity about the exact way in which psychology and psychotherapy relate to spirituality. Anyone who wants to sort out this area of listening would do well to read Wilber (1981).

The political: sometimes the things that are bothering people are just as much political as personal. In such cases it may be advisable to suggest action other than therapy, such as joining a women's group, doing some community organising, blowing the whistle on an employer, going on a demonstration, duplicating a leaflet or whatever. It may also at times be desirable to join with the client in changing a situation which is politically oppressive (Freedman and Combs 1996). So it is necessary to be able to listen at this level, and to be able to hear the political element in what is being said. (We shall be looking at this further in Chapter 10.)

Of all the levels of listening, it is the emotional level which is the most important. It links, in a unique way, the earliest and the latest experience, the deepest and the shallowest, the most refined and the most earthy. If there is one thing the therapist has to learn, it is how to listen, and how to encourage the client to relate, at this level. And it is in the initial interview that this listening needs to start.

Of course, there may be more than one 'initial interview', because not all the essential groundwork will have come out in one session. In the next chapter we shall see how the opening moves in therapy are made over a number of sessions. But in the initial interview some structural decisions must be made, and it is to these that we must now turn.

STRUCTURE

This is an extremely important area, because it sets the scene for the whole of the rest of the therapy. It raises the whole question of what is often called the 'contract'.

The first and most important element in this is to get it clear as to what the meetings are about. Freud always used to explain his basic rule to people straight away – 'Say whatever goes through your mind.' He would embroider on this, and explain it further, but this was the basic contract.

Nowadays we tend to be a bit more aware that the client may have quite limited aims; the idea of an open-ended time-period extending into the dim future may not appeal very much. Also the therapist may not think in the long-term way that Freud did. These issues are problematic and are not to be taken for granted. Wilson (1996) has a good discussion of these issues, saying that there are several choice points where decisions have to be made about whether to continue, and how to continue.

So we need to say quite explicitly what our expectations are, and check the client's expectations to see if they are different. What I do is to suggest that we should go for a year before wondering whether the therapy is working or not. In days gone by, I used to suggest five or six meetings, at the end of which we should reconsider our practice: should we meet more or less frequently, for longer or shorter sessions, or transfer to another therapist, or end the therapy there, or what? I do not do that now, because I came to feel it was unrealistic: very often we forgot to notice the sixth meeting. On one occasion when I did remember, the client felt that I was trying to reject her.

In terms of the actual content of the sessions, I usually give the client a handout which says, among other things:

> In these sessions you will be exploring your own experience. I am just here to help you to do that, by offering the time and space you need. I can offer certain skills which may enable you to do it better or quicker than you could on your own, but basically it is you doing it, not me doing it. And unless you really treat it in that way, nothing much is going to change.

This seems to me a statement of obvious fact rather than of therapeutic policy, but it certainly is a question of policy as to whether you say that, or say something else. What can be fatal here is to make this statement too late. If, at a certain point, once the therapy has started, you say 'What do you think this therapy is about?' or 'What do you think you are doing here?', this will come across as angry and blaming, and probably will be angry and blaming.

It is very important to raise this issue early, because it immediately opens up the crucial area of what the relationship is going to be. If therapy is going to work, the relationship must be one where the client is being honest with the therapist, not censoring, not holding back, not lying. And for this to happen the client must trust the therapist. Surprisingly often, this does not happen. A survey once showed that of all the people to whom one would admit one's deepest secrets, therapists came about tenth on the list! Now it is not possible to deal with this issue completely in the first interview – trust often takes time to build up – but it would be irresponsible not to raise it at all.

Another aspect of this is the question of what relationship I am going to have with the client. And essentially I see this as a professional relationship, where I am taking the role of therapist and the other person is taking the role of client. In my experience this is often a hard point for humanistic practitioners to accept. Often we have a deeply democratic character structure, fostered by the therapy we have been through ourselves, and it offends us to enter into any unequal relationship with anyone.

Nevertheless, the relationship with the client is going to be an unequal one, and it can only do harm to pretend otherwise. This is clear from the practice of co-counselling, a system dear to all democrats, which has a very clear distinction between what belongs to one role and what to the other. It is also clear from co-counselling that this inequality does not depend on mystification or expertise or money – it simply depends on the fact that the client is the one who is working on problems, and the therapist is the one assisting the process. This means that the client is putting forward the least adequate, the sickest, the most needy aspects of self; while the therapist is putting forward the most adequate, the healthiest, the most nurturing aspects of self.

It is important to be clear that you are not necessarily any healthier than the client, mentally or in any other way. You may even be less healthy, in some absolute overall sense, and yet be able to do a good job for the client. During the session, you are laying aside your various hangups and inadequacies, or using them constructively, but you are not exploring them or abandoning yourself to them: this is the task of the client. This can actually be quite a reassuring point, because many people who want to be therapists put it off in the belief that they have to be perfect before they start. You don't. In fact, there is evidence to show that untrained people are just as effective as trained psychotherapists in getting good outcomes for clients (Durlack 1979, Hattie *et al.* 1984, Berman and Norton 1985). It is obviously a good thing to do plenty of personal work on yourself, but it does not necessarily make you a better therapist (Garfield 1979).

In fact, it is often advisable deliberately to adopt a posture of being one-down to the client, and to adopt what the Buddhists call 'beginners' mind'. This kind of flexibility enlarges my range of choices, and means that I am more manoeuvrable in what I do. It limits a therapist very much to adopt always a one-up position, though this is a great temptation for many.

There is, however, an enormous pitfall just here, which it is important not to fall into. Once we agree that the therapist–client relationship is a professional one, which is fundamentally unequal, it is all too easy to then assume that we are responsible for the client's feelings, and for the client getting better or worse. And it is in the first interview that this issue is most confusing and hardest to sort out; yet if you get off on the wrong foot it can affect the whole subsequent course of the therapy.

THE THERAPIST IS NOT A RESCUER

Obviously in the initial interview the major responsibility for gaining rapport, for getting information, for starting off the therapeutic process and for setting the structures is mine. It is my space as a therapist which is being used, my time which is being paid for, and in general I own the situation – it is my set-up, in which I can call the shots in a great many ways. But the one thing I am never – and can never be – responsible for is the client getting better. As soon as I think thoughts like 'I am going to cure this client' or 'I really want this person to get better', I am getting tangled up in a different role altogether, the role of rescuer. And the point is that you can actually be a good therapist, but there is no way of being a good rescuer.

A rescuer wants to control the other person, and get them to be the way the rescuer wants them to be. Now the object of therapy is that the client should have more self-control (autonomy, self-determination, spontaneity, access to personal power and so on, as is explained in Chapter 5), and it is counterproductive to try to achieve this by exerting control over the client. More important even than this, as soon as I have a programme for the client, or a set of aims which the client is supposed to live up to, I am storing up frustration for myself when the client doesn't live up to it, and this frustration is likely to lead to aggression against the client. I will blame the client for not living up to my programme. James Bugental puts it very well when he says:

> One of the most fundamental characteristics of the ideal therapist is a conviction, born of experience as well as of theory, that the intrinsic healing/growth process of the client can be trusted. What this means is that such a therapist knows full well that no one can heal or cure or even directly 'therap' the client. At a gut level, one learns that the only force which can produce genuine and lasting change is the power and thrust of the client toward greater realization of what is potential within. The therapist who knows this deeply does not waste her or his own or the client's time and emotions trying to do what cannot be done: solve the client's problems, guide the client's life choices, or urge forth the client's latent capacities for living more fully. Instead such a therapist concentrates on aiding the client in recognizing and releasing the blocks that keep the *aliveness* uneasily imprisoned within.
>
> (Bugental 1978: 35–6)

This has to do with the whole theory of change. One of the classic humanistic statements on this came from Arnold Beisser (1972), who wrote from a Gestalt therapy standpoint about what he called the paradoxical theory of change. He stated it very succinctly: *real change occurs when people become what they are, not when they try to become what they are not.* It can be seen immediately how well this fits in with the statement of Jim Bugental just quoted. And Beisser goes on to say that the same argument applies to social change too.

This has to do with the whole question of what therapy is about, a topic which we shall return to in Chapter 5. It is not about curing clients. As George A. Kelly beautifully puts it, the key to our destiny is our ability to reconstrue what we cannot deny. Joan was terribly abused in her own home as a child, and concluded that she was worthless. In order to keep her down, she was told over and over again that she was worthless. In therapy she learned that no matter what was done to her it didn't mean she was worthless. It was the change in meaning that did the trick. It was seeing the past differently. And it was something she had to do for herself, not something the therapist could possibly do for her. It is not the therapist's insight that does the work, but the client's readiness to reconstrue, redefine, re-experience, revise, redecide, re-view what happened in the past. And at the end of the process, the client may emerge just ordinary, as in this example:

Tom started to college during the second year he was in therapy. This was the fourth time he'd entered college. Each time before he'd given up because his need to do exceptionally well had foundered on his fear of really trying (for if he really tried and then failed he'd be shown up so terribly; while if he wasn't really trying then of course there was no real test). Now he could say, 'It's a funny experience just to listen to a professor to hear what he's saying. It may sound crazy, but I've never really done that before. I always was listening to prove to myself I already knew what he was going to say or to find out the trick he was going to pull on the exam or with the expectation that any minute I'd discover I really didn't know what it was all about and that I had no business being there at all. Now I just listen, and, you know, it's really interesting, and I get most of it, but not all, and that's all right too.' 'Now I just listen', Tom says. This is the essence of authentic being. The changed concern of authentic being is that concern is directed toward that which one is intending, not dispersed on what one may be disclosing or other irrelevant matters.

(Bugental 1981: 268)

The game of being a rescuer is well described in the Transactional Analysis (TA) Drama Triangle. The rescuer finds a victim who is suffering from a persecutor. But if the victim doesn't respond in the right way, the rescuer starts to experience the victim as a persecutor who is frustrating the whole enterprise, and starts to fight back against this. But to the victim, this seems as if the rescuer has turned into a new persecutor, so the victim has been victimised all over again. The gamelike quality of this set-up can be recognised by the fact that the rescuer is always doing a bit more than he or she really wants to, and the victim is always finding new ways of frustrating the rescuer. The only way out of a game like this is to bring in a third party who can see things a bit more clearly, and sort out the rescuer's hidden desire for control, as well as the victim's hidden desire to avoid all responsibility.

So if you don't want this to develop, it is important to avoid ever trying to rescue a client. You are there to assist the client to do whatever the client is ready and willing to do, not to know better than the client what the client needs. Every time I do something for the client, I stop the client doing it. Every time I take responsibility for the client, I stop the client taking responsibility. Every time I try to help, I get in the client's way.

Whenever someone takes over for me and tells me what to do, I find myself back as a little boy, in a dependent state. When I went to San

Francisco with a friend, she told me where to turn because she knew the streets better. I became very dependent on her, even asking for obvious directions. Actually, when she wasn't along, I got places quite well by myself.

(Schutz 1971: 113)

And this means abandoning two very seductive traps for the therapist – being right and being successful. Every time I want to be right about a client I am limiting the client to my categories and my assumptions. I am setting limits to the client's own process of change, because once I think I am right I will defend my opinion and thus find it harder to change; I won't want to be proved wrong. But in reality I don't need to be right, and I don't want to be right – I just want to stay in contact with the client.

And every time I want to be successful I am secretly working for self-aggrandisement, striding to the far shores of my profession on the stepping stones of my clients. Success and failure are both largely illusion; people develop in quite a wavy and contradictory way, and what is success on one level may often be failure on another level. It is really a mistake to use the words 'good' and 'bad' at all: every failure is a success, and every advantage is a disadvantage. All a client really needs is someone who is prepared to stay with them while they explore the darkest and most difficult parts of their experience. There is an excellent discussion of experiences of success and failure in the book by Dave Mearns and Windy Dryden (1990).

These traps do not only exist in the initial interview – they apply right through the process of therapy. But if the relationship is to get off on the right foot, it is particularly important to keep them in mind during the initial interview.

FREQUENCY AND LENGTH OF SESSIONS

A simpler structural matter is the question of frequency of meeting. Even if a few trial meetings are set up, their frequency still needs to be thought about carefully. On the whole, experience has shown that it is much better to have high frequency at first, and then relax it, rather than to have low frequency at first, and then step it up. It is more encouraging to drop the frequency, more worrying to step it up. And it is a fact that the new client coming for therapy is usually impatient: now that they have taken the decision to do something like this, they want to get on with it as quickly as possible.

Six meetings a week is almost always too much – few therapists, even of the most psychoanalytic persuasion, would have this many. Five meetings a week is traditional in psychoanalysis, but even psycho-analysts have often moved to four or even three meetings a week in recent years, and five is rather a lot for most people. Four meetings is not unusual for psychoanalysts, but it is rare for humanistic practitioners, because the average humanistic session is more intense than the average psychoanalytic therapy session. Three meetings a week is about the maximum for humanistic practitioners, and this would usually be for relatively short periods of time. Obviously the question of money comes in here. Can the client afford three sessions a week? Some compromise may be necessary between what would be ideal and what the client can manage. So very often it seems that twice-weekly sessions are set up at first, which may drop down to once a week later on, when it seems right. Once a fortnight always seems too long for real therapy, though it may be all right for a 'ticking-over' stage where nothing much is happening, but contact needs to be kept for some reason or another – and the same applies to longer intervals. If the client asks for once-a-month meetings, or something like that, it is best to query it. If it is a question of money, it is better to have a batch of weekly meetings and then a break of two or three months.

One interesting issue about this is that the longer the interval, the more time the client will have to use to tell about all sorts of incidents which have happened in the interim. This will then leave less time for the deeper material to be worked on and resolved. So when deep work is required, it is usually best to have a higher frequency of meeting or a longer session, so that the right proportion can be kept between daily experience and deep work.

On the question of length of sessions, there is tremendous variety. Many humanistic techniques, particularly the heavier ones like body work and regression, take the person very deeply into early material; it takes time to go down and time to come back up again. For this reason many humanistic practitioners favour a two-hour or even a three-hour session. I found one client worked best with a one-and-a-half-hour session. Some people working in the primal area have even used anything up to a ten-hour session.

Even with the one-hour session, which is usually most convenient for all concerned, I will always give the full hour, rather than the fifty-minute hour favoured by analysts. The reason for this is that I do not have clients coming as close together as the analyst. Freud used sometimes to have as many as ten patients a day, one after the other, and obviously if you are doing something like this, you need a break between each one to gather yourself together and maybe write up some notes. I read about some analysts in New York who see four clients for forty-five minutes each back-to-back in the morning, and another four in the afternoon. This sounds horrible to me. The much more intensive work of the humanistic therapist needs more in the way of a break than this, and usually I leave half an hour or even an hour between clients, depending on the length of the sessions. So here again it is often best to set up the longer sessions at first, and then move to the shorter ones as and when that seems possible or desirable.

FEES

The last structural matter we shall need to discuss is the question of fees. Obviously this may have been raised already, but it is material for the initial interview, and should be discussed here. At any given time, there is a 'going rate' which the therapist will have adopted on the basis of the current level of prosperity, the amount of his or her experience, the acuteness of demand for his or her services, the practice of other therapists, and so on. But nearly always this is flexible, so that a well-off person can expect to pay more, and a poor person less, than this going rate. Some therapists, including me, simply charge twice the hourly rate for a two-hour session, while others have a special rate for two- or three-hour sessions. Some therapists charge twice the hourly rate for two sessions a week, while others have a special rate for that. It is partly a matter of what kind of practice one wants, and partly a matter of what people can afford. I like to charge fees which are high enough so that I don't feel exploited, and low enough so that I don't feel like an exploiter. This is a matter which can only be settled by a sensitive discussion with the client.

Often the question arises here of 'How long does therapy take?' Evidently this has some bearing on the same fee issue, because a certain amount a week can be found for a short period, but not indefinitely perhaps. I used to be very vague about this, suggesting that symptom relief might come relatively quickly, but that deeper and more far-reaching changes might take longer. Nowadays I say that for any therapy worth bothering about, we should think in terms of a year's work together, before we start to worry whether we are getting far enough. But by the end of the year, we should have dropped down to one hour once a week. This seems to me much more realistic. The psychoanalysts tell people to expect two years' work before starting to think about any change. This is less realistic, because most patients drop out of psycho-analytic psychotherapy after less than a year's work.

A number of research studies have been done on the length of therapy (for example, see Garfield 1978) which all seem to show that the drop-out rate is very high: it is quite common for a client to come for just one or two sessions and not come back, and in a long series of studies the average number of sessions actually achieved was about five. This was mostly in public outpatient clinics, rather than in private practice, but according to Wolberg (1977) ten to fifty sessions is usual in private practice. This makes it all the more important to have a good initial interview, where the client feels welcomed and understood, and where both parties see eye to eye on what needs to be done. It can be seen now why I lay so much stress on building rapport and starting therapy within the initial interview; it is on this foundation that the therapeutic enterprise is built.

BOUNDARIES

There are certain issues which hover round the edges of the therapy which need to be addressed. A humanistic psychotherapist takes no medical or legal responsibility for the client, and does not contact the client's GP unless there is some specific reason to do so. We do not advise on psychiatric drugs, either to take them or not to take them; though of course we may mention that such drugs (a) may interfere with the aware consciousness which is optimal for therapy, and (b) have to be taken indefinitely if relied on to the exclusion of all else, because they deal with symptoms rather than causes.

It is wise for the therapist to take out professional insurance, because clients have become much more litigious in recent years, and damages can be very high in some cases. Because so many therapists are taking out insurance now, the rates have come down from what they were a few years ago.

Anything which falls outside the set framework of the sessions needs to be taken up and dealt with as an issue, even if it is very small. Such things as lateness, attempts to extend the session, gifts to the therapist, visits to the lavatory, late or nonpayment of fees, accidental meetings outside the sessions, phone calls, attempts to hug or kiss the therapist, accidental interruptions to the session – all these need to be brought into the session and dealt with as issues which may affect the relationship and may affect the course of the treatment. This can be done in such a way as not to seem like a criticism of the client, but rather an effort to understand.

The question of gifts depends rather on the value of the gift. A small bunch of flowers may be acceptable, though it should still be raised as an issue – what does it mean? A diamond necklace would be highly suspect, on the other hand. The essence of a gift is that it puts the other person in your debt. It is an attempt to extend the relationship in the sessions beyond the sessions themselves. I remember discussing the gift of a rather expensive pen to a therapist in supervision. We spent about half an hour going into all the pros and cons of accepting it. On raising the subject with the client, it turned out that he had obtained it quite cheaply, and this clarification enabled the therapist to accept it. Some of these questions are really ethical, and we shall return to them in Chapter 13.

One key thing to remember in all these areas is that there is more than one thing going on at any time within the client. Take something as apparently minor as changing the time of a session to accommodate the client. On a conscious, overt, adult level there is no problem about this – the therapist agrees, the client is grateful. But at another level – and here we may talk in various vocabularies about the unconscious, the aware-ness level, the inner child, the alternate subpersonality, the alter ego or even the Shadow – the client may feel a deep sense of the boundaries not being safe, of being given too much power, of being indulged too much, of being chosen and special, or just a vague uneasiness. It is very important for a therapist to be aware of these other possibilities, and not to assume that what appears on the surface is all there is. Sometimes it is good to change the session time to accommodate the client, and sometimes it is important to say no. Only experience – or perhaps good supervision – can inform the therapist as to which is better. We shall be looking at more supervision issues in Chapter 12.

Chapter 4

The opening sessions

Once the initial interview is over, we start the therapy proper. We now know the main lines of the client's problem, and have set up the structures within which it can be tackled. But it still makes sense to start by asking a very obvious question – 'Why do you want this treatment?' Usually something will come up which bears on relationships which the client may not have mentioned up to that point, but which may be highly relevant to the present situation. Of course, this kind of approach may not always be possible or advisable. I once had a very frightened client, who refused to take off her overcoat, sat in a very hunched position, never talked above a whisper, and never spoke unless asked a direct question, then giving the shortest answer possible. I kept on asking questions, offering her choices, feeding back my impressions of her actions, opening up spaces for her to move into, but very little happened until, after the fourth session, I walked up the road with her after the session. She was animated and talkative, and we built up rapport quickly. In the next session she talked freely about her hallucinations and the problems they had caused her, and we decided that some residential work would be more suitable for her than the once-a-week sessions we had agreed on previously. All of these moves are worth looking at in more detail.

BASIC MOVES

Asking questions is an obvious way of getting some kind of response. But open-ended questions are much better for this purpose than questions which can be answered with a yes or no. Get into the habit of always asking questions like 'What happened then?', 'What was the worst thing about that?', 'How did you feel?', 'Tell me all you can about him', 'Can you tell me some more about that?' and so on. Of course, the traditional 'Mm-hm' is always good – some noise to indicate that you are listening with interest and expecting some more. But it is no good asking questions and then not listening to the answers (this is one of the faults common to new therapists who are nervously trying to fill the silence). The object of asking questions is simply to give you something to listen to, as explained in the last chapter. The answers should be followed up in such a way as to convey to the client that you are not only listening but also hearing and understanding the replies.

There is a warning to be given at this point, however, and that is that it is usually best to avoid any question starting with the word 'why?'. There are several reasons for this: firstly, it is basically an aggressive question, suggesting that there must be an answer or explanation known to the client; secondly, it takes the client out of the level of feelings and into the level of abstract intellect; and thirdly, it is asking the client to do something which is really the business of the whole interaction – namely to get insight into the pattern of the client's life choices. In other words, the question 'why?' usually represents an attempt to cut corners in therapy, and it very seldom works. And it usually turns out, in any case, that another approach is much more appropriate and useful. If someone says 'I hate my mother!' we don't ask 'Why?', we say 'Could you express that more fully?', or 'How do you experience that in your body?', or 'Can you bring to mind a time when you felt that strongly?', or 'Would you like to go further into that?', or 'Are there times when you don't feel like that?' All these responses keep the client on the feeling level, and invite the client to go deeper in self-exploration.

There are exceptions to this general rule, and no rule should be left unexamined and untested in any case, but on the whole it is worth keeping to it.

Offering choices is usually good. These are usually things which in a group we would call exercises. But in the individual session they can be strictly tailored to the person. So you might say 'Try clenching your fists when you say that', 'Could you say that louder?', 'Say that again', 'Would you like to stand up and say that?', 'How about lying down and saying that again?', 'Try hitting the cushion', 'What do your hands want to do?' and so on. There are hundreds of these ideas, and new ones can be made up as occasion demands. They all depend on the basic idea of noticing what is going on at a physical level, an idea which was first brought into therapy by Ferenczi in the early 1920s, and greatly developed by Moreno in his quite different tradition. It is most important for the humanistic therapist to be able to pick up and use these physical cues.

Feeding back impressions can be very useful. It should normally be done in a permissive manner, rather than in a dominant way. Thus 'I wonder if there isn't some anger behind that depression?' or 'Is there perhaps someone you are being depressed *at*?' would be better than just 'Tell me about the anger behind that.' It is both appropriately modest (you can never be certain, you are always guessing to some extent) and appropriately comradely.

The general approach of the therapist is to act as a comrade engaged with the client in a common search, a common concern. It is always a question of saying 'You can do it.' You may add 'Here is a hint, try this, use this', but always in a context of trying to increase the client's choices, the client's autonomy. This cannot be done by diagnosing the client, by telling the client what is wrong with him or her, by trying to know better than the client what is going on.

Feeding back impressions can be done in ways which are imaginative, and these are often very effective. The therapist can say 'I had this flash' and then describe a symbol or image of the client, or the client's situation. The therapist can say 'My fantasy is . . . ' and tell about a scene or picture which seems to express in some way what is going on for the client. The therapist may mimic the client's posture or gesture in a way which is funny without being intentionally hurtful.

All feedback can be felt as hurtful or disturbing to the client sometimes, but if it is accurate in the first place, this hurt can be worked through successfully and can add to the relationship rather than taking away from it. It is one form of self-disclosure, particularly when it takes the form 'My feeling is . . . ' and really does reveal the therapist's own feelings.

The issue of *self-disclosure* is an important one, and needs some attention in its own right, particularly in the first few meetings, where it is most likely to arise. There are two extreme views on self-disclosure. At one extreme there is the traditional psychoanalytic view that therapist self-disclosure is out, because the ideal therapist is a mirror, merely playing back the client's unconscious fantasies. On this account, attempts by the client to relate to the real person behind the therapeutic front are always suspect, as being merely attempts to get off the hook, and play some kind of power game instead of doing therapy. At the other extreme, there is the traditional existentialist view that the therapist is first and foremost a real person, and that the whole value of the therapeutic encounter lies in the real meeting of real people in a setting where it is made hard to evade these realities.

Obviously then the psychoanalyst will avoid self-disclosure, while the existentialist will welcome it. But few of us are in the simplicity of these extremes. Most of us are somewhere along the continuum between them, with no clear place to settle and no clear position to go to. I suggest that each situation where this arises be treated as unique, and each therapeutic response be fresh, appropriate and brand-new. But there are some hints which can be given. If the request for information is basically hostile – 'I bet you have never had problems of poverty like mine; how much money do you earn in a year?' – it is usually best just to pick up on the hostility and say something like 'It seems you are angry with me; could you say some more about that?' If it seems to be a request for reassurance, a question such as 'How can you possibly understand childbirth, when you've never been through it?', then it is often possible to emphasise the difference between form and content. It is possible to have the same *depth* of experience, and therefore to be able to go down to the same *level* of feeling or pain, without having had the same specific experience. But you as the therapist have to decide whether it is reassurance the client needs, or something else. You may feel that it is best to give straightforward reassurance first, and then, if the questioning goes on, to deal with the hostility, which by then will be more obvious.

Another type of information which the client may seek consists of personal details about you: are you married or single, how many children have you got, how old are you, what school did you go to, where have you lived, are you gay and so forth. It is your choice whether to give these or not, but it is always best to probe the answer before giving it, by asking what difference it would make. This will tell you whether it was a casual question or a question heavily loaded with meaning and feelings for the client.

A further type of question may be something very immediate and direct, such as 'What are you feeling about me right now?' Rather than giving an impulsive answer to this – the first thing that pops into your mind – or giving a highly controlled answer to this – a diplomatic reply – the best thing is to give a spontaneous answer, reach into your consciousness for all that is going on in you, at every level, and integrate all those feelings, all those considerations, all those values, into your answer. Some research evidence backing up this stand is to be found in Hill (1989). Of course, one possible answer may be silence – there is no compulsion on you to answer at all – but be aware that this can be perceived as a defensive and status-conscious way of dealing with such a question.

Other questions of self-disclosure come up in connection with transference, which we shall be discussing in Chapter 7. Suffice it to say here that this is an area which can be a minefield for the therapist, and it should always be approached with full awareness of what may be at stake.

Opening up spaces for the client to move into is a very important activity for the therapist, and there are a number of ways of doing it. One of the most important is the use of symbols and images. If the client seems to have some problem with heterosexual relationships, you can say 'There are two large boxes on the ground, one with a man in it, and the other with a woman in it. Imagine that scene and tell me what happens next.'

Or if there seems to be a split or imbalance between the left and the right side of the body, you can say 'Exaggerate the difference between the two sides, so that each seems quite separate and distinct from the other. See if you can allow a symbol or image for each side to come into your mind. When you have the two clear, let a dialogue develop between them; what do they say to each other?'

Or if the client wants to escape and be somewhere else, you could say 'Close your eyes and go in your imagination to the place you would most like to be right now. Tell me what happens when you get there.'

These are just examples. Absolutely anything the client says or does can be picked up in this way and a space opened up for him or her to move into. The most general way of all is just to say 'What would you most like to do right now?' Or this can be put more negatively by saying 'Is there anything you are avoiding right now?' This all has to do with the important issue of *tracking* the client. This means staying in contact with the client, following what is going on, exploiting every opportunity to get deeper into the client's experience. This involves a moment-to-moment awareness which is actually a different state of consciousness from that which we use in ordinary conversation. It is not exactly a trance, but it is akin to certain states found in meditation, as Schuster (1979) has pointed out.

AWARENESS

A great deal has been said by various people about the importance of this kind of awareness. Perhaps John Enright (1972) puts it most clearly:

I am quite serious in asserting that most of us, including those of us in the mental health professions, are much of the time, to a surprising extent, not fully aware of our actual present. Much of the content of our consciousness is remembering, speculating, planning ('rehearsing' for our next interpersonal performance), or carrying on a busy inner dialogue (or monologue). More specifically, we professionals sitting with a patient may be diagnosing, 'prognosing', planning our next intervention, wondering what time it's getting to be, etc. – we are only too rarely being really open to our experience of self and other. Those of us who are not seriously mentally ill remain sufficiently in touch with the actual environment to move through it reasonably effectively. We respond to its salient characteristics, but miss so many nuances that our experience of the world and the other is often pale and our memories of it, therefore, weak. Engaged as we are with our own phantoms, we attend only sketchily to the other. Since he then seems rather pale and incomplete, we fill him out with our own projections and react vigorously to these. The resulting encounter often gives a convincing show of life and involvement where, in fact, there is little.

What should we be cultivating, then, instead of this? It is a state of consciousness where we are genuinely open to listen, on all the levels we mentioned earlier. Freud called it 'free-floating attention', and emphasised how it hovered evenly over the client and the therapist, being aware of what was going on in each, and between both. Reik (1948) called it 'listening with the third ear', and emphasised how important it was to stay in touch with the feelings involved, which might be beneath the surface. Rogers (1968) calls it 'intuitive sensing', and emphasises that it is the opposite of having clear-cut constructs – it is a whole person awareness, not just an intellectual awareness. Torbert (1972) just calls it consciousness, as opposed to the mystery-mastery way of thinking which he sees as much more common in our culture. It is hard to describe, but it seems that the essence of it is openness to one's own experience as well as that of the other, in a context of action. It entails a deliberate effort, in the early stages, to switch off one's own usual state of consciousness, where one is trying to be sharp and accurate and focused. It is a kind of deliberate unfocusing, which is well described in the Taoist literature (see Rawson and Legeza 1973). As long as we stay focused and single-minded, we are limited by the categories which our intellect has set up; we are at the mercy of old knowledge which has become fixed and inflexible. When we unfocus, we let in the object, and we let out our other faculties – feeling, intuition, remote associations, creativity.

The most extreme form of this type of consciousness (so that we can look at it in its pure form and then come back to the therapy situation) is to be found in the peak experience as described by Maslow (1973). Probably most of the people reading this will have had one or more of these peak experiences, where we enter what Maslow calls the 'realm of Being'. Instead of grasping and grabbing the world, we find ourselves allowing the world to come in to us, so that we can then flow out and become that world, losing our usual boundaries. Instead of focused perception, we have what Krishnamurti called 'choiceless awareness'.

Schuster (1979) suggests that this kind of awareness can be cultivated by the practice of meditation, particularly those types which encourage mindfulness and witnessing. He says:

> In this way one begins to train the mind to stay in the present moment. Likewise a 'directness of vision' develops as the meditator learns to bypass the intellectual-analytical screen of conditioned thought (Thera 1972). Reality is experienced directly and this results in a resurgence of spontaneity and freshness that has been likened to the unconditioned perception of a small child.

We must not be misled by this last phrase to imagine that this state of awareness is regressive in character, going back to some pristine state before the intellect started to do its work. We can never do that. We have to go beyond the intellect, not try to put the clock back. A small child is not aware of his or her own inner complexities to nearly the same extent that we can be. We have to bring all of ourselves into the present, not leave part of ourselves behind. The intellect is not ditched, it is transcended, taken up into a higher unity which includes it but is not dominated by it. I have explained this at more philosophical length elsewhere (Rowan 1993). But for now it is enough to say that what you should be aiming for as a therapist is to suspend thinking and to stay aware of your experience in the ever-flowing present. If you find this difficult, Torbert (1972) has a sympathetic discussion of what happened in a group who tried this together, which may help to encourage you.

EMPATHY

How does this relate to the more traditional (for humanistic practitioners) category of accurate empathy, so much emphasised by Rogers (1961) and his followers (Truax and Carkhuff 1967) and rivals (Egan 1994)? Truax and Mitchell (1971) define empathy as the moment-by-moment exploration of another human being by viewing that person's world from his or her perceptual and emotional perspective. In other words, we put ourselves into the other person's shoes. This is really a two-step process of acceptance followed by understanding:

> Acceptance does not mean much until it involves understanding. It is only as I *understand* the feelings and thoughts which seem so horrible to you, or so sentimental, or so bizarre – it is only as I see them as you see them, and accept them and you, that you feel really free to explore all the hidden nooks and frightening crannies of your inner and often buried experience.
>
> (Stevens and Rogers 1967)

In this sense empathy is one of the three conditions which Rogers says are necessary and sufficient for good therapy; the other two are therapist genuineness and nonpossessive warmth. The research evidence (Parloff *et al.* 1978) doesn't support the view that this is all there is to therapy, but empathy has been generally accepted as an important nonspecific factor (that is, it runs through all forms of therapy, including psychoanalysis and behaviour modification) which is ignored at the therapist's peril. In 1979 Daniel Hogan, a Harvard-based attorney-therapist, published four scholarly volumes called *The Regulation of Psychotherapists*. They constitute a comprehensive review of research on effective psychotherapy, as well as a history of legal disputes involving the regulation of psychotherapists. In this authoritative work Hogan identifies empathy as the most important ingredient in effective psychotherapy.

The point made over and over again by Rogers is that it is no good being empathetic if there is no evidence of it for the client. In other words, we have to show our empathy by saying something or doing something which shows that we are on the client's wavelength. Interestingly enough, Matarazzo (1978) reports research showing that the therapist must not interrupt the client if a good rating on empathy is to be obtained. The client needs to be heard out, and the response given after a pause.

Empathy, then, has been studied a great deal and a lot is known about it. It is important to emphasise that empathy is acting 'as if' we were the other person, without ever losing sight of the fact that we have remained ourselves. It is therefore much less threatening than what we have earlier called full awareness, where we do run the risk of actually becoming one with the other person, and deliberately run that risk. It is also different from what Watkins (1978) calls 'resonance'.

RESONANCE

Watkins believes that a person has various ego-states. Each of these ego-states is like a person. This is very similar to Berne's idea (1972) about Parent, Adult and Child, and Assagioli's ideas (1975) about subpersonalities, though more similar to the latter. According to this approach, when we are in a particular setting, we put our energy into the ego-state suitable for that situation. In the case of therapy, the therapist sets up an ego-state corresponding to the client and puts energy into that. In that way the therapist can be with the client from the inside, and share the client's subjectivity. So resonance is: that inner experience within the therapist during which he co-feels (co-enjoys, co-suffers) and co-understands with his patient, though in mini-form.

Now this is a pretty startling claim. One of the things which we learn in philosophy classes, and which Gestalt therapists hold particularly dearly, is that no one can feel another person's pain. This is dogma to many people, and it used to be dogma to me too, until a woman once explained to me patiently that a mother who couldn't feel what her baby was feeling would be severely handicapped in her efforts to relate to that baby. If we don't feel other people's pain, it is because we don't want to; it is more easy and comfortable to cut off from them. But any time we want to do it, we can; it is a natural human ability which we all have. Watkins explains it using the analogy of two pianos which are put side by side; if you then hit the 'A' on one piano, the 'A' string on the other piano resonates in sympathy. He goes on to say exactly how resonance differs from empathy:

> Rogers says that empathy means the *understanding* of the feelings of another. He holds that the therapist does not necessarily himself experience the feelings. If he did, according to Rogers, that would be identification, and this is not the same as empathy. Resonance *is* a type of identification which is temporary.
>
> (Watkins 1978)

And similarly, he argues that resonance is not the same as the psycho-analytic notion of counter-transference, which we shall be discussing in Chapter 7. Recently Alvin Mahrer, in his book *The Complete Guide to Experiential Psychotherapy* (1996) has argued very vigorously in favour of his version of this, which he calls experiential listening.

There are three separate things, then, to which the therapist can pay attention in the general area of relating to the client. All of them involve abandoning the ordinary state of consciousness in which we carry on our daily conversations with other people. Empathy does this a little, resonance does this a little more, and awareness of the full kind we have described does it still more. There are various scales for measuring empathy, and Watkins has developed a scale for measuring resonance, but to the best of my knowledge full awareness has not been measured yet.

GENUINENESS

What about the other conditions which Rogers recommends as being essential to the therapy process? Genuineness (which Rogers has also called 'congruence') is a quality of the therapist which consists in being aware of one's own feelings and one's own process, at the same time that one is in contact with the client. It is a question of doing justice to oneself in the same way that one tries to do justice to the client. The therapist is completely open to his or her own experience. It is important to note here the close connection between congruence in this sense and authenticity:

> It is my feeling that congruence is a part of existential authenticity, that the person who is genuinely authentic in his being-in-the-world is congruent within himself; and to the extent that one attains authentic being in his life, to that extent is he congruent.
>
> (Bugental 1981, p.108)

So congruence is a human quality, not a skill to be switched on and switched off. We cannot fake genuineness, and if we try we shall only produce a phoney performance which fools no one.

Note that Rogers is not advocating that the therapist should blurt out feelings at all times but simply that the therapist should be aware of them, and allow the whole situation to determine whether they are uttered or not, and if so, how. The important thing, Rogers says, is to be real.

WARMTH

It has often been pointed out that this demand of Rogers can conflict with his other requirement, that the therapist demonstrate nonpossessive warmth (which he used to call 'unconditional positive regard'). If I am supposed to be real, and what I am really feeling is cold or hostile, doesn't that conflict with the warmth I am supposed to show? Let us see what Rogers (1961) says:

It involves . . . genuine willingness for the client to be whatever feeling is going on in him at that moment – fear, confusion, pain, pride, anger, hatred, love, courage or awe. It means that the therapist cares for the client, in a non-possessive way . . . By this I mean that he does not simply accept the client when he is behaving in certain ways, and disapprove of him when he behaves in other ways.

This attitude of the therapist was phrased by someone else as 'I care, but I don't mind.' That is, I care about you, but when you do something bad, wrong or stupid it doesn't hurt me, it doesn't make me suffer – I won't add my evaluations to your burdens. And this comes out of the basic outlook held by all humanistic practitioners, that each human being, deep down underneath it all, is all right. There is a basic lively health and intelligence there which we can believe in, and rely on. So we may as therapists have all sorts of negative feelings of our own, but these do not contradict our basic respect for the wholeness of the other person.

It is important to emphasise the word nonpossessive in this however. There is a kind of warmth which comes across as very possessive – a kind of seduction, where the therapist is making emotional demands on the client to respond in a warm way. There is a big difference between being warm yourself, and expecting the client to be warm in return. Rogers says: 'It involves an acceptance of and a caring for the client as a *separate* person, with permission for him to have his own feelings and experiences, and to find his own meanings in them' (1961).

This seems clear enough, and perfectly nonseductive, but in practice it seems that quite often the therapist can go much too far *in the eyes of the client*. Frankland (1981) suggests that there are many parallels between courtship and the gaining of rapport in therapy. In both cases there is an initial nervousness which develops gradually into trust; in both cases there is an increase in the giving of more and more intimate information about oneself; in both cases there are body signals of high arousal, such as pupil dilation and colour in the face. If the client is misled by such reactions into thinking that there is a sexual element coming to the fore – a sexual relationship in the making – then this may put them off, even to the extent of making them withdraw from therapy. Frankland also suggests that there are many parallels between the early stages of therapy and what Argyle (1967) calls 'affiliation' – that is, making friends. In other words, the client may pick up the cues given by the therapist as meaning that the therapist wants to be friends; but this is not so, and quite inappropriate expectations may result from this. Friendship is a much more two-way thing than therapy, and also a much more informal thing.

Friends spend time with each other for the company and for relaxation, rather than for concentration on some task, and so this model again would not be helpful for the pursuit of good therapy. Thirdly and finally, Frankland suggests that even more than sex or friendship, the warm approach of the therapist may set up expectations of dependency:

> Analysis of this part of the pattern of non-verbal cues in the therapeutic interaction leads to the quite unoriginal conclusion that many clients will perceive their relationship to the worker in terms of a dependent pattern of caring, modelled on parent–child transactions (1981).

So what he is saying is that the perception of the therapist's behaviour, both verbal and nonverbal, may very easily be diverted in these three ways: into a sexual pattern, into an affiliative pattern, into a dependency pattern. If 'warmth' is taken in the proper Rogerian sense, as prizing the client's separateness and individuality, this is not so likely to arise as if the new (or old) therapist acts in a seductive manner, trying to extract warm responses from the client.

But there is really no way of totally preventing such misconceptions and such misperceptions. Certainly we can become more aware, as therapists, of the implications of our body language, and more aware of our secret desires for intimacy or domination or indeed for sex; but ultimately we cannot stop the client getting the wrong message completely. This is just one of the many issues which can arise between therapist and client, and which all have to be dealt with in the same way – by bringing them to the surface and enabling them to be worked through.

Frankland would no doubt reply to this that he is seeking for relationship styles which are living and potent but which are not essentially friendly, dominating or seductive. And he would emphasise that his main concern is for the new client who does not come back for a second or third interview, rather than for the client who is already coming regularly. Here we must leave the point, but it is evident that it can be a very important one.

DEPTH AND SURFACE

These three variables – empathy, genuineness and nonpossessive warmth – are the established and so-called traditional nonspecific elements in any therapy; in other words it does not matter what approach you adopt, these will be important in any case. But there is a newer one, pointed out most clearly and succinctly by Bandler and Grinder (1975). This is based on a distinction between depth and surface structures in grammar and communication. If we assume that the sentences actually spoken by the client represent the surface structure, and that the deep structure underlying that represents what the client really meant to say, we can look at all the client's sentences as symptoms. Each sentence will reveal in some way the client's own way of distorting his or her own experience when communicating it. But in order for it to be possible for the therapist to detect these distortions, it is obviously necessary for the therapist to be able to compare the surface structure with the deep structure. This the therapist does by looking for gaps in the communication – words which appear to fill the necessary spot in the sentence, but which actually say nothing.

For example, suppose the client says 'I can't relate to people', the therapist immediately notices that the word 'people' actually represents a gap. It is a way of *not* saying who the client can't relate to – a way of covering up feelings which may be painful. But it is precisely these painful feelings which need to be brought out into the open if the therapy is to proceed; they are the main material which needs to be worked with. So the therapist says 'Which people?' or 'Who in particular?' or 'For example, who?' or 'Who is the person you would most like to relate to?' This then takes the client down to a more emotional level, and puts the client in touch more with his or her deep structures – the real meaning of what is being said.

Another example is the case where the client says – 'When you come into a room full of people you feel nervous.' Here there is a gap where the word 'you' is used. It can't mean the therapist; it can't mean humanity in general; it presumably means the client. But it is a way of avoiding the feelings which are personal about this, by spreading them around in an indeterminate way – a kind of mental fog hides the gap. So the therapist would say 'Do you mean that you personally feel nervous?' or 'Who feels nervous?' or 'Could you say that again, this time using the word "I" instead of "YOU"?' or 'See what it feels like to say the word "I" in that sentence.'

This is a very simple technique to use, and it does not contradict the tenets of any form of therapy known to me. It is particularly useful in the early sessions, when you as the therapist may be quite reluctant to use any techniques which seem out of the way or odd.

One of the most important things in therapy, however, is something so simple that it is easy to overlook. It is the therapist being there. If the therapist can be there, then the client can more easily be there too. Jim Bugental puts it like this:

A therapist facilitates the client's fullest use of the capacity for inward searching through (a) identifying the resistances which block the search process; (b) through insisting on the necessity for the client's being as fully and genuinely present as possible; and (c) through persistently taking the client and what the client says with complete seriousness.

(1978: 55)

We shall be seeing more about this in later chapters, but let us just focus for the moment on presence. Ronnie Laing often used to speak about the importance of the therapist being truly present with and for the client. Bugental again clarifies the matter:

Presence is immensely more than just being there physically, it is obvious. It's being totally in the situation . . . Presence is being there in body, in emotions, in relating, in thoughts, in every way . . . Although fundamentally presence is a unitary process or character-istic of a person in a situation, accessibility and expressiveness may be identified as its two chief aspects.

(*ibid.*: 36–7)

Accessibility and expressiveness – how important these are, and yet how rarely they are referred to or properly given their due weight. For a humanistic practitioner, they are crucial. Primarily it is for the therapist to be accessible, and for the client to be expressive; but it is equally important in humanistic eyes for the client to be accessible and for the therapist to be expressive. We have no place for the passive or mirror-like therapist.

All the time in therapy we are trying to get the client to get closer to his or her own experience – all of it – rather than holding it at a distance or suppressing some of it or distorting it. Rogers (1961) has a good discussion of the stages which any therapy goes through, where the client starts by seeing all the problems as external, moves to seeing some internal problems in the past, then moves to seeing some internal problems in the present, and finally moves to seeing that it is possible to live fully in the present. This sequence – from external to internal and from past to present – seems to be common to all forms of therapy. And the technique, of using the surface structure to dig down into the deep structure, seems tailor-made to help this process in a very simple and direct way. Just as presence also leads in this same direction. This leads us on to the whole question of what therapy is about. What is the actual process, and how does it work, and what is it aiming at? This is what we shall look at now.

Chapter 5

Aims

As we saw in Chapter 3, it is important for the therapist not to get attached to the notions of success and cure. These are not things which the therapist can ever be responsible for, and it only leads to frustration and disappointment for the therapist who sets these things at the forefront of consciousness. It is the client doing it, not the therapist doing it.

Nevertheless, it is inevitable that the therapist always has some idea of where the therapy is going. In the moments when teaching is going on, the therapist actually tells the client something about this direction and rationale. But even if this never happens, the therapist does already have some background of theory and knowledge which suggests a certain set of aims.

BACKGROUND CONTRASTS

Psychoanalysis has quite limited aims. The remark of Freud about exchanging hysterical misery for ordinary unhappiness has often been quoted, as also has his dictum about the eventual outcome for the client being the ability to love and to work. Other phrases used include 'Where Id was, there shall Ego be' and 'making the unconscious conscious'. All this suggests that the ultimate goal of psychoanalysis is adjustment to the current social order. As Malan (1979) puts it, the aim is 'changing maladaptive into adaptive behaviour'. Another therapist (Kapelovitz 1976) who seems very typical says: 'The main goal of psychotherapy is to decrease the patient's symptoms while increasing his self-understanding, improving his interpersonal relationships and enhancing his capacity to deal with new problems.' The patient has let his mental/emotional life get out of hand, and now a 'corrective emotional experience' is going to put things right again. Society is basically seen as right, and the patient wrong; it is the individual who must adjust to society, and not the other way round.

Behaviour therapy and behaviour modification also have limited aims. They too see the individual as in need of being put back on the track of normality. The individual has somehow engaged in faulty learning. But what has been learned can be unlearned; new ways of behaving can be induced which will be more adaptive and more adequate to the world which exists. Lakin Phillips (1977) says that behavioural psychotherapy aims at 'skill development, positive problem solving and greater behavioural adequacy'. And of course these disciplines are even more limited than psychoanalysis, since they usually set up precise targets and have no place for the psychodynamic aspects of the person.

In recent years the cognitive behavioural tradition has become much more popular, as is witnessed by such books as Dryden and Golden (1986). This again has quite limited aims. The typical statement is that the client is encouraged to state specific outcome goals, which the therapist endeavours to help the client to achieve. The drawback with this is that the client's goals may be just as much a product of mental distress as anything else about the client. It also assumes that the client is consciously aware of the ultimate goals, which may not be true.

THE HUMANISTIC APPROACH

The humanistic psychotherapist has unlimited aims. What we do is to set the client's feet on a path which has no finite end. This path does, however, have certain recognisable way-stations, and one of these is by far the most significant from the point of view of what can be achieved in humanistic therapy. This is what we call the real self.

The notion of the real self is one of the most characteristic of humanistic concepts. But it is not unique to us. The chart which follows on p. 74 demonstrates that numerous writers have expressed some version of this idea.

What all these investigators are saying is that the ordinary ego which is presented to the world, and which other people know us by, is false. It is a made-up thing, a mask, a fiction. We may have spent many years building it up, and have invested a lot of energy in it, but it is unreal. Benson (1974) calls it the Public Relations Personality, and emphasises how desperately it depends upon other people's opinions. It essentially arises out of an attempt to protect the real self from pain. It puts up boundaries and walls between the various parts of ourselves, so that pain will not be felt, or so that familiar pains are held on to lest they turn into

	Central	Peripheral
C.G. Jung	Self	Persona
A. Adler	Creative self	Guiding fiction
P. Federn	Id	Ego-states
F.S. Perls	Self	Self-image
R. Assagioli	I	Subpersonalities
D. Winnicott	True self	False self
H. Guntrip	Primary libidinal ego	Internal objects
R.D. Laing	Real self	False self
A. Janov	Real self	Unreal self
J. Love	Primal intent	Conscious will
R.E. Johnson	Real self	Symbolic self
P. Koestenbaum	Transcendental ego	Empirical ego

something worse. A common way of representing this is by way of the concentric ring diagram (see Diagram 5.1). This diagram can be made much more complex. Lowen has one with four rings, Perls one with five, and Elliott has one with ten, but the basic principle can be well illustrated with these three.

Diagram 5.1

Most of us are quite conscious, as soon as it is pointed out, that our positive self-image is an illusion, but our next thought is that underneath this we are bad. Each person has a different notion of what this badness is, but the three most common feelings about this are:

(a) If they knew how nasty (evil, bad, horrible, hating) I really am, they would all hate me;

(b) If they knew how inadequate (weak, worthless, inept) I really am, they would all reject me;

(c) If they knew how needy (insatiable, sucking in and then destroying, attracting and then devouring) I really am, they would all avoid me.

In extreme cases, we may even believe all three of these things at the same time! All three of them pertain to the false self and its definitions of the world.

It is because we are aware (perhaps vividly, perhaps only vaguely) that we are bad behind our façade of goodness, that we resist therapy. The discoveries we might make, once we start questioning our false front, might be too terrible to bear. The false self defends itself against such discoveries. And so people put off therapy like they put off going to the dentist – until the pain gets to be too much to bear.

But humanistic psychology says that underneath all this positive and negative stuff there is the real self, which is perfectly OK. We will have to work through the good and bad stuff to get there, but this will be all right, because the bad stuff is just as illusory as the good stuff. It, too, was just a story we made up and lived out for neurotic reasons. It is no more fundamental, no more basic, than the positive self-image which it balances.

Our prime aim, then, in humanistic psychotherapy, is to enable the person to get in touch with their real self – to gain an actual experience of the real self. And so we encourage clients all the time to question all – all without exception – of the taken-for-granted images of themselves, having only quite a limited degree of respect for their defences.

DEFENCES

This question of defences is one of the key areas where we differ from the psychoanalysts, and it is easy to see why. Psychoanalysis, as put forward by Freud, has no notion of the real self. (Though this is not true of some of the later people such as Horney and Winnicott). Consequently it takes the negative self-image as being the basic truth about the person, and sees the person as a permanent battleground for good and evil. The good Ego must be strengthened and buttressed against the evil Id. Certainly the way of doing this is not the blind suppression which we find so often prescribed by more ordinary teachers, but a much more sophisticated 'know your enemy' investigative weakening process which involves getting to know the Id much better; but still defences are going to be necessary, only perhaps healthy ones like sublimation or suppression rather than unhealthy ones, like projection and repression.

But we don't have any need for defences in our system, because the person would only be defending themselves against their own real self – and there is obviously no point in that. So our policy in regard to defences is continually to chip away at them, in a manner and at a speed which is only limited by the need to maintain rapport between therapist and client. We obviously don't want to be hurtful to the point where the client breaks off therapy. And in this respect we are exactly like the psychoanalysts: we pay a lot of attention to the quality of the relationship. I suspect that the same is true of a good behaviourally-oriented or cognitive psychotherapist, even though it forms no part of their theory.

Humanistic psychotherapy, then, is a process of questioning all that is false in the person, and its object in doing that is to lay bare what is true in the person, in the confidence that what is true in the person is always OK.

THE REAL SELF

So what is this real self, and what does it feel like to open it up? This whole area has become a lot clearer since Ken Wilber (1980, 1981) defined the centaur level, as distinct from the mental-ego level on one side and the transpersonal level on the other. What we are dealing with mainly and essentially in humanistic psychotherapy is this centaur level. This level is variously referred to as the 'integration of all lower levels' (Sullivan *et al.* 1957), 'integrated' (Loevinger 1976), 'self-actualising' (Maslow 1968), 'autonomous' (Fromm 1941, Riesman 1954), 'with individual principles' (Kohlberg 1969), 'growth oriented' (Alderfer 1972), 'integrating persons' (Mahrer 1989) and so on. Broughton (1975) in his research found that this stage was one where 'mind and body are both experiences of an integrated self'. And Wilber (1980) says: 'This integrated self, wherein mind and body are harmoniously one, we call the "centaur". The centaur: the great mythological being with animal body and human mind existing in a perfect state of at-one-ment.' What this achievement of integration brings with it is a great sense of what the existentialists have called 'authenticity'. And indeed the existentialist thinkers have done a great deal to outline this stage in some detail. According to general existential thought, when an individual's self is taken fully as autonomous, he or she can assume responsibility for being-in-the-world. And if we do this we can, as Sartre put it, choose ourselves. Here are some other existentialist texts to give the flavour:

The 'I' casts off its shells, which it finds untrue, in order to gain the deeper and authentic, infinite, true self.

(Jaspers 1931)

Before his death, Rabbi Zusya said: 'In the coming world, they will not ask me: "Why were you not Moses?" They will ask me: "Why were you not Zusya?"'.

(Buber 1961)

Free and alone, without assistance and without excuse.

(Sartre 1959)

Rogers is one of the great fathers of humanistic psychology, and he certainly saw the matter in this way, as can be seen in all his writings. Here is a passage in which he is most explicit about this:

> I have been astonished to find how accurately the Danish philosopher Søren Kierkegaard pictured the dilemma of the individual more than a century ago, with keen psychological insight. He points out that the most common despair is to be in despair at not choosing, or willing, to be one's self; but that the deepest form of despair is to choose 'to be another than himself'. On the other hand 'to will to be that self which one truly is, is indeed the opposite of despair', and this choice is the deepest responsibility of man.
>
> (Rogers 1961)

What we are saying, then, is that the real self which we are aiming at in humanistic psychotherapy is not something very abstract and hard to pin down – it is situated very concretely both in the empirical realm of psychological research and in the conceptual realm of philosophy. It is contrasted very sharply and clearly with the aims of other forms of therapy, though it is closest to existential psychotherapy, as described by Friedenberg (1973):

> the purpose of therapeutic intervention is to support and re-establish a sense of self and personal authenticity. Not mastery of the objective environment; not effective functioning within social institutions; not freedom from the suffering caused by anxiety – though any or all of these may be concomitant outcomes of successful therapy – but personal awareness, depth of real feeling, and, above all, the conviction that one can use one's full powers, that one has the courage to be and use all one's essence in the praxis of being.

And this means that there are certain things which the real self certainly is *not*. It is not the transpersonal self, the higher self described by Assagioli (1975) and others. It is not the ultimate all-embracing God of Christianity, Judaism or Islam. It is not the ultimate formless void of Eastern mysticism and the perennial philosophy. It is simply the real self – that which was buried and put away as being too weak and too vulnerable for everyday life. We put it away, very often in a moment of panic or terror, because that seemed the only way to survive. We developed enormously effective systems of blocking it off and pretending it was not there. But at certain moments – often called peak experiences – we get back that freshness of experience, that marvellous sensitivity to the world.

When we get close to the real self in therapy it feels awfully dangerous to go any further. This is for two different reasons: firstly, the way in lies through all our most negative self-images, which have been experienced as painful and shocking, and so we are scared of meeting even more, even dirtier secrets as we dig down further; and secondly, there seems to be something 'ultimate' about the real self, so that when we get to it, it seems like a breakthrough into a whole different world. We are promised that this different world will be better, but it is the difference which appals us. It seems that we almost have to die to get there. In fact, Alvin Mahrer (1996) has been quite explicit about this.

Getting close to the real self, then, almost inevitably brings with it feelings which have to do with extreme good and extreme evil, with Heaven and Hell, with death and destruction as well as with life and growth. And in fact, contact with the real self is often experienced as a breakthrough. Finding suddenly that we are able to let go of all those false pictures of ourselves which the mental ego took for granted can bring feelings of bliss or ecstasy. An example:

> Then one cold Saturday in February we had an all-day [primal] marathon and I had the most profound experience of my life. On that day I fell in love for the first time. It was the first time because my head, heart and body were involved. I was no longer stone cold rigid and unavailable. I experienced my own beauty that day, as a woman, as a person. I really felt it on the inside. I loved everyone *as they were*. With each person and with each moment I was different. I saw their perfection and I also saw their limits. I was not judging. I was just appreciating. I went through a door to a place I could only call whole, clear vision. A sight that sees all undisturbedly. The endless self judgements had quieted. I was. I felt very young, open, vulnerable, not afraid and at peace.

It doesn't have to happen that way, but I have seen that sort of thing happen many times in therapy, and it is genuinely impressive when it does take place. A common image for this process is the dark tunnel which we go through, sometimes in a boat. The darkness which we have to go into may seem very frightening and very hard to enter. But once the journey actually begins, it then seems easier than we thought. We see a light at the end of the tunnel, and when we come out, it is into a bright world where a sun or star or moon illuminates everything. We then rise to that light and become one with that light. It is then that we experience the ecstasy.

Now these images – both the descent into darkness and the ascent into white light – are essentially spiritual images. They are found in many accounts of religious experience of a mystical kind worldwide (e.g. Cohen and Phipps 1979). And this has deceived many people into thinking that this ecstasy is an experience of God. Obviously this attracts some people and repels others; it is hard to be unbiased about something like God, which has aroused so much passion and so many wars down the centuries. But when we look more carefully at the matter, we find that any breakthrough into a new awareness or a new consciousness brings with it these same feelings of exposure to danger, of possible death, of falling through the bottom into infinite emptiness. And so at this relatively early stage on the spiritual path, where all we are discovering is the real self, it is important not to kid ourselves into a belief that we are entering some high mystical state. It is really what the Buddhists call the 'pseudo-Nirvana' (Goleman 1978). This is rather a put-down phrase, and there is really nothing pseudo about the experience, so long as we do not mistake it for what it is not. Actually it is very important, because it allows us, for the first time, to have a genuine experience of who we are, underneath all the trappings and all the roles. Dick Anthony and his colleagues state that these are 'glimpse experiences' on the psychospiritual path, and very much worth having (Anthony et al. 1987). Who we are is perfectly ordinary and perfectly ecstatic at one and the same time. The earlier experiences of the real self – which tend to last for short periods only, which is why they are called peak experiences – are often more ecstatic; the later experiences of the real self become more ordinary, partly because ecstasy becomes more ordinary, and partly because we are getting ready for the next breakthrough.

This is important too: the discovery of the real self is not the only and final breakthrough, as the diagram earlier in this chapter suggested. We can go on working on ourselves, if we want to or need to, either in the same way (psychotherapy) or by using methods like guided fantasy, meditation or prayer. And in these ways we can experience even bigger and more difficult breakthroughs (see Diagram 5.2). However, because this book is about therapy and not about the committed path of spiritual development, we shall not deal with these higher levels here. The interested reader is directed to Ken Wilber (1980), where these matters are dealt with in admirable clarity.

the real self

the higher self

the divine self

the Ultimate

Diagram 5.2

James Bugental (1978) has an interesting discussion of these matters, and talks about levels of therapeutic goals. Level 1 is adjustment – the minimal removal of symptoms without any real change of outlook. Level 2 is coping effectiveness – the idea here is that the person can cope better than before. Level 3 is ego renewal – the person feels refreshed and more able to face the world. All these three are labelled as deficiency-motivated – that is, they go from a need to a goal in a very direct way. All forms of therapy have to cover these levels, but the humanistic practitioner prefers the ones following these stages. Level 4 is growth in personal and interpersonal actualisation – the person has moved on from one outlook to a new one, where the old ego dominance is not so strong. Level 5 is existential emancipation – this is what we have referred to as the centaur level, the discovery of the real self. Level 6 is transcendence – we are ready to move on in our psychospiritual development. This second set of three levels is labelled as growth-motivated. This seems to me a practical and helpful set of distinctions, and obviously the form of therapy will differ depending on which level one is tackling.

The real self, then, is not an ultimate stage of development. It is not strange, alien or mystical. It is just the innermost and truest part of the separate individual, seen still as a separate individual. It can be described as the existential self, or the integrated bodymind centaur. And as such it offers a centre for the full integration of the person, as has been very thoroughly discussed in Mahrer (1989), particularly in his chapter on the 'optimal state'. What this means is that the usual splits which are found in so many people, between body and mind, intellect and emotions, duty and inclination, top-dog and underdog and all the rest, can now be healed very simply. It may take a little time to work through all the implications of this healing of the splits, and there may be some painful choices to be made along the way, but the essential barriers to full integration have now been removed, and the process is not so hard as all that.

And this means that the person now experiences a sense of personal power (Rogers 1978) which is quite different from the old kind of power associated with the mental ego. Power at the mental-ego stage is always power *over* other people; power at the real-self stage is power *with* others. And this means that the whole person is acting at once, with no splits, no reservations and no holding back; this is the 'spontaneous will' described by Rollo May (1969).

Yet sometimes it can be quite ordinary, as we saw in Chapter 3. The way Bugental puts it is modest indeed:

> Intensive psychotherapy of the sort discussed in this book is not a problem-solving technique. Not infrequently, the client at the end of several years of hard, costly, demanding work will recognize, 'I still have the same hang-up I had when I came, but somehow it seems different now, smaller, less threatening. It's like it's remained the same, but I've grown so much larger, so it doesn't seem so important or bothersome any more.'
>
> (Bugental 1981: 60)

This is also amazing, but in a much quieter way, which does not arouse the same high expectations as some of our earlier formulations. Perhaps all we can say is that the person who realises their own reality is in a better position to choose, to learn, and to be, and to be with another person.

This is the aim of humanistic psychotherapy.

SOME QUESTIONS ANSWERED

Q. It all sounds very male to me. All this autonomy and independence. A mother with a baby couldn't afford such luxuries.

A. In describing something as tricky as the real self, I didn't want to obscure the main lines by bringing in too many qualifications and implications. But you are right to be suspicious. Some humanistic practitioners have gone much too far in emphasising autonomy at the expense of everything else. The most famous of these was Fritz Perls. In his teaching he constantly emphasised 'moving from other-support to self-support', and his 'Gestalt prayer' is all about independence. In his life he was unable to have close relationships with other people – his wife found it best to live 3,000 miles away on the other side of the country. And in his death it is related that, sick and in hospital, he was taped up with tubes coming out of him and being given oxygen, when he tried to get out of bed and the tubes started to pull out, and the nurse said 'Dr Perls, you have to lie down.' He looked at her and said 'Don't tell me what to do!', and died.

I think the positive moral of this story is that we need nourishment as well as autonomy. Just because we have found our real self doesn't mean we don't need nourishment. And self-actualising people, as Maslow suggested, can be good choosers choosing good food, good companions, good work, good art and so forth, which will be beneficial, both to them and to those around them. So, we can be good at providing ourselves with the nourishment we need, not ignoring or setting aside any of our needs, and not denying our dependency needs. It seems much more important to satisfy our dependency needs in an elegant way than to pretend we don't have them at all.

Q. Isn't it very dangerous socially, to encourage this kind of personal power?

A. No, because during the process of working with the real self, consciousness changes. The mental ego is mainly either existence-oriented or relatedness-oriented (Alderfer 1972). If existence-oriented, then the main concern is with power, mastery and control. If relatedness-oriented, the main concern is with conformity to people or standards. But in either case the main motivation is fear. The concern with power, the concern with conformity and standards, are both based on a dualistic conception of the world, where one part is supposed to control another part. And the reason why A has to dominate B is because A is afraid of B. Diagram 5.3 gives possibilities for what might fill the role of A and what might fill the role of B.

A	B
Rulers	Ruled
Conscious	Unconscious
Mind	Body
Intellect	Emotions
Parents	Children
Whites	Blacks
Men	Women

Diagram 5.3

When we emerge into the integrated world of the real self, however, all this changes. Instead of a dualistic world we see things in terms of ecological systems. Instead of fear being the dominant emotion, we can be open to a whole wide variety of feelings, all of which can be allowed into conscious awareness. Instead of trying to control emotions, we let them all have their say, but in such a way that they flow and integrate with all of the other things which may be going on, such as ideas, aims, needs, ideals, motives, other emotions and so on. Our new diagram might look more like Diagram 5.4. We can explore the whole of our land – it all properly belongs to us. We start out from safety, but in order to grow we need to make journeys away from Mother's Knee. Each time we move towards the dangerous sea, we break down existing structures, and every time we move back towards the safe sea, we build up

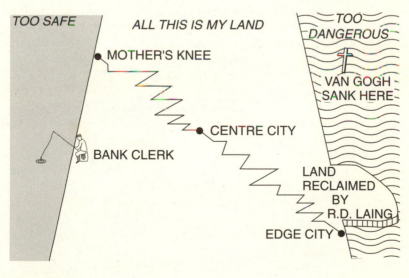

Diagram 5.4

structures. We make our home at a point which is not too safe and not too dangerous. If we want to make an expedition towards the dangerous coast, it is a good idea to take a guide – someone who has been there before. It is possible, as R. D. Laing did, to reclaim some of the land from the sea; it turns out to be not as dangerous as we thought, once someone has the temerity to do what is necessary. But it is also possible to go too far out, and not to be able to get back – perhaps this is what happened to Vincent Van Gogh.

If we can see the world in this way, the question of personal power becomes much more easy to handle. We are just not so panicked by the issue. It becomes something we can discuss without being scared all the time about the implications. Just because this new personal power has been gained by a total integration of the person, it takes more into account than the old mental ego was ever able to do. And because more is being taken into account, action is more rational (in the best sense of that word) and more adequate in social terms. We can act spontaneously and well at the same time.

Q. You talk about the mental ego as if this was something we could just dump and get rid of. Does this mean we have to be egoless? I have never met an egoless person.

A. It is certainly true that we have to put the whole mental ego into question in a radical way, without any reservations. The mental ego wants to reduce things to its own terms so that it does not have to change in any fundamental way. It likes to reduce things to a formula or form of words, so that it can say 'The real self is nothing but . . . ', and retain its equanimity. But the point is that the real self has to supplant the mental ego as the centre of the person, as Wilber explains (1980) in detail, and that this feels like death to the mental ego. No wonder it objects! No wonder that even a really healthy mental ego becomes quite irrational when faced with this prospect. So the doubts which you feel about the real self cannot ever be resolved by mental-ego language and explanations – only by experience, and experience which seems very unsafe and very risky, going from the known to the unknown. And this is the same for each further breakthrough along the path.

Work by Hall (1977), Miyuki (1979) and Marlan (1981) suggests that it makes sense to say that the ego is never given up – all that happens is that false images of the ego are abandoned, and we end up with a new and improved ego. In one sense the real self is non-ego; in another sense it is the very core of the ego. Edinger (1960) calls this the basic paradox of therapy. If this were true, it would mean that the mental ego is transcended and transformed, rather than left behind. It is not dumped or got rid of – *it just feels to it as if it had been*. Wilber is very clear (1980) about this process, and talks about the death-seizure of the mental ego. But this is an illusion; the ego does not really die – it just has to change, by removing some of its boundaries, some of its assumptions, some of its identifications.

Q. You said that the aims of humanistic therapy and growth were unlimited, but now it seems as if the real self is itself limited; it is not the end of the road at all. Yet this is all you are aiming at, isn't it?

A. Yes, you are right. There is a contradiction there, but it is a creative contradiction. By saying that the aims are unlimited, we wish to make it clear that if someone wants to go beyond the real self, that is fine with us. We may not be so much help at that stage, because the person may be looking for a spiritual teacher rather than for a therapist, though in fact the best spiritual teachers often seem to behave rather like the best therapists, as Alan Watts (1961) and Levin (1981) both point out. But some humanistic practitioners do in fact go into the transpersonal area which lies beyond the real self. Transpersonal psychology forms a kind of bridge between what is properly psychological and what is properly spiritual. Psychosynthesis (Assagioli 1975) is very much in that position, making heavy use of symbols, which are ideal for this Janus task of facing towards the psychological for one set of people, and towards the spiritual for another set. But it seems clear that moving on from the real self to the higher self is just as problematic, just as difficult, just as much of a breakthrough, as moving on from the mental ego to the real self was. In fact, more so.

Chapter 6

Ways and means

Over the past thirty years or so, an enormous number of new techniques have been introduced by humanistic practitioners. In this chapter we want to look at just the main categories of work, giving references to more detailed sources as appropriate.

One way of breaking up this field is that used by William Swartley, in a privately-circulated handout from 1977 (see Chart 6.1) which takes the four functions mentioned by Jung – sensing, feeling, thinking and intuiting – as the basis for division. This does not mean that Jung is a humanistic psychologist – simply that he has contributed a usable idea.

SENSING

Many of the humanistic techniques start from the body. As we saw in the last chapter, the integration of mind and body is crucial to the aims of the humanistic practitioner, so it is not surprising that the body can feature so directly in therapy. Wilber (1979) points out that our whole culture encourages us to see ourselves as sitting on our bodies as if we were a horseman riding on a horse:

> I beat it or praise it, I feed and clean and nurse it when necessary. I urge it on without consulting it and I hold it back against its will. When my body-horse is well-behaved I generally ignore it, but when it gets unruly – which is all too often – I pull out the whip to beat it back into reasonable condition.

Indeed, Wilber goes on, our bodies seem to just hang on underneath. We don't approach the world *in* our bodies but *on* our bodies. We are up here, in our heads, and it is down there. Our consciousness is almost exclusively head consciousness – we *are* our heads, but we *own* our bodies. There is a boundary between us and our bodies – a boundary which is like a fissure, a split, or as Lowen (1967) calls it, a block.

Chart 6.1 Historical components of primal integration (William Swartley, PhD) 1977

Primary process techniques

Techniques which depend primarily on Jung's:

Secondary process techniques

Sensing function	**Feeling function**	**Thinking function**	**Intuiting function**
	Cathartic Method Breuer and Freud 1880–1889 An active provocation of emotional abreaction via hypnotic suggestion	*Psychoanalysis* Freud 1900–1939 Passive, non judgmental acceptance of **verbal** behaviour in order to get material for rational analysis of dreams, transference, and similar unconscious behaviour	*Analytical Psychology* C.G. Jung 1875–1965 Intuitive and semirational analysis of dreams, active imagination
Birth Trauma Theory Otto Rank (student of Freud) *Trauma of Birth* 1924			
Psychodrama J.L. Moreno 1892–1974 Structured provocation of acting our emotional behaviour on a stage		*Child Analysis* Melanie Klein 1920–1960 London (student of Ferenczi) Rene Spitz 1945–present	

Chart 6.1 continued

Primary process techniques

Character Analysis
Wilhelm Reich
1920–1957
Systematic provocation of emotional discharge via massage of chronic muscular tensions

Bioenergetics
Alexander Lowen
(student of Reich)
1965–present
Further systematised Reich's use of the body in psychotherapy, especially with bodily stress positions

Gestalt Therapy
Fritz Perls
(student of Reich)
1936–1970
Combined stage techniques with an active dream analysis technique

Client-Centred Therapy
Carl Rogers
1951–1987
Introduced a more active acceptance of emotional during psychotherapy

Secondary process techniques

Group Analysis
W. Bion
1948–1979
Tavistock Clinic
(student of M. Klein)
Analysed the psycho-dynamics of the interaction between the members of a group of patients

Group Dynamics and T-Groups
Kurt Lewin
1920–1947
Introduced feedback of group dynamics of the group

Directed Fantasy
Robert Desiolle
1938–1966
Paris
(influenced by Jung)
Technique permits much active participation of the therapist during the therapy via manipulation of symbols

Chart 6.1 continued

Implantation Trauma
R.D. Laing
1976–1989
Introduced importance of the implantation of the fertilised egg on the uterus 8 days after conception

Encounter Movement
1963–present
Combined T-groups, Gestalt Therapy, Carl Rogers' value systems, Maslow's humanism, oriental religions, etc. into a group which accepted a wide range of behaviour

Transactional Analysis
Eric Berne
1910–1968
Simplified Freudian theory for use in groups

Psychosynthesis
Robert Assagioli (friend of Jung)
1920–1974
Popularised transpersonal values and related techniques

Primal Therapy
Arthur Janov
1970–present
Popularised the re-emergence of cathartic techniques

Developed and systematised his method to include:

First Line Primals
(bodily sensations such as a 'birth primal')

Second Line Primals
(emotional catharsis)

Third Line Primals
(Freudian-type insight)

Primal Integration
Developed by the Staff of the Centre for the Whole Person
(Broder, Freundlich, Smukler, Swartley, etc.) 1962–present

Combine all the above techniques plus additional techniques:

Sensing Techniques
1 Primal Massage of muscular 'triggers'
2 Intensification of symptoms
3 Massive skin contact

Feeling Techniques
1 Intensification of
a. acting out
b. transference
c. incest

Thinking Techniques
1 Deconditioning of interpersonal phobias

Intuiting Techniques
1 Completion of dreams with guided fantasy
2 Acting-out a fantasy
3 psycho-ritual
4 Group-guided fantasy
5 Pre-conception primals

Chart 6.1 continued

Sensing function	Feeling function	Thinking function	Intuiting function
Usual phylo-genetic order of development of the functions:			
1st to develop	2nd to develop	3rd to develop	4th to develop
Usual centre in the brain (of the right-handed person) of the functions:			
Lower brain stem	Limbic system	Left hemisphere	Right hemisphere(?)
Usual SYMBOLIC centre functions in the body:			
Sense organs, especially in the skin and internal senses	'Guts' (stomach) Heart	Head (brain)	'Third eye' or above the head
Typical symptoms of fixated development (blocked maturity) of the functions:			
Birth trauma Maternal deprivation syndrome Surgical trauma Umbilical affect Depressive position	Hysteria Incest trauma Oedipus complex Paternal deprivation	Pseudo-rational symptoms: Obsessions Compulsion Delusions Paranoia	Blocked creativity and/or religious development

Chart 6.1 continued

Preferred Treatment of fixated development (blocked maturity) of the functions:

Abreaction of painful sensations followed by substitution of positive sensations	Abreaction of painful feelings followed by substitution of positive feelings	Analysis of transference dreams and free association Ego states	Guided fantasy Art therapy Meditation Dance therapy Sand play

Goal of treatment of fixated development (blocked maturity) of the functions:

Complete a sensation and replace with new sensations	Complete an emotional reaction and replace with new feelings	Change a destructive logical conclusion	Change a symbol

Major limitation of techniques outlined above:

Catharsis alone does not change behaviour without re-education (second-chance family)		Insight does not necessarily change behaviour	Creative and religious development does not necessarily change other behaviour

So all the 'sensing' approaches start off by encouraging awareness of the body. One of the simplest ways of starting this is the Gestalt approach, where you ask the client simply to pay attention to what is going on right now:

Get in touch with [whatever is coming from your senses] from inside, gently – like getting acquainted with it. Stay in touch like a spotlight that doesn't push anything around and doesn't keep anything the way it is. 'Stay in touch' means so lightly that if somewhere else in your body calls – any kind of pain or tension or discomfort – you can move to it, as easily as moving your eyes from a window to the door. Let the pain be. If it becomes more intense or less intense, let that happen – or any other changes. Let be what is . . . No straining, no pushing, no *trying* in that sense . . . No jumps, jerks, pushing, persevering or holding on.

(Stevens 1975)

This is a good method of approaching the body, because it is non-threatening in its invitation. It can lead to deep feelings coming up sometimes, but that is not the aim. The aim is simply that the body be allowed to exist and have its say. Awareness is enough.

Another very simple way of getting in touch with the body is to get the client to try the three-step exercise of Masters and Houston (1978):

1 Take an imaginary walk, trying to notice what you do while you are walking. Come back to where you started, and reconstruct what you did.

2 Now actually get up and walk around, paying close attention to your movements and sensations. Come back to where you started, and recollect what you did in detail.

3 And now be aware of your present position and sensations in detail.

Again this is very simple and non-threatening, but a few questions will be enough to show how out of touch we are with our bodies. Questions suggested include the following:

When you got up in imagination, what did you do? When you started walking, which foot took the first step? When you turned, did you turn to the left or to the right, or perhaps left on one occasion, to the right on another? Whatever you did, it will have been the same as what you normally do when you walk. While the left foot and leg were going forward, what were you doing with the left arm? As you were walking, what part of your foot made contact with the floor first, and what part left the floor last? . . . When you got up to start walking, did you use one or both arms to help you, how did you use them, and did you use first one and then the other, or one more than the other? Did you push down harder with one foot, and if so, which one? As you walked, what were the feelings in the ankles, the knees, the hip joints, the shoulder joints? How extensive were the movements in the joints? How freely did your arms swing? Did you notice what direction you turned in, and what you did with your hands and arms, your shoulders, your neck and head, and your eyes, when you turned? Were you aware of your breathing, whether it was free or whether you held your breath as you tried to concentrate on your movements? Were you, until now, aware of your breathing as you tried to answer these questions?

This is a very simple exercise, yet most people are shocked to discover how few of the questions they can answer. This demonstrates how little attention we normally pay to our bodies. Becoming aware of this is one of the first steps towards changing it.

Of course this simple awareness of the body, which seems so easy, but which actually has been made very difficult for us by our cultural assumptions, has been noticed by Eastern thinkers. The Buddhist concept of mindfulness is particularly relevant here, and also Gurdjieff's concept of self-remembering, derived from Sufi thinking.

The humanistic therapist, however, sometimes goes further than this, and actually touches the body of the client. The skin covers us all over; it is the oldest and most sensitive of our organs, our first medium of communication, our boundary and protection:

> In the evolution of the senses the sense of touch was undoubtedly the first to come into being. Touch is the parent of our eyes, ears, nose and mouth. It is the sense which became differentiated into the others, a fact that seems to be recognised in the age-old evaluation of touch as 'the mother of the senses'.
>
> (Montagu 1978)

As babies, we all have strong needs to be held and touched and cuddled. If these needs are not met, we may go through life looking for the touch we missed. Marc Hollender's research, as reported in Montagu's excellent book referred to above, demonstrates this very explicitly. More informally, Harvey Jackins (1965) said that everybody needed four good hugs a day to keep mentally healthy. Eric Berne (1972), speaking in metaphors, says 'If you are not stroked, your spinal cord will shrivel up.'

So when the therapist touches the client, something very powerful can be set in motion, and it always needs to be carefully considered. The psychoanalytic point of view is that touching is always sexual, and that it puts too great a strain on the transference. There were great battles between Freud and Ferenczi over this issue. But because we have a different attitude to transference (see Chapter 7) we do not have to rule out touching.

However, it is essential to recognise that there is a sexual aspect to touching, and that you as a therapist need to have worked through your own feelings about being touched in therapy before starting to touch anyone else. And it is important that just because touching is sexual, that does not mean that it is necessarily genital. As Alan Watts once pointed out, sex is like a long French loaf: one end is the lightest possible contact, like a warm handshake or a peck on the cheek, and the other end is full sexual intercourse with orgasm. We often make the mistake of thinking that if we go further than the one end, we have to go all the way to the other end, in an automatic kind of way. But in reality there is all the rest of the loaf to be explored and used – all sorts of degrees of non-genital sex. We are entitled to all of that – not just the two ends.

Touch can be used in therapy in a number of different ways. Lowen (1976) makes the interesting point that a client often has a great need to touch the therapist, but feels that this is not allowed:

> To overcome this taboo, I often ask a patient to touch my face while he is lying on the bed. I use this procedure after I have opened up some of the patient's fears. Bending over him, I am in the position of a mother or father looking at the patient as a child. The hesitation, the tentative gesture, the anxiety this manoeuvre evoked was surprising to me at first. Many touched my face only with their fingertips, as if afraid to make full contact with their hands. Some said they were afraid of being rejected; others said they felt they had no right to touch me. Without encouragement few felt they could bring my face close to theirs, although this was what they wanted to do. In all cases this procedure went to the depths of a problem that could not be reached by words alone . . . Getting in touch with me as the therapist may enable clients to get more in touch with themselves, which is the goal of the therapeutic endeavour.

This leads on to another use of touch which is very often useful. If the client is crying, and seems to need encouragement to go deeper, it is often good to reach out and give a light hold to the shoulder or upper back. This gives reassurance of the therapist's presence and support without interrupting the flow of feelings. It is important not to hold or cuddle the client at such times, unless the client actively seeks it out. Holding the client with a lot of body contact can stop the flow prematurely. Let the emotional discharge build to a climax and resolve itself through catharsis (Nichols and Zax 1977). *Then* warmth and cuddling may well be in order, though not necessarily so.

Another use of touch is to go directly into muscles which are tense. Usually the client can point to the tense spot and guide you to it. With experience, you can feel it for yourself. One approach developed by Gerda Boyesen (1970) is to apply gentle circular strokes to the tense areas. These are brief and there is a pause between strokes so that the body has time to react fully. The client is encouraged to breathe from deep down in the abdomen. More about this technique is to be found in the excellent chapter by Clover Southwell (1988). It must be emphasised that *none* of the techniques mentioned in this chapter should be carried out by anyone untrained in their use. Boyesen gives the case of a young woman who experienced ten days of almost constant nausea, vomiting and diarrhoea after her shoulder had been treated in this way.

With tense muscles, another approach (developed by Reich and taken further by Lowen, Kelley, Keleman and others) is to press firmly on the tense part.

> For example, screaming is blocked by muscular tensions in the throat. If a firm pressure is applied with the fingers to the anterior scalene muscles along the side of the neck while the person is making a loud sound, that sound will often turn into a scream. The scream will generally continue after the pressure has been removed, especially when there is a need to scream. Following the screaming, one moves into [the conscious ego layer] to determine what the screaming was about and why it was necessary to suppress it.
>
> (Lowen 1976)

The view here, of course, is that the muscles have been used in the client's defensive manoeuvres, and that by working directly on the defences in this way, we can get very quickly to what is really going on. And in fact this approach does very often get into deep material very fast – sometimes too fast for the material to be accepted and integrated, so that the client gets very scared. The therapist must again be thoroughly familiar with these sudden and profound effects, if this technique is to be used effectively. Variations on this are helpfully described by David Cranmer (1994) and by William West (1994). Breathing is of course an important issue in body work, and William West says: 'Over my years of work as a Post-Reichian therapist I have rarely found anyone who could breathe well, easily able to inflate both chest and abdomen.' I would confirm this from my own experience.

An even deeper form of touch is used in Rolfing. Ida Rolf (1978) invented a method which she called 'structural integration', which involves correcting all the ways in which the body has become distorted through experience, actually rearranging the muscles at a deep level. This is very specialised and needs very specific training. As done by Ida Rolf herself, it caused a good deal of pain, but some Rolfers recently have developed a more gentle form of it, which does not cause pain at all. A related form of therapy is Postural Integration, and Jack Painter (1986) has written an excellent account of this.

There are other body approaches, such as those of Kurtz and Prestera (1977); Moshe Feldenkrais (1972); Matthias Alexander (1969); Lulu Sweigard (1974); Magda Proskauer (1977); Lillemor Johnsen (1979a, b, c, 1980) – an excellent summary of these may be found in Dreyfuss and Feinstein (1977). In contrast to this approach is the body work developed by a few German women, including Elsa Gindler, Magda Proskauer, Marion Rosen, Ilse Middendorf, and Doris Breyer (Moss 1981). Their work promotes mind/body awareness and integration using such techniques as movement, touch, natural breathing, sensory awareness, and voice work. These are much more nonstressful and nonpainful practices. Some of the earlier work was very 'masculine' and almost violent, but in recent years we have all relaxed and become more 'feminine', relatively speaking.

Some valuable positives and negatives about working with the body are contained in Chart 6.2, which is largely derived from Dreyfuss and Feinstein (1977).

Since about 1985, there has been much more suspicion of touch in therapy, because of the increased awareness of sexual and other childhood abuse first drawn to our attention by Alice Miller. Book after book came out detailing the things which can go wrong in therapy because of sexual exploitation of the client by the therapist (Russell 1993). In addition to that, clients have become more litigious and aware of their rights, and therapists no longer feel as invulnerable as they did. Petruska Clarkson (1995) has a whole section on the 'vengeance of the victim', where she says that 'a clinical practice is now developing which I would call "defensive psychotherapy"', where therapists deliberately censor themselves in the light of possible later criticism. She says that in the USA some insurance companies will not insure a therapist against malpractice if they touch their clients at all.

Chart 6.2 The body

MY BODY IS ME
One of the key insights of the centaur phase is that the self is one with the body. This represents a healing of the split between mind and body which is so common in Western experience and theory. Overcoming this split is a very important stage in development.

MY BODY IS A MAP OF MY PAST
We respond to life events with our whole bodies, and if the events are traumatic the body often records those events by certain patterns of tension. We hold the tension by tightness or flaccidity in certain parts of our bodies. This results in extra sensitivity or extra insensitivity in those parts.

MY BODY IS A MAP OF MY LIMITATIONS
Moreover, this can also result in a whole pattern of holding, which becomes a character type. There are eight basic character types in this sense.

MY BODY IS A MAP OF MY POTENTIALS
My deeper potentials, which are the key to my development, are registered in my body. Working on my body inevitably puts me in touch with these potentials.

MY BODY IS A MAP OF MY UNIVERSE
If I am in contact with myself, I am in contact with my world. The relationship I have with myself is the relationship I have with the world. It starts with me. And it also seems to be true that by simply paying attention to this, transcendental experiences will also come to me.

WAYS PEOPLE GROW
There are two main things we can work on in working with the body: unhindering and unfolding.

Unhindering
Here we are working with the person's hangups and problems – the things they are are aware of and dissatisfied with. The body may be badly aligned and in chronic tension. Or it may simply be that there is a lot of blocked energy of one kind or another, which needs to be released.

Unfolding
The natural potentials of the person will come forth as growth work progresses. Awareness is one of the most important things here. And nurturing relationships are also important.

DANGERS AND TRAPS
There are a number of traps it is easy to fall into when working with the body.

The destroy-the-defence game
Always keep in touch with what the client is really ready for, and don't push on at a pace which is fine for you but too much for the client. Don't pull green apples.

Chart 6.2 continued

The flying chair
Be careful that you only use techniques you are really familiar with yourself. Otherwise you may release much more energy than you expect,
frightening yourself and the client.

Flying high without ground control
It is important to be grounded when working with high-energy techniques.
One good rule, for example, is to keep eye contact at all times, and not to
let the client go off into unknown spaces.

Liberated soul for a day
Pushing for peak experiences without working through all the problems
and impasses of ordinary therapy can produce experiences, all right, but
they do not last. It is better to work gradually through, arriving at peak
experiences in their natural order.

The laying on of the trip
Don't get too enthusiastic about a method which works well with one
person. It is not necessarily the best thing for the next person. Take your
cue from the client, not from the last workshop you went to.

My guru is better than your guru
Don't be intolerant of other systems than the one you learned first or best.
Every approach is good for some people and not for others.

But it is possible to work with the body without touching it. An
interesting version of this is to be found in the work of David Grove
(Grove and Panzer 1989). He will take a bodily sensation such as
tightness in the chest and work with it on a metaphorical level.

> *Client*: I have a tightness in my chest.
> *Therapist*: And you have a tightness in your chest. And when you
> have tightness in your chest, that's tightness like what?
> *Client*: Like a rock.
> *Therapist*: And a rock. And when it's like a rock, what kind of rock
> is that rock?
> *Client*: A hard rock.
> *Therapist*: And a hard rock. And when it is a hard rock is there
> anything else about that hard rock?
> *Client*: Nothing can break it.
>
> (Tompkins and Lawley 1997)

The therapist then continues to explore the symbol of the hard rock by
asking further questions, until some kind of transformation takes place.
This is a surprisingly effective way of working, and works simply by

taking the bodily sensation seriously and working very directly with it, taking it where it needs to go.

The work of Arnold Mindell also works without necessarily touching the body, but just following the promptings of the physical sensations experienced by the client. His excellent and very helpful book *Working with the Dreaming Body* (1985) is packed with examples of how he works on this level.

FEELING

This is the approach where we start from feelings. Probably the best-known of all the humanistic approaches is Person-Centred therapy. Carl Rogers (1961) emphasised the healing quality of simply paying real attention to the client's feelings. We have already seen in Chapters 3 and 4 how important this approach can be in the early hours of the therapeutic relationship. It can of course be made the basis for the whole therapy, but many practitioners feel that it is too slow for them. Akin to the Rogerian approach is the Gendlin (1969) approach, which he calls 'focusing'. This is based on the idea of the felt experience as a kind of summing-up of the whole weight, size and pattern of a particular person or situation. The theory here is that the felt experience is prior to any analysis or intellectual elaboration, and that if we can get a shift at that level, we can do what is essential in therapy. This shift in experiencing is ultimately what therapy is all about; it is not a matter of having better conceptualisations at an intellectual (what we earlier called the mental-ego) level. So the client is encouraged to feel meanings rather than just intellectualise about them.

Another approach which is superficially similar to Rogerian counselling and therapy and to Gendlin's focusing is Harvey Jackins's 're-evaluation counselling'. This way of working, which is more informally known as co-counselling, lays great stress on emotional discharge as the key to therapeutic change. And because it is a method developed by Jackins (1965) for use by lay-people with just forty hours of training, it lays a great deal of emphasis on positive feelings and a light touch. One of the key differences between the co-counselling approach and the Rogers or Gendlin approach comes in the treatment of self-put-downs. The earlier approach is to go down with the client into his or her bad feelings, on the grounds that it is only when these have been fully explored that the positive impulses can be voiced. The Jackins view, however, is that the counsellor should lighten the darkness by contradiction (getting the client to say the opposite, or to repeat the accusation in a funny way, or to boast about the fault); or validation, where the client has to say how good or right or marvellous he or she is. This brings about a *balance of attention* between the distress material and the current situation here in the room, and this is the optimal condition for therapeutic change to take place. Jackins is admirably clear and succinct as to what he is about, and has done a lot to demystify therapy. A good account of some of the current versions of co-counselling which have developed in recent years is contained in the two special issues of *Self & Society* which appeared in 1980 (vol. 8, nos 4 and 5).

One of the most-used of the feeling therapies is Gestalt therapy, as developed by Fritz Perls (1969a,1972,1975). It is important to realise, however, that what most humanistic practitioners use is not Gestalt therapy in its pure state, but rather certain specific techniques lifted out of Gestalt therapy and used in a much more eclectic way.

Gestalt therapy in its pure state focuses almost exclusively on the here and now. How is the client sitting? Breathing? What are the client's hands doing? Eyes? Feet? All these things are part of who the client is and how the client functions. The tone of voice is very important: the hesitations, the changes in pitch and volume – listening to the music as much as to the words. 'We have to become aware of the obvious. If we understand the obvious, everything is there' (Perls 1976). Perls didn't ask the client in his demonstrations what the problem was; he got the client to talk about the here and now, and then worked directly on what came up. Neither did he tell the client what the problem was – he just encouraged to emerge whatever was ready to emerge.

This is not the place to describe Gestalt therapy in detail. All I want to say is that what most humanistic practitioners do is simply to use one of the techniques from Gestalt therapy: that of the empty chair or cushion. Perls used to use chairs, because of his generation and history, but it is really better to use cushions, because they are more flexible and make more distinctive and colourful anchors. All you do as a therapist is to wait until some conflict emerges, as 'on the one hand this, on the other hand that' or as 'part of me wants to do this, and another part of me wants to do that', and then to put one side of the conflict on one cushion, the other side on the other, and let a dialogue take place between them. Anything can be put on a cushion – people, things, events, times, qualities, expressions:

Okay, I would like you to put phoniness in that chair; talk to phoniness . . . Now let's finish up by putting that smirk in the chair. Talk to your smirk . . . Put the old man [in the dream] in that chair and compare him to me. What are the similarities, what are the differences? . . . Can you talk to that memory once more? Change seats. Be the memory . . . Say, bye-bye memory.

(Perls 1976)

This is an enormously flexible technique, which can be used at the drop of a hat. It is used in self-help groups (Ernst and Goodison 1981) a great deal, and comes very easily once it has been experienced. Some people initially find it very artificial, and say they can't or won't do it. The answer to this is always to use it for the first time with a naïve client when the client has already said something like 'It is as if there were two voices inside me'; this makes it really easy to get into this way of working.

Another way of getting round objections to this empty chair technique is for the therapist to role-play. This is one of the techniques also used in co-counselling, and it is quite easy to do. Let us say the client is talking about his or her mother. You can say 'Imagine that I am your mother, and talk directly to me.' This gets the benefit of eye-contact as the action proceeds, which for some clients is more powerful anyway.

Feelings usually appear in the first instance in mild ways. It may be just one word or phrase that seems to have a little extra charge behind it. Both in co-counselling and in Gestalt therapy one of the most basic moves is to ask the client to repeat such a word or phrase, continuing with it as long as there is energy behind it. This often results in a deeper feeling being expressed, which was not apparent at first. A great deal of therapy consists in turning molehills into mountains: the reason why this works so well is because they really were mountains in the first place – they were just pretending to be molehills. The best account of the actual psychodynamics involved here is to be found in Mahrer (1989).

One of the best ways of picking up something small and amplifying it is through the use of images. I do this a lot. For example, Jean had the experience of feeling a weight in her stomach, with waves going through it – something like an orange, with green waves flowing past it. I got her to draw this with felt pens on paper. I then put the paper on a cushion and got her to talk to it, and then talk back, in the usual Gestalt dialogue. This resulted in a very strong interaction, which led into a piece of deep work.

You can even use images when the person is stuck completely. Bill was bothered about women, but could not get any clear line on what was going wrong. I asked him to imagine two large boxes. One contains a man, the other a woman. What happens next? He told how they climbed out of the boxes, the man fucked the woman, then departed. What did the man feel? Disappointed and unsatisfied. This opened up the area for a much deeper exploration than we had been able to do up to that time. Shorr (1972) has a whole host of suggestions along these lines, which are very usable in brief and informal ways.

A similar and even more effective approach is that of Allen (1982) which I have been using recently. Joe complained of a pain in the neck. I asked him to focus on the exact pain, and ask it a question. He asked 'What are you?' I then said – 'After repeating the question three times with intensity, relax and let go into a place of not-knowing, where you don't know the answer and you are not trying to figure it out or logically deduce it. [Pause] Now be aware of the next experience that comes up for you, and get in touch with it as openly as possible. [Pause] Now draw or write on this sheet of paper what you have experienced.' Then I put the drawing (of a gateway, in this instance) on to a cushion and invited Joe to talk to it, and this became a very valuable dialogue.

More recently, David Grove has been describing a way of using imagery which has the power to work completely through a trauma without the therapist needing at any time to know what the trauma actually is. He turns the physical experience in the present into a metaphor, and then works with the metaphor, using what he calls 'clean language' – that is, language which does not assume anything, which does not put any idea into the client's mind, and which sticks to the age to which the client may have regressed. Grove and Panzer (1989) have a clear account of how this is done, and make it clear that this approach is particularly suitable for cases of sexual abuse in childhood.

It is important in all this work to make it easy for the client, so that there are no awkward transitions. It is very disruptive if the client suddenly decides that the whole exercise is nonsense or artificial. So you build into your instructions just sufficient scaffolding to hold the thing up. For example, Ellen talked about having a fog between her and other people, and I wanted to put the fog on the cushion. So I said 'Let's imagine that we can put the fog on to this cushion [bringing the cushion into position] and that by some miracle you can talk to it, and it can talk back if it wants to.' If she had said 'I don't know if I can do that', I would have added 'Just imagine it's a character in a play, called "Fog", and it's coming on to play its part.'

What we are trying to do all the time is to bring something which is hidden out into the open a bit more, so that we have a chance to see just how big or small it is, how important or unimportant, how shallow or deep, how much feeling is attached to it or bound up with it.

Similarly if a word or phrase is uttered with a certain gesture, you can ask the person to exaggerate the gesture more and more, until the feeling behind it comes out. What we are trying to do all the time is to get down to the roots of the affect tree. The lower we go down on the tree (see Diagram 6.1) the more basic and single-minded are the feelings, and the closer we are to the real self. The crucial step is the realisation of total aloneness – 'I'm all I've got!' This brings a feeling of excitement, which is perhaps the most basic feeling of all. But it can either be negative excitement – how terrible, how awful, how dreadful – or positive excitement – what joy, what bliss, what ecstasy! It is this switch from negative to positive which is the most fundamental move in therapy. As Mahrer (1989) puts it, we have to embrace and love our deeper potentials; the moment we can genuinely do this, they change from negative into positive. For an example of this sort of thing, see Example 6.1.

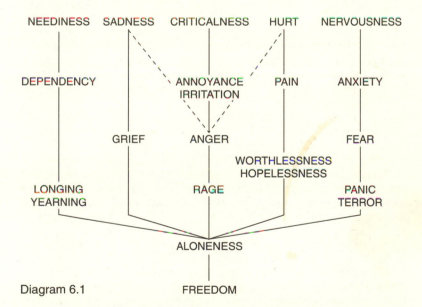

Diagram 6.1

One of the best and most direct ways of getting back to this point is through the process of regression. In regression we take the client back to the earlier days of life. The person who has done most to establish the importance of regression is Arthur Janov, and his book *The Primal Scream* (1973) is one of the most moving documents in the whole literature of therapy.

Example 6.1 The 'I am' experience

In the hope of making clearer what it means for a person to experience his own being, we shall present an illustration from a case history. This patient, an intelligent woman of twenty-eight, was especially gifted in expressing what was occurring within her. She had come for psychotherapy because of serious anxiety spells in closed places, severe self-doubts, and eruptions of rage which were sometimes uncontrollable. Her mother, in periods of anger, often reminded her child of her origin, recounted how she had tried to abort her, and in times of trouble had shouted at the little girl, 'If you hadn't been born, we wouldn't have to go through this!' [In therapy, she had this experience.] It is reported here as she wrote it down from memory and notes two years later.

I remember walking that day under the elevated tracks in a slum area. Feeling the thought, 'I am an illegitimate child.' I recall the sweat pouring forth in my anguish in trying to accept that fact. Then I understood what it must feel like to accept, 'I am a Negro in the midst of privileged whites.' Or 'I am blind in the midst of people who see.' Later on that night I woke up and it came to me this way, 'I accept the fact that I am an illegitimate child.' *But* 'I am not a child anymore.' So it is, 'I am illegitimate.' That is not so either: 'I was born illegitimate.' Then what is left? What is left is this, '*I Am*'. This act of contact and acceptance with 'I am', once gotten hold of, gave me (what I think was for me the first time) the experience 'Since I Am, I have the right to be.'

What is this experience like? It is a primary feeling – it feels like receiving the deed to my house. It is the experience of my own aliveness not caring whether it turns out to be an ion or just a wave. It is like when a very young child I once reached the core of a peach and cracked the pit, not knowing what I would find and then feeling the wonder of finding the inner seed, good to eat in its bitter sweetness . . . It is like a sailboat in the harbour being given an anchor so that, being made out of earthly things, it can by means of its anchor get in touch again with the earth, the ground from which its wood grew; it can lift its anchor to sail but always at times it can cast its anchor to weather the storm or rest a little . . . It is my saying to Descartes, '*I Am, therefore* I think, I feel, I do.'

It is like an axiom in geometry – never experiencing it would be like going through a geometry course not knowing the first axiom. It is like going into my very own garden of Eden where I am beyond good and evil and all other human concepts. It is like the experience of the poets of the intuitive world, the mystics, except that instead of the pure feeling of and union with God it is the finding of and the union with my own being. It is like owning Cinderella's shoe and looking all over the world for the foot it will fit and realizing all of a sudden that one's own foot is the only one it will fit. It is a 'Matter of Fact' in the etymological sense of the expression. It is like a globe before the mountains and oceans and continents have been drawn on it. It is like a child in grammar finding the *subject* of the verb in a sentence – in this case the subject being one's own life span. It is ceasing to feel like a theory toward one's self . . .

[Case vignette from Rollo May (1983) *The Discovery of Being*, New York: W W Norton]

But the best explanation of what regression is all about is to be found in Stan Grof (1975). He says that you don't just find an emotion hanging around loose, as it were. It is attached to a situation, and forms a definite pattern, which he calls a COEX (short for constellation of condensed experience). Now the important thing about a COEX is that it is one of a long line, a chain of similar experiences. Events from different life periods are linked together by the common feeling which runs through them – an identifiable felt sense. And the links lead back to the oldest experience, usually traumatic, of the sequence. The oldest event that forges the prototypical pattern forms the nucleus of the COEX – the core of the whole neurotic system.

When encouraging a client to regress, it is not necessary to give them LSD, or to hypnotise them, or to make them breathe in a particular way, or anything else of that nature. All that is necessary is to give the client permission to regress as far back as necessary.

For example, a client might talk about a small incident at work, being criticised by a superior. The feeling associated with this could be expressed in the words – 'It's not fair.' The client is then invited to get in touch with this feeling, to experience the weight of it, the size of it, the colour of it, the texture of it, the sound of it, the taste of it. Then comes the request 'See if you can allow yourself to go back to another time when you had that same feeling.' The client might then go back to a time in adolescence, and be asked to get in touch with the feeling again, expressing it as appropriate in order to get a better felt sense of it. Then the suggestion again, to go back further, and so on. In this way we are, as it were, climbing back down the ladder, using the COEX units as rungs. And we may get back to the primal trauma, with the results that Janov has so graphically described. In an interesting book relating psycho-therapy to physiology, Janov (1977) distinguishes between third-line primals (verbally-oriented, dating from the period of about four years old and upwards), second-line primals (largely referring to events taking place in the preverbal and highly emotional early years before that), and first-line primals, concerned with physical survival at the earliest times. This is a very important idea, which ties in with research on the brain

(MacLean 1973). It is also important in making it crystal clear that much of our experience is preverbal, and that language is not primary or fundamental to experience.

We do not always get back to a single 'grand-slam' event, however, and it would be wrong to expect this, in line with our earlier warnings against being oriented towards results and success. All we are trying to do is to encourage the client more and more to open up the inner world. That is therapeutic in itself, because it enables the client to re-own more and more of that rich emotional world which had been cut off and denied. Or as Mahrer (1989) says, to get in touch with his or her deeper potentials.

Grinder and Bandler (1981) have an ingenious trick which can be used with clients who balk at a particular scene, and will not describe it, because they know it is going to be too painful. You get them to begin the experience and then step outside of it so that they see themselves going through it. They hear what was going on at the time, but they watch themselves go through the event as if they were watching a movie. Or you can even go further:

> If you want to be really safe, have them *watch themselves watching themselves* go through the experience, as if they were in the projection box at a movie theatre, watching themselves watch the movie. If you have them go through an event this way, when they remember it later on, they won't remember the terror.

This is particularly suitable when events like rape or war-wounding are involved, or any incident which resulted in the client losing consciousness. You don't want the client to lose consciousness while regressing, because that interferes both with the therapeutic process and with the therapist–client relationship. This is why the approach of Grove and Panzer (1989) already mentioned is so valuable and important.

People in the Gestalt tradition are often very suspicious of the idea of regression, because they want to pay much more attention to the here and now. Similarly with people in the existential tradition – although one of the best discussions of the value of regression is to be found in Laing (1982, Chapter 12). But all therapists of all persuasions find that their clients spontaneously regress from time to time, and it is well to know how to handle regression even if it is not regarded as something to aim at. The Gestaltist Frank-M. Staemmler (1997) has an excellent discussion of this whole question, making a number of very careful distinctions. Similarly Petruska Clarkson (1995) has a good account of the relationship which is set up in the consulting room when the client regresses: she calls this the reparative or developmentally-needed relationship.

THINKING

The thinking therapies are again very varied, but what they have in common is an emphasis on insight and clear thinking as the starting point in therapy.

Humanistic psychotherapy tends rather to avoid this area, in spite of the efforts of Albert Ellis (1970) to classify himself under the humanistic banner, and the way in which transactional analysis (Berne 1972) has been used in part by many humanistic practitioners.

Both psychoanalysis and behaviourism have more to say about this thinking function than does the humanistic approach, and of course the cognitive approach even more so. This is very clear from a book which somebody once showed me, in which the same case notes of the same client were given to three therapists, and asked to share the process they would go through in diagnosing and treating this client. The humanistic therapist treated this task in quite a different way from the psychoanalyst and the behaviourist. He started by talking about his own response to the whole idea of relating to a piece of paper instead of relating to a person, and ultimately rejected the whole task, in a very interesting way.

But there are ways in which the humanistic practitioner does often start from the thinking function. The main one of these, perhaps, is simply the patient digging-out of the client's system of beliefs. Often we cannot even begin to work with a client until an interlocking and self-supporting structure of beliefs has been exposed.

Bill had a belief system in which there were only two types of women he could be attracted to: beautiful women and women with problems. He couldn't get to go out with the beautiful women, so he had to go out with women with problems. But women with problems were too much for him, and made him impotent. The thing is that as soon as this type of absurd system is brought out into the open, it is so obviously self-defeating that the very awareness sets in motion a process of change, which can then be used as appropriate.

Claire had a system where washing-up was a chore so boring that she couldn't do it, couldn't find the energy to do it. But she couldn't go out of the house until the washing-up had been done. So she would wander round the house with her shopping list, not being able to do the washing-up and not being able to go out either. This was quite literally an imprisoning system.

Beck (1979) points out that people often have a story that they keep telling themselves, a kind of running commentary going on in their heads. He calls these 'automatic thoughts'. Surprisingly often, these are self-put-down thoughts – 'they won't like that' and the like.

Ellis (1970) has collected a whole anthology of such thoughts, stories which people tell themselves in order to avoid ever winning or being happy.

I should be thoroughly competent, intelligent and achieving in all possible respects.

I must be loved by everyone for everything I do.

What I have done is awful or wicked, and I should be punished for it.

If something once strongly affected my life, it should go on doing so indefinitely.

I must have certain and perfect control over things.

There are many more of these statements, guaranteed to keep you miserable.

One of the best books showing how people's belief systems are constructed to be self-defeating is by Dorothy Rowe (1978). The heart of this book on depression is a set of nine case histories, told almost entirely through extracts from therapy sessions. I think I would disagree with Rowe when she just regards the statements such as 'I despise myself', 'My husband spoiled my life', 'Animals are better than people' and so on as propositions. I would regard them as *decisions*, made at some specific time under some specific pressure, and linking back to more fundamental decisions, such as 'My mother is part of me', 'I don't trust women', 'I don't know what love is', 'If I am on my own I cease to exist' and so on, also made at some specific time under some specific pressure.

Greenwald (1974) has taken the view that all therapy is about decisions like this. Find out what decisions the person has made about their life, and you will be able to go back and change those decisions. This is similar to Berne's idea (1972) that what you need to know is the person's script: 'A script is an ongoing program, developed in early childhood under parental influence, which directs the individual's behavior in the most important aspects of his life.' The client is almost always unwilling to give up the script, because it makes sense of life. Without the script, the world would no longer make sense, and would become a frightening and unpredictable place. But it ultimately has to be given up if therapy is to proceed. In Mahrer's terms, we have to be prepared to surrender our operating potentials in order to realise our deeper potentials.

This is now very close to the neuro-linguistic programming (NLP) ideas of Bandler and Grinder (1979). They say that each thing that a person does is done for a reason, because it seems the best choice possible in the circumstances. If we want to change a neurotic pattern of behaviour, we have to find out what it is doing positively for the person, and then we find out how the person could get the same result by more healthy means. In other words, we go back and question the original decision to operate in that way. This is a very sophisticated form of decision therapy which they call 'reframing', and it is particularly useful where a very visible and overt pattern of behaviour can be found, such as a phobia or obsession.

As well as these approaches via the thinking function, there is also the question of 'direct teaching' in the therapy session. Many humanistic therapists are very opposed to teaching, saying that it is untherapeutic to give explanations or to attempt to persuade the client of anything. But when we examine the matter more closely in practice, we find that therapists of every persuasion do a good deal of actual direct teaching in the session. They tell clients what to expect, or what their experience might mean.

One of the best examples of this is in rational-emotive therapy (RET) where Ellis (1970) talks to clients about the ABC theorem:

ACTION ⟶ BELIEFS ⟶ CONSEQUENCES

When you do something to another person, he tells the client, its effect on that person depends entirely on the beliefs which that person has about what your action means. You may try to punish a three-year-old for some transgression of your household rules, for example, but unless the three-year-old has a notion of what a rule means (which most of them do not as yet) he or she will merely experience you as being in a bad mood, or being inexplicably disagreeable, or proving once again that he or she is bad or worthless. (RET has now been renamed as REBT – rational-emotive behaviour therapy (Ellis 1995).)

Similarly, if you try to reward someone, it will only work as a reward if it is something that the other person believes to be valuable and interesting. Otherwise it will be experienced as just another odd or even oppressive act – as for example the famous white elephant.

By teaching the client this theorem, we can give a very useful hint as to how to take up the most productive stance in therapy: the stance which says 'I create my world.'

Now we have to be very careful about this notion, which is used so consistently and thoroughly by central humanistic people such as Schutz (1979) and Mahrer (1989). Let us stay with it for a moment, because it is so important. The standard misunderstanding which arises is for people to think that we must then approach clients, and other people generally, by saying in effect, as Jill Tweedie once put it, 'You're wretched, mate, because you chose to be wretched. So rot.' To understand why this is wrong, and not our position at all, we have to distinguish between saying that I create my world, and saying that *they* create *their* world. This is the difference between first-person use and third-person use.

In first-person use, I say 'I create my world,' and this can be an incredibly liberating thing for me to say and fully believe. It can give me the energy to lift myself up by my own bootstraps – or more accurately, it can give me access to my own energy, which was there all the time. Charles Hampden-Turner (1977) movingly describes the Delancey Street project, a house for ex-convicts in San Francisco. It is full of people who are victims of society, if that phrase ever had any meaning, and yet he says that for each person there, it was only at the moment that they said 'I create my world' that they could change their destiny. Once they had said that, they could create a healthy community with a genuine capacity for healing and for survival. Few of us are buffeted by fate as much as the men and women in Delancey Street; for most of us it is easier to take control of our own lives. And this is one of the main effects of personal growth – this ability to say: this is my life, and I run it. In doing this, we are not denying that the world is complicated, or that we are subject to many pressures. We are just saying that *we decide* which pressures to respond to, and how to respond to them. Different people respond differently, choose differently, as Mahrer (1989) has so brilliantly laid out. But if I pretend that I have no choice, I am just copping out, avoiding the issue, letting myself off the hook, and therefore not learning anything, not changing. As someone once said, the distinguishing feature of all victims is that they tell themselves that they have no choice.

Taking this attitude, of taking responsibility for creating my own world, is not like hiding behind a role. It is more exposed, more honest, more risky. It is responsive as well as responsible. It makes me feel like a complete human being. When I do this, it makes me into a person, and takes me away from behaving like a thing. I become an origin rather than a pawn; an end rather than a means. So I value this as a key part of the whole message of humanistic psychology.

But look what happens when I move into third-person use. I change it just slightly, it seems, and say 'He creates his world,' 'She creates her world,' 'They create their world.' Immediately this turns me into an observer, a commentator, even a judge. I am standing outside the person and the situation, and making myself superior to them both. And I am implicitly withholding any help, assistance or sympathy I might be capable of offering: it is a *cold* thing to say. It is a statement which removes me far away from the person and the situation: it is nothing to do with me.

And so the third-person use of this kind of phrase is a denial of solidarity, a negation of community. It is also a contradiction of my own responsibility for the situation which people find themselves in; I am not owning up to my part in the social situation in which a person may be suffering. I am a bystander, in the terms which Petruska Clarkson (1996) has so clearly laid out.

So there is nothing healthy or productive at all in the third-person use of this statement. It is not conducive to growth at all – neither mine nor that of the other person. So using such a statement in a third-person way *is not part of the philosophy of humanistic psychology at all.*

Now, in the light of all that, what are we to say about the statement in its second-person form – 'You create your world'?

It must depend on context. In a context where I am identified with you, or empathetic with you, or very close to you, a situation where you trust me and feel my support, it may be just what you need. It may be the spark which ignites you. Even in this situation, however, it will be most effective when you see it for yourself; and the least effective thing I can do is to lay it on you as a truth. The nearer to first-person it gets, the better it will be.

But in a context where I am not at all close to you, and where you do not trust me at all, such a statement will be seen as an even greater reason for distance and mistrust. In that situation, it will seem more and more like the third-person use, and will be useless and even harmful.

And there is one more thing to say about this issue before we leave it. The statement of self-responsibility, even in its good first-person form, is often taken quite wrongly as a statement of one-sided autonomy, some kind of a claim that I don't need other people any more. Nothing could be further from the truth; the people at Delancey Street, for example, support each other in a very striking and effective way. The point is that *you alone can do it, but you don't have to do it alone.* Both sides of this new statement are true, and they must not be separated from one another. Autonomy is important, but love and mutual support and nourishment are important too.

It can be seen how closely we are approaching the ideas of existentialism. And there is indeed a form of therapy called existential analysis (or sometimes *Daseinsanalyse*) which is on the borderline of humanistic therapy. The reason why it is not squarely within the humanistic territory is that it does not believe in the use of any techniques. This makes it the purest form of therapy there is, in a way, and yet there is a curious contradiction about the whole thing. By just sitting there and 'being authentic', the existential therapist is not far away from the original psychoanalytic model pioneered by Freud. There is the same silence, the same sense of frustration and deprivation for the client, and the indications are that it is just as slow (Shaffer and Galinsky 1974). Yet existential therapy is developing too, and a more recent text (van Deurzen-Smith 1997) makes it clear that even though existential analysts are still suspicious of questions and interpretations, they do still use such things on occasion.

A fascinating dialogue between Martin Buber and Carl Rogers shows how similar and yet how different are the existential approach and the humanistic approach. Buber (1965) makes it clear that for him Rogers is too technique-minded. Rogers is still trying to do something, whereas Buber says that being is more important than doing.

As I say, this is very pure and very simple. But in practice it is very boring and slow, and also, like most of the 'thinking' approaches, it completely ignores the body. The result is that violence tends to erupt outside the therapy room, because it can find no expression inside. Humanistic psychotherapy wants to make the best use of all the skills available, on whatever level they may be.

INTUITING

Here we are concerned with work that starts from the transpersonal level. In other words, we are concerned with the spiritual aspects of the client. These include intuition, the higher self, higher archetypes from the collective unconscious and so on. In practice, this means using symbols a great deal, sometimes to supplement language and sometimes to replace it.

Work with dreams often touches on this area. For example, Ernst and Goodison (1981) describe work on a dream involving an 'androgynous figure from Mars, supple and radiant in white and silver'. On being asked to 'get into and be' this person (in the usual manner of Gestalt therapy) the dreamer realises that this is her spirituality, which she has repressed and been scared of. Similarly Perls (1976) gives a fully worked example of a dream (Madeline's Dream) where it is quite clear (and even more so from the film which was made of this piece of work) that the client has got in touch with her spirituality.

How do we detect when we are beginning to work in this area? Grof (1975) gives a good hint when he says that we are looking for 'experiences involving an expansion or extension of consciousness beyond the usual ego boundaries and beyond the limitations of time and/or space'. He has a whole list (Grof 1988) of such experiences and shows how they can be ordered and classified.

But as well as just waiting for this kind of material to come up spontaneously, we can work directly to evoke it. This is often done in psychosynthesis (Assagioli 1975) where guided fantasy is used a great deal. Through guided fantasy we can introduce symbols to the client which can be useful in opening up spiritual areas, to the extent that the client is ready for that and needs that. Assagioli has a discussion of four critical stages in spiritual awakening, which can happen at any age. A more up-to-date rundown, with some excellent examples of guided fantasies to use, may be found in Ferrucci (1982). Stevens (1971) gives us an excellent manual of guided fantasy, and a number of fully worked-out examples. Usually in this work, an upward journey takes us towards the spiritual (what Assagioli calls the 'superconscious') while a downward journey takes us into the personal unconscious. But these are just conventions which suit a patriarchal culture, and there is no reason why an upward journey should not represent the more materialistic and superficial types of consciousness, and a downward journey represent descent into the depths of spirituality. Stanton Marlan (1981) has suggested that attention to the depths of the psyche is actually a more valid way of exploring spirituality than any of the more usual aspirations to the heights.

Hillman (1979) has made a striking and very disturbing extension to this way of seeing the matter. He suggests that it is wrong to treat dreams merely as clues to day-world problems. Before going into Hillman further, let us look at this question of dreaming.

In the area of dreamwork, there are traditionally three broad ways of working. The first is to see dreams as having to do with the past. This is the psychoanalytic approach. The work on dreams is then retrospective, using the dream material to guess at what is coming up from the unconscious, distorted and censored as it usually is.

The second way of working with dreams is to see them as about the present. This is the approach of Gestalt therapy and existential analysis, as well as of Corrière and Hart (1978) with their idea that as therapy continues, the client comes more into the active central position in the dreams they have.

The third way is to see them as about the future. This is the Jungian approach, where the work we do is prospective, and refers to our aspirations and our directions in life. The dream is seen as referring to our journey towards individuation.

It is important to realise that these different approaches to dreams can all work because the dream is symbolic. A symbol can and does stand for layer after layer of different things. For example, a Tarot card like the Wheel of Fortune symbolises, on the most gross and material level, the ups and downs of life. On another level it is about being able to 'stop the world' and sit on top of all the cycles. On another level it is about going to the still centre and resting there, part of the movement and yet not moving round. On another level it is about standing back and being able to look at the whole Tarot card. And this is just a beginning – there could be a million other interpretations, any one of which might be the best on a particular occasion. This is why there is no way of working on a dream without the client being present.

Coming now to the Hillman revolution, what Hillman (1979) does is to say that all of these methods without exception are wrong. What we need to do instead, he says, is to treat the dream-world as a world in its own right. The world of the dream is a night-world, different from the day-world. It is a soul-world, a spiritual world which needs to be done justice in its own terms. Instead of interpreting the dream symbols, we must live with them and get to know them and learn how to relate to them:

It is not what is said about the dream after the dream, but the experience of the dream after the dream. A dream compared with a mystery suggests that the dream is effective as long as it remains alive . . . It is better to keep the dream's black dog before your inner sense all day than to 'know' its meaning (sexual impulses, mother complex, devilish aggression, guardian, or what have you). A living dog is better than one stuffed with concepts or substituted by an interpretation.

(Hillman 1979)

By really getting into the underworld in this way, Hillman says, we deal with what the dream really has to offer, which is our own soul. He calls therapy soul-making rather than analysis:

Growth lets the soul do its own thing, like a plant. This organic mystique implies minimal work. Soul-making, too, has a mystique, the mystery of death, which encompasses organic growth and employs its images in the work of soul. *Making* is a term which reflects what the psyche itself does: it makes images.

(Hillman 1979)

This is radical stuff, and far removed from the usual ways of seeing the matter. Even more radical is the still unpublished work of Peter Wilberg, which he calls 'Inner Theology':

You 'sleep' or 'slip' into a free identification with other times and spaces, other selves, other bodies – other threads of your activity being, other likelihoods of identification with. These other likelihoods of your activity of identification with are other threads of it, and woven in your dreaming – you call them 'dreams' or 'dream selves'. But *for* these other identification threads, each of which is imbued with its own *now*, a now that may not fit 'your' tenses, you are the other likelihood of, you are the 'dream self', you are a 'past' or 'future' that is dreamt and re-identified with now. The fabric of what you call 'sleep' is an identification texture consisting of dreaming and of being dreamt, of breathing and of being breathed. In this identification paradox the identification tensions of consciousness are released. And yet the identification texture of sleep is not 'unconscious' but superconscious, spanning all your identities known and unknown.

(Wilberg 1979)

It is obvious that we are getting into deep water here, and indeed only a small part of what is now called the transpersonal area of psychology and therapy falls within humanistic psychology.

BORDERLINES

Ken Wilber (1979) has given an admirably clear account of where the borderline falls. He says that there are three broad areas of human development:

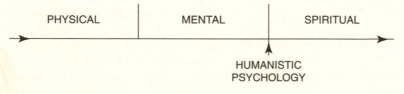

For the mental area, he says, psychoanalysis is appropriate but slow; other approaches include reality therapy (Glasser 1965), rational-emotive therapy (Ellis and Harper 1975), psychocybernetics (Maltz 1960), self-psyching (Werthman 1978), mental adjustment (Putney and Putney 1966) and transactional analysis (Harris 1969). To which we might add cognitive therapy (Beck 1979), personal construct therapy (Fransella 1972), neurolinguistic programming (Bandler and Grinder 1975), cognitive-behavioural therapy (Dryden and Golden 1986) and communication therapy (Fisch *et al.* 1982).

For the spiritual area (the transpersonal) he says that the Jungian approach is appropriate but slow; other approaches include journal workshops (Progoff 1975), awakening intuition (Vaughan 1979), psychosynthesis (Assagioli 1975), meditation (White 1972) and yoga (White 1979). To which we might add creative psychotherapy (Banet 1976), enlightening Gestalt (Enright 1980), past lives therapy (Netherton and Shiffrin 1979) and LSD therapy (Grof 1980).

If we now expand the borderline between the two in the manner suggested by Wilber himself, we get this picture:

In order to get from the mental-ego area into the real-self (centaur) area we have to go through the biosocial bands – a difficult and somewhat traumatic transition in many cases – involving the radical questioning of our social roles and our self-image.

In order to get from the centaur area into the spiritual area, we have to pass through the transpersonal bands – again a difficult and somewhat traumatic crossing in many cases – and this involves a radical questioning of the real self. The chart already given in Chapter 1 (see p. 16) shows what a difference this makes. So all in all, what this adds up to is that the thinking approach, mainly concerned with the mental ego, and the intuiting approach, mainly concerned with the spiritual, both fall largely outside the main area which the humanistic psychotherapist is concerned with. The humanistic practitioner is mostly concerned with the sensing and the feeling approaches.

Unfortunately for our peace of mind, however, this does not get us off the hook. Because the client is a human being, he or she may be at any point of development, or may be partly here and partly there. It is all too common for people to try to work at more advanced levels when they haven't dealt with the basic ego stuff yet. Being able to talk about the mental ego in lofty terms doesn't always mean that it has been adequately dealt with. So the humanistic therapist needs to know and be able to work with these other levels even though they have different and incompatible aims.

The beautiful thing about dreams, however, is that they can be worked with *at all levels*. We can do mental-ego work on dreams, as the Freudians do; we can do real-self work on dreams as the Gestaltists do; we can do transpersonal self-work on dreams, as the psychosynthesis people do. But in all cases we shall need to get the client to remember and record dreams, and keep a dream diary. The best set of instructions for this is to be found in Garfield (1976), who says:

> Remind yourself before going to sleep that you will remember your dreams . . . Knowing that you have just completed a dream, the next step is crucial: Don't open your eyes! Lie still with closed eyes and let images flow into your mind . . . When you feel as though your dream recall is complete in the position in which you awoke, move gently into other sleeping positions which you use, with eyes still closed, and you will often find additional dream recall . . . record your dreams, preferably with eyes closed [Garfield explains how to write in the dark], in the order that you recall them . . . record a unique verbal expression immediately . . . Note your unique productions first . . . Try to at least identify the elusive elements of your dreams . . . Share your dream experiences with a friend, if possible, as well as recording them . . . Select titles for your dreams from their unique character-istics . . . As you practise valuing, recalling and recording your dreams, you will increase your recall. Your dreams will become more vivid, complete and relevant to waking life.

To close this chapter on techniques, let us just note that the humanistic practitioner has a wealth of methods available. There is no shortage of techniques and methods. But it is important to have the aims and implications of the techniques clear in your mind.

Chapter 7

Transference

One of the key differences between psychoanalysis and humanistic psychotherapy concerns the concept of transference. Psychoanalysts regard transference as the single most important element in any therapy which goes deep enough to change the whole character structure. Humanistic psychotherapy and psychoanalysis share the aim of changing character structure, but differ on method – psychoanalysts deny that any method other than transference can go deep enough to achieve this goal.

What is transference? Transference is the inappropriate repetition in the present relationship of what was important in a person's early development. Fenichel (1945) described it happening when 'the patient misunderstands the present in terms of the past'. Jim Bugental says: 'The transference is a patterned way of being in the world that involved a significant other and that is reactivated in the patient's relation to the therapist' (1981: 138). The most common form it takes is of the client having strongly positive – perhaps erotic – feelings towards the therapist, or else strongly negative feelings. The illusory quality in these feelings becomes very visible in certain cases: for example, a woman brought her therapist a blue tie 'to match his wise blue eyes'. When she presented it to him, he first pointed out that he had brown eyes, and then took her over to the mirror, so that she could see her own eyes, which were blue. 'Whose wise blue eyes are we really talking about?' was the next question.

So in transference the therapist quite often turns into a loved, hated or feared parent. The client then reacts to that projection rather than to the therapist as a real person.

This is a phenomenon recognised in psychology generally, and not just in psychoanalysis. The co-counselling people call it 'restimulation', and Madison (1969) calls it 'reintegration'. His definition of reintegration is 'The unconscious mechanism by which brain-stored traces of past experiences are located and aroused by the contemporary situation and interact with incoming sense data to codetermine ongoing psychological processes.' Unravelling this jargon-like account, what Madison means is that certain traumatic experiences build up in the child a resonating 'echo chamber', so that certain incoming actions of people 'turn a whisper into a shout'. A relatively slight incoming stimulus (in energy terms) can quickly touch off and arouse powerful energising systems.

So there is nothing peculiar to therapy about this – it is going on all the time in everyday life. Part of our reaction to many events in our lives is under our conscious control, and part of it comes from unconscious forces. We all have these echo chambers in our minds, so that certain words, gestures, actions which have the right 'vibration frequency' have the power to evoke a powerful 'noise' in us. The therapy situation merely brings this to our attention more, makes it harder to avoid or deny. The humanistic approach recognises this fully:

> Transferences may be designated as positive or negative. A positive transference would be made by clients when they project their feelings of affection or dependency to the counselor, perhaps perceiving him or her as a loving, helpful father or mother. A negative transference would be made by clients when they project their feelings of hostility and aggression. These transference feelings change form, sometimes quite suddenly.
>
> (Brammer, Shostrom and Abrego 1989: 203)

Transference is there, whether we like it or not, and whether we know it or not. The only question is, what are we going to do with it?

The psychoanalysts say that we have to foster it and concentrate on it, because it is here and now. It is the neurosis come alive, dancing in front of our eyes: here is our best chance to look at it and deal with it. And this is the only way to get this alive, here-and-now quality.

HERE AND NOW

All forms of therapy which are at all effective must work in the here and now. Making the absent present is the secret of real change. Psychodrama does it by role-playing and counter-role-playing the problem, so that it comes to life in the present. Gestalt does it by getting the client to talk to the person direct, rather than talking about the person. Primal does it by allowing the client to go back and re-experience the actual traumatic events, re-living them in the present. Psychosynthesis does it by having the client go through a fantasy in front of the therapist, in which the therapist may actually participate. Rogers does it by tuning in to the feelings of the person as they are now being expressed overtly or covertly. Existentialists do it by bringing their own responses to the surface, and working with them in relation to the client. There are probably hundreds of methods, many of them still undescribed, for bringing relevant material into the here and now.

So we do not need transference in any exclusive way, because we have so many alternatives to it. And in fact many humanistic practitioners fight shy of transference, don't like it, don't want to know about it and generally deny it. Perls calls transference 'bear-trapping', which is a pretty hostile and dismissive phrase. Janov says 'The Primal therapist does not deal with transference . . . In fact, the patient–therapist relationship is ignored entirely' (Janov 1973). In co-counselling, it is not supposed to matter who your counselling partner is – one is interchangeable with another. Moreno uses the word 'tele' instead of transference and sees it as relevant to the other group members rather than to the psychodrama director. Medard Boss, on the existentialist side, sees transference as destructive to any real relationship between therapist and client, and says that the patient will hate the therapist as long as he or she is restricted to the limited perception of a child–father or child–mother relationship. Eric Berne says 'This is crossed transaction Type 1, which represents the common form of transference reaction as it occurs in psychotherapy, and is also the type of transaction which causes most of the troubles in the world' (Berne 1973). Mahrer says that the transference requires a relationship between the therapist and the client, and he advocates the abandonment of such a relationship.

This is all very dismissive, and I do get the feeling that most humanistic people don't like the idea of transference and countertransference going on in the relationship between therapist and client. Why should this be?

I think the main reason is that we believe that the exclusive reliance on transference by a therapist means a very narrow and one-sided imbalance in the relationship. The therapist becomes nothing more than a parental authority figure, and the patient becomes just and only a child. This gives the therapist too much one-sided power in the situation, which cannot be challenged. It can put the therapist in the position of never being wrong. Everything which may be uncomfortable or ineffective in the relationship can be attributed to the patient's neurosis; and if the patient wants to get out of such an unequal situation, this can be interpreted as just another piece of resistance. I think that's what we don't like about the Freudian set-up. And I think that's basically justified, as far as it goes; I think we are right to reject that way of working as undemocratic and ethically wrong.

What I am saying is that the permanent and inbuilt imbalance of the relationship where the analyst refuses to enter into any equal contact with the patient – and indeed insists on calling the person a *patient* – does peculiarly lend itself to manipulation (not that the psychoanalysts are the only manipulators – the behaviourists, the communication people and the NLP people are just as bad in their own ways). It is the exclusive attention to the transference all the time which does this. This is a fixed and limited stance to take up, which prevents a whole host of desirable therapeutic moves from being made.

But in fact there is nothing unique to psychoanalysis about most of this. All single-minded therapies, which hold tight to one particular technique, also offer only a narrow selection of roles and moves. And all therapy puts the therapist into a position of power and potential manipulation. To take one simple instance, male therapists are often accused of sexual exploitation of their female patients. But this accusation is by no means restricted to psychoanalytic therapists – it seems to extend right across the spectrum. It is one particular form of manipulation which happens to be a bit more visible than many others.

And in all forms of therapy it is easy for the therapist to become infallible, making any difficulties in the relationship be caused by the patient's neurosis; this is not at all peculiar to the Freudians. *The therapist holds all the aces, whether s/he wants to or not.* This is the crucial truth about transference, which the Freudians are aware of and the humanistic psychotherapists run away from.

So because we don't want to work with transference exclusively and totally, this doesn't mean that we don't need to deal with it at all. Seeing as it is going to arise – and it does indeed arise, in every therapeutic relationship in some way, and so does countertransference – we may as well get to know what it is and how it works. We must make it clear, however, that we think that the position taken up by some psycho-analysts, that all therapeutic relations are transferential relations, is extremely unhelpful and conceptually confusing. The humanistic position is well stated by Bugental again:

> This term is sometimes loosely used as though synonymous with the 'therapeutic relation'. This misuse seems to me to lead only to confusions. In this book, the term will be used only to refer to distortive or parataxic aspects of the therapeutic relation.
>
> (Bugental 1981: 64)

Certainly people like Reich, and Elizabeth Mintz, and Frank Lake, do recognise that transference and countertransference are there, whether we like it or not, and they have found very good ways of recognising it without letting it take over all the time. Frank Lake (1966) actually says that if any relationship at all is strong enough to be personally helpful in facing up to the crises of life, 'it is also deep enough to evoke the hope that life's more painful personal crises, buried alive for many years, may also be transferred into it for solution'. And Mintz (1972) has a very clear picture of how, in a group situation, the therapist can move into and out of transference positions in a very effective way. But it seems very difficult for humanistic therapists to realise how deep transference can go, and how impossible it is to evade it in a one-to-one relationship – and particularly one which is prolonged. Petruska Clarkson has a very good discussion of this, in which she distinguishes between four different types of transference, and says:

> In most cases experience proves that the psychotherapist does not have to be a blank screen in order for the patient to enter into a transference relationship. In fact, even some self-disclosing psycho-therapists who pride themselves on their presence, openness or authenticity are used by clients and patients in ways which can be regarded as transferential.
>
> (Clarkson 1995: 77)

This latter point is, of course, a possible point of entry for an alternative view. Some of the humanistic people go in for brief psychotherapy just because of this. I seem to remember seeing in a book on humanistic work some time ago the idea that because transference resistance arises more and more as the therapy proceeds, one should aim at having just a few sessions, rather than continuing for years. This is obviously a tempting idea, and I think there is something in it, but it does bring to mind an argument I had with a Freudian once. I was saying that the reason why psychoanalysts were so sold on the idea of transference was because of their fear of the Id and the unconscious. By keeping their parental end up, they were able to avoid being scared by eruptions from the unconscious, because they were able to take control of the session just by failing to respond to questions or anything else. To which he retorted that the humanistic therapists were scared too – only what they were scared of was a long relationship with one person. To avoid this, they went in for groups, for brief psychotherapy, for a lot of travel and for imputing an infinite amount of responsibility to the patient!

Now this book is in itself a refutation of that accusation. It may have been true for some people at some time in the past, but the humanistic practitioner of today is certainly able and willing to conduct long-term psychotherapy now, designed to help the client change in a completely open-ended way. This means the transference issues are going to arise. What are we going to do with them?

INTERPRETATION

The Freudian answer is that we have to interpret it. At once the humanistic hackles go up. Rogers was against interpretation, Perls was against interpretation, Janov was against interpretation, Moreno was against interpretation, Mahrer is against interpretation, every man and his dog is against interpretation in the humanistic camp. So let's go on to have a good look at that one too.

The brute fact of the matter, as it seems to me, is that humanistic therapists engage in just the same process as interpretation, but do not call it that, because it follows a different model.

There are two steps in making an interpretation. The first step is to notice that something is going on, to decide that here is an area worth probing. For example, a young man may refer to his girlfriend in very dependent terms, which may make the therapist think 'I wonder if he is seeing his mother in her, and trying to get from her what he couldn't get from his mother?' It is a possibility which is worth exploring, because if it were true, this would go back to very early material in the Freudian oral stage. This is, then, the first essential stage in interpretation – picking out something as worth paying attention to.

Step two is to get the client to pay attention to it too. Unless both of you are paying attention to the same thing, no interpretation is going to be at all effective. So you take the last thing the client did which was relevant, and you hold it up for the person to see in some way. If you're a Rogerian, you say 'You're kind of *imploring* her to pay some mind to you.' If you're a Gestaltist, you might say 'On this cushion is sitting your mother. Try saying the same thing to her.' If you're a co-counsellor, you might say 'Try saying that again a few times and see what comes up.' If you're a primal therapist, you might get the person to lie down and hold up their arms and repeat the last request a few times, such as 'I want more from you.' And if you're a psychoanalyst, you might say 'It is as if you were really talking to your mother,' or possibly 'Do you feel the same way about me?'

Now I can't see how any of these responses are not of the nature of interpretations. They all put the therapist's guess into the client's mind in some way or other, more or less directly. And sure, there are all sorts of moves one might want to make between step one and step two. One might want to get the client to focus more on the general area before deciding exactly how specific to get. But this is just as true of the psychoanalyst as it is of the humanistic practitioner. But the therapeutic responses just outlined are not interpretations, because of the different theoretical models behind them. The person-centred therapist is empathically tuning in to the emotional undercurrents. The Gestaltist is noticing the change in the tone of voice. The co-counsellor is seeing an opportunity for emotional discharge. The primal therapist is picking up on the regressive quality of the utterance. In all these cases what is happening is what Alvin Mahrer calls the carrying forward of the potentials for experiencing:

> Therapeutic change occurs when there is a carrying forward (deepening, enhancing) of the experiencing occurring right now in the patient. The experiencing may be at the surface, operating level, or it may be deeper within the patient. The process is one of letting it happen more, more fully, more deeply, with greater depth and breadth and saturation.
>
> (Mahrer 1986: 3)

So when I said earlier that the way to deal with the transference was to interpret it, I meant it just as widely as that. Step one is to notice that positive or negative transference is going on, and step two is to bring it to the client's attention in some way.

One thing which I often do, for example, is to get the client to sit on the cushion or chair I have just been sitting on, and comment on what has been going on from that position, as me. This has the effect of bringing out any fantasies the person may have about my reaction. In co-counselling, one of the standard recommendations is to ask the other person at certain times 'Do I remind you of anybody?' This is a very direct way of asking about transference, although it only works if the client is conscious of what is going on.

But of course the best place for working at problems to do with transference is in a group. As Thomas Szasz pointed out long ago, it's awfully hard to deal with something like this in a one-to-one situation. If the client says 'You're cold and you really hate me,' the therapist can interpret this to be something about the client's father or mother, but there could be some truth in it, and this would never get dealt with. But in a group, there are other points of view which can be brought to bear, doing justice to the reality as well as to the fantasy.

I'm not saying that a group is infallible at all. Some very funny dynamics go on in groups. I read an article a few years back by a group leader, where he was pointing to the difficulty of handling such a situation. He used to say innocent-seeming things such as 'Jim says I've been picking on him in a hostile way. Did other people see it like that?' The group stays silent or gives ambiguous answers, because of unconscious dependency on the leader – and poor Jim has been screwed all over again! But I am saying that in a group there is at least a chance, if the thing is honestly tackled, that more different realities and perspectives can be tapped.

When I'm leading a group, and someone picks on something I've done or said, what I do is to ask my co-leader, or a group member whom I trust, to take over and facilitate the interaction. And then I go into it prepared to find out something about myself as well as about the other person. I don't think the idea of transference should be used in such a way as to make the therapist infallible.

Now a Freudian might say that to stand down and interact like another group member would be unwise, because it would be threatening to the group members, knocking away the basic safety structure of the group. The therapist is responsible for the work and boundaries of the group, and to step down in this way is to abdicate that responsibility, or at least to attempt to do so.

RESPONSIBILITY

And this brings us back to the question of responsibility. We saw earlier that one of the criticisms which analysts bring against the humanistic therapist is that the latter is seen as imputing unreal amounts of self-responsibility to the client or group member. And the question the Freudian asks is 'You brought this person into the consulting-room, or these people into the group room. The fact of transference, which you have now admitted to, means that they are now dependent on you – that they are handing you all the aces. Yet you are saying to them that they have to be autonomous at one and the same time. How can they be both? And what are *you* responsible for?'

I think this is an important question, and I've given it a lot of thought. To take the last question first, what the humanistic practitioner is responsible for is *being there*. I think there's an implicit promise, which can easily be made explicit, that the practitioner will be fully present. And I think that's all. By doing this, the practitioner does all that is in his power to encourage the client to do the same. As the therapy proceeds, the client is more and more able to be there too, to be fully present in the room. But if the client had no ability at all to be there in the first place, any therapy would be impossible.

It is the same with autonomy. In the average therapy situation, it may be true that dependency is on top, and the autonomy underneath, but it is the autonomy I am trying to speak to, and encourage to come forth. These are very crude terms I am talking in, and there is a lot more going on than that. We all know that one of the best ways of getting rid of a symptom is by paying more and more attention to it, driving it to its utmost – I am not in any way advocating an unrealistic ignoring of the power of the surface appearances. There is a certain balance in the attention to what is obviously there on top, and what is there less obviously underneath. But what I am contending for is a full recognition that there is something already there in the client which we can speak to and which is healthy. If we lose sight of this, we are losing sight of something central.

I don't think I'm saying anything here which a Freudian would not also say. I feel more and more that the differences between us and the Freudians are minor rather than major.

So when we say, as Perls or Schutz do very directly – 'You are responsible for yourself in this group,' we are not saying anything ridiculous or different from what a Tavistock consultant is saying much more implicitly. It doesn't mean that we don't recognise the fact of transference or resistance, and it doesn't mean that we are abdicating our responsibility to be there. But I sometimes wonder whether we are always as aware as we might be of the phenomenon of counter-transference.

COUNTERTRANSFERENCE

This is where I project my own material on to the client, and have just the same kind of positive or negative reactions, because of early stuff which has not been fully worked through. It is valuable and realistic to point this out, and I think again this whole thing has been underestimated until recently by humanistic therapists. It seems to arise most of all with clients who understand the therapist very well, and know how to get him or her going in some way or other. There are pages and pages of warnings about the seductive client, and now more and more about the seductive therapist.

But it is because of the phenomenon of countertransference that I think it's important for anyone working in this field to have their own therapist or group, where they can work out their feelings about their clients. This is now something which seems to be agreed by all psychotherapists and all counsellors of whatever persuasion. As Tim Bond (1996) urges, this is not only a technical point, but also an ethical one. What we all seem now to be saying is that we need to work on our countertransference and become much more aware of it. If we don't work on our countertransference very much, it means that we have no first-hand experience of transference, and are therefore less likely to understand it fully when it does arise.

It is for this reason that the Association of Humanistic Psychology Practitioners lays down as a condition of membership that a humanistic therapist must have a supervisor, and must continue to work on himself or herself. At last we have recognised that this is a crucially important area, which must be taken care of if good therapy is to be carried out.

It's strange in a way that we have neglected this area in the past, because it is we who have developed the classic answer to it – the idea of self and peer assessment. Here a group of practitioners get together – and this has been done with doctors, dentists, co-counsellors and a variety of other people – and agree on criteria for monitoring each others' practice. John Heron (1981a) describes this method fully, and has given a number of lectures and workshops on the subject. But co-counselling is also a resource for the therapist in practice. All s/he has to do is to find another therapist of similar persuasion, and agree to share, say, two hours a week with them. Then all the problems of countertransference with clients can be worked out in an atmosphere of mutual trust, support and confrontation. If both of these people belong to the same group, things which may go wrong between them can be brought up in the group. This recourse, of mutual supervision in a pair, does not have to be done according to the principles of co-counselling: it is recognised in a number of fields quite independently. It is called the collegial–peer approach, and is well described by Allen Hess (1980).

Another recourse is, of course, formal supervision of some kind. This is often provided in some forms of training, and may often be continued after the training has ceased. The advantage of this is that the supervisor has had more experience, and may be able to give very simple bits of advice, or warnings about what to expect next. This has been developed to an enormous extent in recent years, with courses and books proliferating, and leading to the emergence of extremely well-worked-out texts such as the one by Elizabeth Holloway (1995). The disadvantage is that any kind of authoritarian set-up can work against the basic humanistic outlook of equality. 'Communication is only possible between equals,' as Hagbard Celine put it so well.

So a more favoured method among humanistic practitioners is the peer review group. This is a group of therapists who meet together at regular intervals to discuss cases and work on their reactions to clients of various kinds. Due to the wealth of experience available, a great deal of learning can take place. A peer review group is the same as the 'peer group supervision' model described by Fizdale (1958) and Watson (1973). The group members need to be mature and at the same general level of competence. In addition, they have to respect each other professionally, and be interested in improving their own skills. A good discussion of this whole area is to be found in Aponte and Lyons (1980), and a more up to date one in Gaie Houston's (1995) list of configurations.

As with any other supervision group, the work can be done at various levels, from the most didactic to the most feeling-oriented. On the whole, it is found that more trust builds up in the group if it is allowed to be more feeling-oriented when appropriate. But it is important for each member to insist on getting the form of feedback which is most useful for them personally. (See Appendix A.)

It must not be assumed, however, that countertransference is just a problem to be overcome. It is also a positive advantage, to be cultivated and used. Racker (1957) says that the emotional response of the therapist is often a more accurate clue to the psychological state of the client than is the therapist's conscious judgment. Singer (1965) goes so far as to say that it may well be the case that all important insights into another person are ultimately brought about by carefully examined personal reactions to the person. Brammer *et al.* have a stimulating list of things to look for in trying to decide whether we are suffering from countertransference or not:

Signs of countertransference feelings

1 Getting sleepy, not listening or paying attention, or not hearing a client's messages.

2 Thinking, 'I feel all right about this topic and should feel upset; but I don't.' (If there were no anxiety present, why would the counsellor even think about it?)

3 Finding it difficult to shift positions or experiencing one's self 'tighten up'.

4 Becoming sympathetic rather than empathic – overly emotional about a client's troubles.

5 Selecting certain material to reflect or interpret and wondering afterward why this material rather than some other material was interpreted.

6 Consistently interpreting or reflecting too soon or incorrectly.

7 Consistently underestimating or missing the client's depth of feeling.

8 Feeling an unreasoning dislike or attraction for the client. Getting angry at the client.

9 Being unable to identify with the client. For example, when the client feels upset, the counsellor feels no emotional response.

10 Overidentifying with the client, as in becoming aggressively sympathetic when the client cites maltreatment by an authority figure.

11 Discovering a tendency to argue with the client, becoming defensive, or otherwise vulnerable to client criticism.

12 Feeling that this is a 'best' or 'worst' client.

13 Being preoccupied with the client in fantasy between sessions, even to the extent of thinking of responses to be made.

14 Being habitually late in starting interviews or running over the hour with certain clients.

15 Attempting to elicit some strong affect from the client by making dramatic statements.

16 Being overly concerned about the confidential nature of the work with clients.

17 Feeling the compulsion to do something active; hence, making too strong an impact with 'shotgun' interpretations and suggestions.

18 Dreaming about the client.

19 Being too 'busy' to see the client or complaining of 'administrative duties'.

20 Working excessively hard with clients to the point of fatigue, then complaining of overwork.

(Brammer, Shostrom and Abrego 1989: 217–18)

What do we do, then, when we notice such emotional reactions in ourselves, directed toward the client, which seem exaggerated or suspect in some way?

The first thing is always to be aware of it. If we are too defensive, we shall never even notice it. For example, when the client is talking about something of great interest, and is quite absorbed in it, I sometimes find myself falling asleep. I used to criticise myself for this and try to keep awake. This sometimes resulted in a real struggle – my eyes wanting to close and me trying desperately to keep them open. But through working on this I began to notice that in such situations I was really feeling that the relationship between me and the client had gone dead. In other words, we were no longer working in the here and now, where all real therapy is done. There was no therapy going on. Once I became aware of this, I was in a much better position to do something about it.

The second thing, then, is to do something about the counter-transference responses we are now aware of. There are a number of choices here, and it is important not to do something automatic:

(a) We can just notice it and lay it aside for future work in our own supervision or peer review sessions, or indeed in our own therapy;

(b) We can let it sensitise us to issues which may be floating just beneath the surface. For example, a group leader once told me that whenever he started to be sexually attracted to a woman in one of his groups, he found that Oedipal material came up from her within the next hour;

(c) We can put it to the client and stimulate a reaction thereby. For example, I have said to a client 'I'm getting a strong feeling of phoniness, as if I don't believe a word you are saying. I can't take seriously what you are saying now. I wonder why that should be?' If I am right, the client will break down and admit that some other feelings are more important; if I am wrong, the client will get angry. Either way, I have got the interaction into a more meaningful stream. This kind of confrontation (like any other kind of confrontation) can only be done effectively if I have got a good level of trust and rapport with the client;

(d) We can just act it out. For example, I sometimes feel like falling asleep, as mentioned earlier. And sometimes I just let myself fall asleep. In each case where I have done this, the client has got angry, and this has been extremely useful in bringing a here-and-now relationship into being, much more productive than what was going on before. But again a good working alliance needs to have been built up before doing this kind of thing.

The most difficult thing of all, of course, is where we are not aware of the countertransference. It may only be later, if ever, that we realise that what went wrong in the therapy was our own countertransference reactions. So here are some of the things to look for.

Defensive countertransference is the most general type, and occurs when the client triggers off the therapist's unresolved struggles with areas such as dependency, sexuality or aggression. Flescher (1973) says 'the therapist's unconscious readiness to accept or refuse specific material is an important suggestive factor in stimulating the patient to surrender or withhold such material.'

Aim attachment countertransference is about the therapist's motives. Unconscious needs for success, power, omnipotence or money can distort the therapeutic relationship; so can desperate searches for love, recognition and admiration. Other things of this kind which can enter in are saviour and rescuer fantasies; voyeuristic impulses; the need to feel superior by working with sick or inadequate people; and attempts to alleviate guilt feelings by helping others. All these are worth looking out for, as Slavson (1953) has suggested.

Transferential countertransference happens when the therapist responds as though the client is a parental figure or a sibling figure or suchlike. For example, if the client is silent and withholding, the therapist may have feelings stirred up of parents and not being able to get through to them.

Reactive countertransference arises when the therapist responds to the client's transference distortions as if they were real. I had a client who used to accuse me from time to time of having lured him into therapy when he didn't know what he was doing. If I had replied to him by defending myself or explaining what had really happened, this could only have come from reactive countertransference. Instead, I invited him to work on his feelings about that, with good results. Similarly, a young therapist was very upset by being criticised for dressing in a sloppy way, and was even more hooked by criticisms of the room she was working in. She actually started to see the room in the same critical way as the client, instead of simply regarding it as a good opportunity to explore the client's feelings about sloppiness, untidiness and imperfection.

Induced countertransference is where the therapist takes up a role suggested by the client's transferential behaviour. For example, a dependent client may send out strong take-care-of-me signals, which the therapist may respond to by giving advice, answering questions, giving reassurance and so forth – in other words, acting like a parent. This is feeding the neurosis, not changing it. There is an interesting misunderstanding which can arise here, about the meaning of the word 'humanistic'. As used by analysts and many others, the word often just means 'sloppy'. For example, if a client comes in with a huge bandage on, or tells us that a parent has just died, these people say that the 'humanistic' response is to express sympathy and to comfort the client, while the 'analytic' response is to probe the client's feelings about these matters. This is not my terminology in this book. Some humanistic therapists would act in the former way, and some, including me, in the latter. I would agree totally with Brenner (1979) where he says:

> It is true enough that it often does no harm for an analyst to be thus conventionally 'human'. [In expressing sympathy to a patient whose father has just died.] Still, there are times when his being 'human' under such conditions can be harmful, and one cannot always know in advance when those times will be. As an example, for his analyst to express sympathy for a patient who has just lost a close relative may make it more difficult than it would otherwise be for the patient to express pleasure or spite or exhibitionistic satisfaction over the loss.

This seems to me absolutely right. A therapist is a therapist, playing a very strict role (this is one of the things which co-counselling has made crystal clear) and to step outside this role is to ask for trouble.

Identification countertransference is where the therapist overidentifies with the client, entering into a covert alliance with the client's neurotic aims. You can become aware of this whenever you find yourself blaming others for the client's difficulties. Loeser and Bry (1953) say that this is the most common form of countertransference. It can also take a negative form, where the therapist avoids areas which are reminiscent of the therapist's own problems.

Displaced countertransference occurs when the therapist displaces feelings from his or her own personal life on to a client, or when feelings towards one client are displaced and acted out on another. Also the therapist may displace feelings towards a client on to people in his or her personal life, such as family or friends. This is the source of that common experience of therapists that 'all my clients seem to have the same problems at the moment'.

Some writers on this subject (e.g. Freundlich 1974) say that there is such a thing as conflict-free countertransference, which is a mature relationship between therapist and client which is not driven by historical needs and fears: 'It is characterised by autonomy, mutual respect, spontaneity, cooperation and an absence of exploitation and manipulation.' I would just call this liking the client, or good therapist–client communication, rather than any kind of countertransference. There would seem to be no need for any further therapy at this point.

PROJECTIVE INDENTIFICATION

Something which must not be confused with countertransference is projective identification. In times gone by, this was regarded as something rather unusual and particularly difficult to handle, but today it is regarded much more as something which occurs quite frequently but is not always well handled. The difference is that while countertransference is the therapist's stuff, projective identification is the client's stuff. What happens is that the therapist comes to feel something which seems very strange and alien, and may be quite upsetting. On checking for countertransference feelings, nothing seems to fit or apply, while on the other hand it seems that it may well be something to do with what the client does not want to feel, and is resisting, but is projecting into the therapist. So the therapist is feeling it for the client. Since the client cannot then have access to it, what has to happen is that the therapist somehow brings it to the notice of the client. Here is an example:

> I recall listening to a graduate intern's report of his clinical progress and noting how relaxed and clear he appeared to be. Everything seemed in order. I began to suffer a terrible stomach ache. I supposed the problem was mine, something I'd eaten or some piece of my own personal work. I decided to tell my supervisee that I had a stomach ache that had come on suddenly. I asked him if he was sitting on something he wasn't talking about. He thought for a moment, then stared at me, then burst into tears. My stomach ache began to abate. There was in fact a terrible piece of business going on in his life that he had tucked away so carefully that in coming into my office he'd forgotten it for the time being. My sharing candidly with him prompted clear self-disclosure. What I felt was a way of seeing. And my seeing brought him back to himself.
>
> (Baldwin 1997: 95)

In general, the right way to handle this kind of thing seems to be to see the session as a kind of container, in which the therapist and the client (or the supervisor and the supervisee, in the example given above) can both be safe if the material is shared in an appropriate way. Scott Berry makes a good point in talking about people who come into counselling because of being diagnosed with a life-threatening disease, such as HIV/AIDS.

> Projective identification may play a role in the initial encounter with a newly diagnosed person. Specifically, questions may transfer a large amount of emotional energy from the client: 'Why is this happening to me?' and 'How do I keep on living?' At such cathartic emotional points, when the client simply needs to be held, some counsellors find the fantasy 'I am a container for some of these feelings' helps both client and therapist bear the initial shock. In some cases there may be a shared fantasy between them that the sessions somehow hold the client's pain.
>
> (Berry 1996: 310)

Again this needs to be shared if it is to be therapeutic, and this is very much in line with the general humanistic rubric of openness and self-disclosure. But it does not have to be done so directly. One more example may be helpful, this time from a Jungian who has written a great deal about transference and countertransference. He is talking about a client who kept sending him to sleep.

> What I did was to ask her if at that moment she might have the feeling that she was far away, or even isolated from me. And in fact she was then able to say that she had the impression she was blabbing about completely uninteresting things in which she could naturally not expect me to be interested, and thus felt more and more unsure of herself . . . Further analysis of our situation showed that she found herself constantly having to fend off an ever-increasing need: a deep yearning for a mirroring selfobject. This need had been deeply buried and was now slowly coming to light . . . since it was connected with early traumatic memories of disappointment, it was coupled with fear and had to be repressed.
>
> (Jacoby 1984: 55)

So again the therapist is feeling something which really belongs to the client, and which the client is warding off. The idea of projective identification comes of course originally from the Kleinian school, and is well described in Hinshelwood (1989).

Chapter 8

Resistance

We saw in Chapter 5 that the aims and underlying assumptions of humanistic psychotherapy are very different from the aims and underlying assumptions of psychoanalysis. For Freud, the Id is fundamental bedrock. For us, the real self is the equivalent foundation.

Yet it is curious how virtually all the people who broke away from Freud, whether the break came early or late in Freud's life, did come to believe in the real self, as something healthy and trustworthy. Some of them did so while making huge revisions in the theory, while others did so with very little change at all. And this suggests that the idea of the real self may not be so remote from Freud after all – maybe it is really very close to Freud, rather than being at the other end of a long line.

Suppose, for example, we look at Paul Federn (1952), a psychoanalyst of the 1930s and 1940s. He has an outer layer of the person which he calls the ego-states, rather similar to Eric Berne's ego-states or Assagioli's subpersonalities, and an inner centre which he calls the Id.

REAL SELF AND ID

Where would it take us if we simply said that Freud's Id was the real self? At first it seems quite ridiculous. The Id is seen in psychoanalysis as the basic foundation of all motivation in the individual. It is an extraordinarily dramatic concept. It seems to be impossible to describe it without excitement. It is a 'seething mass', 'primitive', 'repository of primitive and unacceptable impulses', 'completely selfish and unconcerned with reality or moral considerations', or 'unorganised chaotic mentality'. Freud's own words are 'a cauldron of seething excitement'. The Id works on the pleasure principle – that is, it uses primary process thinking, attempting to discharge tension by forming an image of the object which will remove the tension. There is no time in the Id – past, present and future mix without distinction. The laws of logic and reason do not exist for the Id, so that contrary wishes can exist side by side quite happily. One thing can stand for or symbolise other, incompatible things, and so on. If the Id were a person, it almost sounds as if he or she would be mad!

I don't want to exaggerate this, because Freud talks in one place quite positively about 'the Id's will', but certainly Freud and his commentators see the Id at least as unreliable, not to be trusted.

Contrast this with what people say about the real self. Jung says 'The self is our life's goal, for it is the completest expression of that fateful combination we call individuality.' Reich says that the deepest layer of the human personality is a place where the impulses are no longer distorted and pathological, but spontaneously decent. Maslow says that

> self-actualisation means experiencing fully, vividly, selflessly, with full concentration and full absorption . . . At this moment the person is wholly and fully human . . . Peak experiences are transient moments of self-actualisation. They are moments of ecstasy which cannot be bought, cannot be guaranteed, cannot even be sought.

Janov says that 'to be totally oneself is a spectacular feeling'. And as the Maitreyana Upanishad puts it, 'Having realised his own self as the Self, a man becomes selfless . . . This is the highest mystery.'

These seem to be two very different things, then, don't they? The Id and the real self are both supposed to be somehow at the base or centre of the person, and to represent the person's most fundamental bedrock, but it is as if one were black and the other white. Or as if one were a mess, and the other a jewel. And yet . . . And yet there is something which doesn't fit about that way of putting it. And what doesn't fit is that getting in touch with the real self is very scary. Everyone seems to agree that it's a good thing, and well worth getting in touch with, and yet everyone avoids getting in touch with it like mad. People appear to be just as scared of it as they would be of the Id.

The way this comes out is in the phenomenon which Freud called 'therapeutic resistance'. What Freud discovered was that people came to him saying they wanted to get rid of their neuroses, and then proceeded to hang on to them and grab on to them and dig their heels in to keep them in every way possible, and even found whole new ways of expressing them better. And this was easy for him to understand, because he could see how people would naturally want to avoid admitting all the nasty impulses coming up from the Id – all about desperately unsavoury things like incest and destruction and horror and fear. So he felt very comfortable about resistance and devoted a lot of time to thinking about it.

But humanistic psychotherapists find plenty of resistance too. I've been around most kinds of therapy in my time, and I've certainly felt it in myself and seen it very clearly in others. And it arises in just exactly the same way as it does for the Freudians – people come to a group or an individual session to work on their problems, and then proceed to avoid them, sidetrack them, not know how to work on them, get interested in other people's problems, smoke a lot, drink cups of tea, go to the toilet a lot and all the rest of it. And then maybe start working, but find that the therapist isn't doing it right . . . But humanistic psychotherapists don't talk much about resistance at all. Rogers only mentions it as a temporary stage in the life of a group. Perls plays it down and treats it as just another split in the personality. Corsini says that it only really arises in long-term therapy, so he advocates short-term therapy. The NLP people say, 'There is no resistance, there are only incompetent therapists.'

But there is one person who does justice to the whole thing, and shows us where the answer might be, and that is Reich. I didn't realise until recently that Reich's whole early approach was being worked out in a seminar which he ran at Freud's request, which was mainly devoted to the study of resistance. And the way he came to look at it was that the human personality is something like an onion, with layers. The deepest and innermost layer – the centre – was what we have been calling the real self, healthy and fundamentally OK. But surrounding it on all sides was another layer just like what we have been calling the Id – a layer of distorted impulses and dangerous fantasies.

What we are saying, then, is that from his deep and extensive studies of resistance, Reich (1950) came to the conclusion that the real self was 'inside' the Id. This would mean, if it were true, that in order to get through to the real self, the route would go through the Id. This radically changes the definition of the Id, though not its nature. Instead of the Id being seen as the biological bedrock of the personality, it is seen as just another false self – a set of mistakes we have made about ourselves. But each of those mistakes may need to be picked up, and seen, and dealt with, before we can leave them behind or transform them. So there is no way, either for Freud or for Reich (or for us), of avoiding the need to deal with that layer. (Compare our account in Chapter 5.)

If this way of putting it is anything like the truth, as I believe it is, then resistance is understandable once again. The reason why we avoid the real self is because we have to walk through hell to get there. This means that we can accept the Id as a perfectly valid description of the way things appear, and of what we have done to ourselves and had done to us. It does have to be dealt with, just as Freud said it did. Only when we have done that, instead of just going back to our boring old over-socialised ego, we can go on to the ecstasy of the real self. It was James Bugental who made the link with existentialism. He says: 'Resistance is the name that we give to the general defensive wall the patient puts between himself and the threats that he finds linked to being authentic. Resistance is anti-authenticity' (Bugental 1981: 103). So the real self is the authentic self. And the way to it comes through a thicket of threats. One of the most important aspects of resistance is the way we can let our catastrophic expectations get in the way of the work. One of the best accounts of this is by Beth Erickson (1993), and Chart 8.1 is largely derived from her work.

Brammer, Shostrom and Abrego have a very good discussion of resistance, and one of the things they say which has really stuck in my mind and resonated there, is: 'The job of the therapist is not to overcome this resistance, but to explore it, because it can reveal the answer to the question – "How does the client hide his or her secret?"' (Brammer *et al.* 1989: 225). This idea of hiding secrets, and of this being a useful skill as well as whatever else it may be, is very close to the ideas of Reich mentioned earlier.

TYPES OF RESISTANCE

These authors go on to say that resistance may vary from rejection of therapy and overt antagonism on the one hand, to subtle forms such as hesitation and inattention on the other.

For example, the client criticizes the counselor, expresses dissatisfaction with the results of counseling, fails to hear or to understand the counselor, comes late or fails to keep appointments, remains silent, forgets the fee, engages in intellectual discussion using complex psychological terms, expresses negative attitudes toward psychology, desires to end counseling prematurely, is unproductive in associations or with unfamilar material, introduces irrelevant topics, makes unreasonable demands on the counselor, is pessimistic about counseling, or expresses skepticism about interpretations. The client's resistance may take less aggressive forms as, for example, agreeing unequivocally with everything the counselor says, refusing to get emotionally involved, being overly cooperative, prolonging a dependency transference, maintaining persistent facetiousness, forcing the process into a semantic wilderness of abstractions and philosophical notions, pressing the limits of the relationship by asking for overtime, perhaps, and expressing strong interest in the counselor's personal life.

(Brammer *et al*. 1989: 224)

What does this mean in practice? Well, for me it means that I can now go to all the wealth of knowledge and experience which therapists of all persuasions have built up over the years about resistance, and learn a hell of a lot from it. For example, we can now distinguish five different kinds of resistance.

Repression resistance is just due to the person not being aware of all the games they are playing. The unconscious defences remain unconscious because of the weight of repression still operating on them. This is the most common and basic kind of resistance. The client is fighting against becoming aware of painful feelings which are coming up, and may suddenly switch to a different subject, or switch off altogether.

Secondary gain resistance is all about the set of satisfactions the person gets from being neurotic – all the advantages you get, like gaining attention, avoiding things you don't want to do anyway, getting looked after and treated specially, and so on. This is all about the dangers of improvement:

If one loses weight, one will have to alter or buy a whole new wardrobe; if one feels more confident, others may then not hold back on unleashing criticism they have withheld 'while you were down'; in performing better sexually one may feel impelled to make up for lost time and neglect other necessary activities, or one's partner might not be able to keep up; and so forth.

(Fisch *et al*. 1982)

These drawbacks are very real, but they are often pooh-poohed by the client at the conscious level, even though they do affect behaviour. *Superego resistance* comes out in the client's unconscious need for punishment or rejection. We would of course not use a word like 'super-ego', which belongs to a different theoretical position. It would be for us just another instance of Mahrer's (1996) disintegrative relationships between operating potentials and deeper potentials.

This feeling is painful, but muted. It is an uncomfortable feeling, but soft and subtle. It consists of a little internal whimper, a delicate inner voice which says, 'You should not do this; that was a real mistake.' It is the voice which psychoanalysis attributes to the superego, and which humanistic theory attributes to the deeper potential which is blockaded in the service of preserving the self.

'The self' in Mahrer's quote here means the unregenerate neurotic self, the self which does not want to change, the unexamined operating potentials.

Repetition-compulsion resistance is that where the person maintains their fixed patterns in spite of all the insights and catharses they may attain to, and which seem to be deep and genuine. This is a particularly difficult form of resistance to handle, and it gave rise to Freud's idea of the death instinct. It can be a particularly frustrating one for the therapist.

Transference resistance is where the client tries to get from the therapist true love, or a magical cure, or tries to be like the therapist, or is competitive with the therapist, and so on. We can easily see how this can arise, from our discussion of transference in the previous chapter.

THERAPIST RESPONSE

Jim Bugental (1978) has a very good analogy to show how we should think about resistance. He says that when we are travelling on a motorway and come to road works causing a diversion, and find ourselves on side roads which are much slower, we are disappointed and inconvenienced. But if we are a member of the crew working on the road and come to that same set of road works, we say 'Aha, this is what I am looking for.' So it is in therapy, he says. We are looking for what interferes with the free flow of awareness of the full creative potential of consciousness (1978: 89).

What I have learned from all this is that the best thing for the therapist to do is to interpret the resistance. We saw in the last chapter how widely that has to be understood by the humanistic practitioner.

One of the best ways I have found of doing this is to personify the resistance and talk to it, and let it answer back. This is a good humanistic recourse. Mahrer says very directly:

> While the patient is 'resistant' to the deeper process, the deeper process has no 'resistance' to the patient, so the interaction is free to occur. The problem of 'resistance' is solved by giving the integrative, 'unresistant' deeper process a form and shape and voice with which to interact with the patient.

> (Mahrer 1986: 115)

Chart 8.1 Catastrophic fears

1 *Catastrophic fear of abandonment (being left bereft)*
'If I open myself to people and let myself love them and then they leave, I will feel abandoned and bereft again as I did before. So I won't really let people in, because they inevitably will leave anyway. And then it won't hurt so much when they do.'

This makes it very hard for the client to trust the therapist, and therefore the whole therapeutic task may be put in jeopardy. It may also cause problems with partners and other people who want to be close. It has often been found that women have this fear more than men.

2 *Catastrophic fear of merger (being swallowed up)*
'If I let people in, they will engulf me, swallow me up, and I won't have a life of my own ever again. So I'll just not ever let anybody close.'

This can be particularly difficult with a partner who has a fear of abandonment, because any moving away to secure my own space will be perceived as rejection. It has been found that men have this fear more than women.

3 *Catastrophic fear of exposure (sharing too much and then being rejected)*
'If I show people who I really am and they don't like what they see, they will reject me and I will be devastated. So I will just keep all my feelings and most of my thoughts to myself.'

This may sometimes be mixed with a fear of being a vampire – someone who attracts people and then destroys them in some way. This can get very complex at times, and the person may get so confused that they shut off altogether. This again makes therapy very difficult.

4 *Catastrophic fear of one's own destructive impulses (rage)*
'If I let people close to me, eventually they will do something to get me angry. So since I can't trust what I'll do, I'll protect them from getting hurt and myself from the humiliation I would feel if I did hurt them by keeping everyone at arm's length.'

This again is something more common with men than with women. It more often causes problems with partners and other intimates than it does with the therapy, but it may come up as a resistance in therapy as Reich found.

5 *Catastrophic fear of attack (persecutory attack and annihilation)*
'If I let people close enough to make them angry, I'll be destroyed by them. So I'll control every relationship by keeping everyone far away from me. Then I won't ever get hurt again.'

This seems to be more common with women than it does with men. It can seriously interfere with the process of therapy, because if one never leaves oneself open to attack by the therapist, one is not going to get very far.

Mahrer has his own way of carrying this out. I find a good way, which is compatible with most of the usual ways of working, works as follows.

Step one in this is to wait until the person comes up with an image of the resistance: 'It is like a wall'; 'It is like a porcelain bath with no way out'; 'It is like a fog'; 'It is like a huge door'; 'It is like a huge ball with hooks on it'; 'It is like a death skeleton', and so on. Step two is put it on the cushion or chair. This may be done quite directly, and it has worked well just like that; but more recently I have started to get the client to draw a picture of it, and then put the picture on to the cushion. This acts as a very powerful 'magnetic' focus of attention, which seems to bring the thing alive more vividly.

Step three is to talk to it. What I usually say is 'Wait until you can really see it there on the cushion, and have a real sense of its presence. When it is really here, start saying any words which come up, without thinking about them or censoring them, addressed directly to it. Let's suppose that by some miracle it can hear you, and talk back if necessary.' If the client doesn't accept this, and argues that a fog can't talk back, I simply say 'If it makes it easier, just imagine that it is a character in a play, labelled "Fog". This character comes on and represents Fog, and talks as if it were your Fog.' This then gets over the logical objection, which is of course just another aspect of the resistance itself. Once the talking starts, let it continue for some time.

Step four is to get the client to change over and sit on the other cushion (putting the drawing under the cushion so that it doesn't get torn or crumpled too much, if one is being used). I say 'Take a moment just to get into the feeling of *being* that character. Sit the way it would sit, breathe the way it would breathe, think the way it would think, feel the way it would feel, and just *be* it more and more. And when you are ready, see if there is anything you want to reply. [Name of client] is sitting there on that other cushion. S/he has just been talking to you, and saying various things to you. [Perhaps repeat some of them.] See them sitting on the cushion. Notice how they are dressed, what their expression is, how they are sitting and all that. And then see if there is any response you want to make.' It is important to put it in this permissive way, because sometimes the resistance won't talk, and it is important not to rule this out.

When the resistance has talked back, the dialogue carries on. People sometimes ask 'How do you know when to get the person to switch from one cushion to the other?' The basic answer to this is that you must allow the client to finish with one cushion before moving to the other, other-wise you can miss important spontaneous material which may emerge. It is like a conversation, and as with all conversations, eye contact is used as punctuation; so when the client pauses and looks at me, I know it is time to switch over.

Sometimes when the interaction has moved into its middle phase, I hurry things up a bit, by just waiting until one important phrase is uttered by one side or the other – something that if replied to will move the interaction along – without waiting for the client to give the signal. But this needs to be very carefully considered, because it puts the therapist into a more pushy and controlling position, and it should be abandoned as soon as possible. The client should always feel as if it is *them* doing it, and not that the therapist is doing it.

There are obviously many other ways of dealing with resistance. Sometimes it is enough just to talk about it directly – things like arriving late, forgetting appointments, leaving one's cheque book behind, can all be directly faced and commented on. For example, when a client is late by a quarter of an hour or more, a good question to ask is 'When was the first moment when you knew you were going to be late?' After all, if it were an examination which only took place once a year, and on which one's whole future depended, one would not be late no matter what. So it is largely a matter of choices and priorities, and that is where resistance comes in.

James Bugental has a very full and clear discussion of resistance. He remarks on how it can reveal not only what the person is doing in the session, but how they relate to the outside world. And in order to track a particular type of resistance, he advocates tagging it. This idea of tagging is not well known, but seems to be very important.

> Tagging the resistance is a matter of again and again pointing to the resistive pattern as it is occurring. This means that the pattern chosen for therapist attention must be one that is manifested frequently and is interfering currently with the client's inquiry into her own subjectivity. This means also that it is usually best to select only one such pattern for attention at any given point . . . With accelerating frequency the therapist needs to point to the client's dependence on this way of managing his in-the-moment experience . . . As the client becomes aware, through the tagging, of how frequently she relies on the pattern, the tagging needs to be extended to show how it affects the work.
>
> (Bugental 1987: 184)

How one deals with resistance says a lot about one's own personality as a therapist, and also about one's aims. The more limited one's aims, the less resistance is going to matter. The more far-reaching one's aims, the more resistance is likely to play a major role. But the therapist can certainly exaggerate and overemphasise resistance – Reich himself was a classic example of this. He would have angry shouting matches with his clients, because that is the kind of person he was. He was a good therapist, but he probably aroused more resistance than was really necessary.

Our approach is not to oppose the resistance, but to let it speak, let it have its day. Usually it thinks it is doing a great job in protecting the person from non-survivable threat. But of course in reality the threat *was* survived – otherwise the client would not be here today – so there must be some flaw in the logic of that.

Usually there are two levels involved: at one level there was an external threat which needed to be defended against; at another level there was a destructive response, where the client went beyond defence into attack. Most therapists, myself included, would say that the first came first, and the second second. Melanie Klein says that the second comes first. But either way, feelings of guilt will be associated with the second part, because the person being attacked by the infant client is usually the mother, and you just naturally feel guilty about trying to destroy your mother.

So the pain arises from intolerable threat and intolerable guilt, in some painful combination. No wonder that, as we get closer to this syndrome, resistance increases. All that I, as a therapist, can do is to work through this material myself, in my own therapy, and then encourage the client to follow my example.

Chapter 9

The process of development

At the end of the last chapter we started touching on the question of theory. If we want to do good therapy, we must have some notion of what is going on inside the person. Obviously our ideas about what works in therapy must be based on our ideas about where problems come from. The psychoanalyst has a clear set of ideas about the Oedipus complex, about the Id, ego and superego, and about the psychosexual stages of development. The behaviourist has a clear set of ideas about stimuli, responses, reinforcement and extinction. The cognitive therapist has a definite set of ideas about automatic thoughts and so forth. The humanistic practitioner is in a more difficult position, because there are a number of separate disciplines within it, each with its own notion of development, often not very well worked out or spelled out.

In my own work, I find I have three different theories which I use at different times. In the first edition of this book I had to say that I could not see how they could be reconciled, but now I can. Each of the three seems to have something which is missing in the others, and which is true and has to be taken into account in any adequate way of looking at these matters. And I now think they fit together in a convincing manner. The three are: primal integration theory; Mahrer's humanistic theory; and Wilber's transpersonal theory. Let us look at each of these in turn, and see what they have to offer.

PRIMAL INTEGRATION

In this theory we say that neuroses and psychoses often come ultimately from early trauma. At some point in our history we meet a situation which is intolerable – it is too painful to be borne. And at that point we resort to a defence which is generally known as splitting.

Frank Lake (1980) is clearest of all about the different levels of stress and the different levels of trauma which result from them. The highest level he calls 'transmarginal stress' (after Pavlov's research terminology) and it is this which leads most catastrophically to the splitting defence. Lake shows how by applying his four levels of stress to Grof's four stages of the birth process (1975) we get sixteen cells which between them account for most of the neuroses and psychoses seen in clinical practice. But the person who has spoken most eloquently about these matters is Janov (1973) who says:

> This separation of oneself from one's needs and feelings is an instinctive manoeuvre in order to shut off excessive pain. We call it the split. The organism splits in order to preserve its continuity. This does not mean that unfulfilled needs disappear, however.

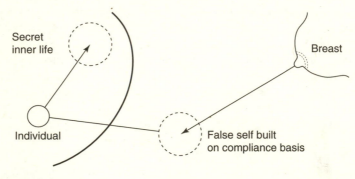

Diagram 9.1

This process has been well diagrammed by Winnicott (1975) (see Diagram 9.1). He says that after a trauma where splitting takes place:

> The infant gets seduced into compliance, and a compliant False Self reacts to environmental demands and the infant seems to accept them ... The False Self has one positive and very important function: to hide the True Self, which it does by compliance with environmental demands.

So the split is a defence against the annihilation of the experiencing subject. This is the same process which Balint (1968) talks about as the 'basic fault'. He points out that we are probably not talking – though we may sometimes be – about a single event: 'The trauma itself, of course, is not necessarily a single event; on the contrary, usually it amounts to a situation of some duration caused by a painful misunderstanding – lack of 'fit' – between the individual and his environment.' This very early splitting is a source of psychosis as much as of neurosis, particularly where the split is deepened and confirmed at a pre-verbal stage. So we should never be surprised when psychotic material comes up in any form of therapy. And this means that we as therapists need to work through our own psychotic material first, if we are not to be overpowered and overwhelmed by the depth of feeling involved in these very early traumas.

How early are they, in fact? Different researchers give different answers to this. Duval and Wicklund (1972) see the major trauma happening at about three years old; Mahler *et al.* (1975) see it happening at about one year old; Klein (Segal 1979) and the rest of the object relations school put it within the first six months of life; Grof (1992) and Lake (1980) say that it most often happens at birth, and have a lot of evidence to support their contention; Noble (1993) and Feher (1980) say that it can happen in the womb; Mott (1969) and Laing (1976) say that it can happen at implantation; Sadger (1941) and Peerbolte (1975) say that it can happen as far back as conception; and Roger Woolger (1990) is willing to go back into past lives in order to find the major trauma which has to be dealt with. One of the best and most fully thought-out accounts of all this material is to be found in Firman and Gila (1997): John Firman comes from the psychosynthesis school, but has a wide-ranging set of sympathies and is very well-read in these matters.

It doesn't seem to matter very much what we believe about this – it is what the client believes that matters. As long as we as therapists keep an open mind, we can go with the client to wherever the client needs to go. The important thing is that crises in the person's life tend to re-activate the defences which were used before. This means that we have to go back down the chain of crises to find the original trauma or traumatic situation.

The basic thought, held by many different theorists, is that crises form a series, such that the way the early crises are dealt with form the pattern for dealing with new crises as they arise. This position has been put forward most classically by Erikson (1965), but Grof (1975) has his version, the NLP people have their version, and so on. Janov (1977) says it this way:

> In the maturation of the brain each new trauma is represented and then re-represented holographically on higher and higher levels of the brain neuraxis. In this way a Primal chain is developed, with later traumas reactivating related first-line Pains. What this means is that at

each stage of brain development an imprint of the trauma occurs, and as the brain develops each imprint joins other related imprints of traumas, the early imprints becoming connected to the later ones. This fusion and representation continues to occur and becomes more elaborate and complex as maturation goes on.

Janov is here trying to work out what must be happening at a neurophysiological level. I don't think we need to get too hung up about the details of that, but it is important to show that in principle the brain is capable of working in this way, starting back before birth, to produce a chain or relay system of experiences which we can use in therapy like a kind of rope-ladder, going down step by step. Verny (1982) has collected a good deal of research which again shows that very early memories are indeed possible, and Chamberlain (1988) has demonstrated convincingly that many people can remember their own birth.

Once we have this basic split into the real or true self and the unreal or false self, it becomes easy to grasp how false selves can proliferate, thus producing the phenomenon which is variously known as subpersonalities, ego-states, complexes, internal objects, little 'I's and so forth (Rowan 1990, Firman and Gila 1997). I call them subpersonalities, because that seems to be most useful for therapy purposes. One of the best descriptions of how this happens comes from Freud:

> A portion of the external world has, at least partially, been abandoned as an object and has instead, by identification, been taken into the ego and thus become an integral part of the internal world. This new psychical agency continues to carry on the functions which have hitherto been performed by people in the external world.

Here Freud is, of course, talking about the superego. What we are now saying is that there are many separated superego-like regions in the child's psychic space, each of which has its own energy and its own rules. These are the subpersonalities.

There is much more which could be said about this process of development, but the main lines are now clear. As can be seen, this approach is not very far removed from psychoanalysis, particularly the position of the object relations school, or the middle school, as it is sometimes known. But the theory as laid down by Grof, for example, is much more flexible than the work of the object relations school, and not so hampered by the need to avoid any mention of perinatal experience or spiritual development. I find it very useful and helpful in my work, and very much in tune with the work I have done on myself. I have written it up more fully elsewhere (Rowan 1988b) and a more recent chapter on primal integration has been written by Juliana Brown and Richard Mowbray (1994). Those who think it is not very humanistic are too much influenced, I would suggest, by the fact that the early classics of the humanistic approach did not mention it. But they were writing before most of the current information, some of it very recent, came to light. Consequently, they missed out on something very important which we who come later do not need to ignore.

MAHRER'S HUMANISTIC PSYCHODYNAMICS

Mahrer (1989) again is more recent and original. According to him, instead of talking about the self as if it were present from the start, we should talk about a primitive personality field out of which a self only gradually emerges, a year or more after birth. So there is no way that early traumas can happen, because there is no one there for them to happen to. This is the logic; but the practice is subtly different. In Mahrer's therapy (1996) he continually takes the client back into earlier experiences, and some of them are extremely early, going back into perinatal scenes. There is clearly someone there, someone experiencing life in the womb, life during the process of birth. So there is a self after all at these early times. My own view is that a threat to life brings a self or ego of some kind into being. Before that I may have been part of a field, or part of a symbiotic unity or a pleroma or whatever, but as soon as my life is threatened there must be me who is being threatened and someone or something else which is doing the threatening. Mahrer calls these 'catastrophic incidents' and agrees that some people call them traumas. And none of Mahrer's clinical evidence contradicts that.

Mahrer talks throughout about 'infantness'. Usually an infant means a baby who can't yet talk, but by using the word 'infantness' instead, Mahrer makes it possible to say that the *idea* of the infant can extend back to a year or two before conception in many cases (or even further back in more unusual cases). So the infant is being constructed by the parents as part of their external world before he or she comes on to the scene in any tangible form. And similarly at the other end, the parents can continue this idea of infantness long after the child can talk.

So the primitive personality field consists (in the usual case where father and mother are both present) of the operating and deeper potentials of the father and the mother, plus infantness.

What does Mahrer mean by potentials? This is one of his major theoretical innovations, and we must look carefully at his account:

> Each potential constitutes its own zone of experiencing, more or less distinct and independent of the other potentials. It is as if each potential is its own mini-world of experiencing. In this sense, we are indeed multiple selves, multiple consciousnesses, even multiple personalities. Each potential has its own centre, its own self system, its own personality.
>
> (Mahrer 1989: 29)

This makes it clearer. We are talking about something resembling sub-personalities, ego-states, complexes, internal objects, little 'I's once again. This enables us to feel that we are on familiar ground to that extent. So when he talks about relations between potentials, it is like talking about relations between persons – only this time they are internal persons:

> The nature of the relationships among potentials is the major determinant of problems. A disintegrative relationship among potentials is probably the major factor in the occurrence of bad feelings, in the occurrence of bodily pain and suffering, in the construction of a person's unhappy world and . . . as the key determinant of human problems and pain . . . Our theory turns to the disintegrative relationship among potentials not only for 'neuroses', but for the whole spectrum of human suffering.
>
> (*ibid.*: 28)

The primitive personality field, then, going back to our discussion of early development, consists of the parents' potentials and the positive or negative relationships among them, plus infantness. And this space, as it were, of infantness, gets filled by the physical baby and infant as and when it appears, and by the embryo and foetus before that. This means that the infant has no potentials of his or her own:

> Bluntly, the potentials of the infant are the relevant potentials of the significant figures. That is, the potentials of the infant are those potentials of the figures within the primitive personality field which pertain to the infant. The same reasoning places some of the relationships of the significant figures within the larger conception of the infant. That is, the relationships among potentials of the infant are those relationships among the potentials of the figures within the primitive personality field which pertain to the infant.

The disintegrative or integrative nature of these relationships becomes the nature of relationships within our larger definition of the infant's primitive personality.

(ibid.: 622–3)

This is reminiscent of the Freudian saying that the superego of the child comes from the superego of the parent, in quite an unconscious way, and at first it sounds as if this is a one-way thing. It sounds as if Mahrer is sinking the poor infant quite vanishingly into the personality field set up by the parents. But he is far more subtle than that. He is saying rather that this primitive personality field, while set up in the first instance by the parents, can be seen from various perspectives once it is set up:

In contrast to our common system of thought, humanistic theory suggests that the definition of an object varies with the context. What mother is depends on our context of understanding. Within the context of mother, mother is one thing, the centre of a given context. Within that context, baby is an extension of mother, a constructed component of her world. But when we switch to the context of the infant, and hold the infant as the centre of that context, then mother becomes a constituent of baby . . . There are . . . as many perspectives as there are participants.

(ibid.: 622)

Having set up this notion of the primitive personality field, and the perspectives within it, Mahrer goes on to say firstly that the process of development of the infant into a child and into an independent adolescent and adult depend on the dissolution of the primitive personality field, and secondly that the parents have a lot of power and resources, if they care to use them, to prevent this dissolution taking place.

So Mahrer is saying that the symbiotic relationship between mother and child, which has been referred to by Stanislav Grof (1992) and others, goes back a lot further than psychoanalysts say, and involves the father as well as the mother. Anxiety, for example, does not start with feeding or with birth – it may be present before the moment of conception, and may become intense for the infant at any point where it affects one or both parents. This is such an unfamiliar idea that we need to look at one piece of evidence at least:

As reviewed by Joffe (1969) the research first indicated a high correlation between maternal smoking and infant prematurity, especially when prematurity was defined in terms of birth weight. This research was interpreted as suggesting a causal relationship between maternal smoking and premature birth. Subsequent research, however, reported similar high correlation between premature low birth weight and *paternal* smoking!

(Mahrer 1989: 677)

The research by Rottman (1974) reported in the classic book by Tom Verny (1982) – and indeed much of the other research in the same book – points in the same direction. Rottman tested pregnant women for the conscious and unconscious attitudes they had towards the child they were carrying. This gave four possibilities: consciously and unconsciously positive (Ideal); consciously positive but unconsciously negative (Ambivalent); consciously negative but unconsciously positive (Cool); and consciously and unconsciously negative (Catastrophic). At birth, the babies of the Ideal mothers were physically and emotionally healthy, and thrived. The babies of the Ambivalent mothers tended to have behavioural and gastrointestinal troubles. The babies of the Cool mothers tended to be apathetic and lethargic. And the babies of the Catastrophic mothers tended to be premature, low-weight and emotionally disturbed. The rather similar research of Lukesch (1975) showed that the fathers were implicated too.

So this primitive personality field, which includes both parents and the infant, is powerful indeed. And it carries on its work of constructing the infant without needing the awareness of the participants. The entire scene may be carried on without anyone being conscious or even half-sensing what is going on. In constructing this field, parents can use any one or more of four basic methods or mechanisms:

Inducing behaviour from scratch – 'By organizing the primitive field in a very particular manner, only certain infant behaviour can occur as the other side of the behavioural coin.' For example, if the parent engages in a high rate of interaction with a baby, at least three types of response are automatically induced (Beckwith 1972). The infant has no way of avoiding this.

Developing behavioural nubbins – The baby does something small, a hint of some later action, if taken in a certain way. The parent then takes it as a fully developed indication of that later action, and treats it in such a way as to turn it into that action. 'Mother will see before her a baby who is demanding immediate gratification, who is demanding that things be done right now; she will not see a mere behavioural nubbin, a whimper or a little cry.'

Attributing intentions to behaviour – 'All the baby has to do is to behave in the most ordinary ways. Indeed, baby's role is so easy that often all baby is required to do is *not* behave in some way . . . Any infant can be interpreted as behaving in a cold and unresponsive manner.' The number and variety of actions which can be attributed to very young babies is extraordinary, only limited by the imagination of the parents. But once an interpretation has been made, the actions of the parents are such as to confirm and reinforce their interpretation, and this is very effective because of the extensive contact of the parents with the baby.

By being part of the field that is the infant – Here the connection is intimate and inescapable. It is not a causal connection, but a relation of identity. It is an 'almost magical relationship between the behaviour of infants and the personality processes of parents'. For example, Glauber's research (1953) found that very young stutterers were acting out their mother's tendency to stutter. All the material on the family as a system can now be seen in this light.

These, then, are the four methods, and by using them the parents have the power to imprison the young child within the primitive personality field long after it could have been dissolved. (All this material comes from Mahrer 1989, Chapter 14.)

Some of Mahrer's most moving and distressing material concerns the way in which parents maintain the field and stop the child's own self from emerging, even right up into school age and beyond. If they want to do this they must:

(a) maintain ownership of the child's behaviour, (b) maintain ownership of the child's external world, (c) maintain ownership of the child's relationship with himself, and (d) prevent escape from the encompassing primitive field.

(Mahrer 1989: 723)

To stop a child developing a sense of self, parents can initiate the child's behaviour, take over the child's behaviour, take ownership of the child's thoughts, prevent the child from defining its centre of attention, serve as model and leader, take over the child's perception of reality, neutralise the child's attempts to own its own behaviour, disqualify attempts to define equal stature relationships and so on. They can determine the nature of the child's external world, they can uncouple the child's behaviour from consequent changes in the external world, they can stop the child owning any part of the external world. And this is just a list of the headings for (a) and (b) above – we do not have space here to do more. Mahrer goes on to give many moving examples of all this – a part of his work which I found very painful to read. It all sounds horribly familiar. He tells of how children's thoughts are monitored, contradicted, twisted and fed back in distorted ways so that the child doesn't know if he or she is coming or going: 'Little wonder that some adults have practically no memory of huge slabs of their childhood; they were engaged in responding to parents, in carrying out what parents got them to do, in never owning their own behaviour' (*ibid.*: 730). The parents will tend to hold on to the primitive personality field in this way to the extent that it is expressing in a successful way their own potentials and the disintegrative relationships among them. If there is a disintegrative relationship between the parents' potentials, then to that extent they will want to project their conflicts into and on to the child. So the dissolution of the primitive personality field depends upon the parents achieving some measure of integration:

> If parents do not let go, then the self cannot occur. The act of dissolving away the primitive field is more than the passive freeing of shackles. It is an *active* step in the development of the sense of self . . . If the parent hasn't achieved intactness, the parent cannot enable the child to achieve intactness.
>
> (*ibid.* 760–1)

Mahrer is very acutely aware of the difficulties involved in the process of emergence into selfhood, to the point where it sometimes seems a miracle that anyone ever achieves it. But of course this fits with his insistence that virtually all of us have some disintegrative relationships with our deeper potentials – this results very clearly from our experience within the primitive personality field. But there are ways out, both for parents and for children. Here is an example, one of many given in Mahrer's book:

> From the beginning, Helen was mother's closest companion and confidante. Helen did not exist as a person, though she was six years old. She was run by mother, encompassed and owned by mother. When mother was ready to undergo her own personal change, she entered into the kind of psychotherapy which brought to an end her owning of her child . . . As the bonds dropped away, as Helen came forth out of the primitive field, little by little, in subtle ways, Helen's mother felt sad. Mother knew that Helen was not, and had not been, the perfect companion. In many ways, Helen had no understanding at all of her mother. Helen preferred to have other friends, and was not really interested in hearing mother's thoughts and feelings. Each tiny

increment in the dissolving of the old field had its own entitled bit of sadness as mother became a new person with a new daughter. It was a good sadness, accompanying the dawning personhoods of both Helen and her mother.

(ibid.: 762)

Now this is a striking, simple and self-consistent theory, and it has many merits. It is profoundly social, and it leads to a view of psychodynamics which is very usable in therapy. But there are three things I disagree with in it.

The first is the overemphasis, as it seems to me, on the idea of parental pressures in forming the infant's personality. Although the resources of the infant are relatively restricted by comparison with those of the parents, it does have some resources, as all parents well know. And in my view the infant is always interpreting the world from its own perspective, right from the start. This is of course allowed for in the quotes above, but Mahrer never really does justice to the infant's point of view, and seems to lose touch with his own insights.

This ties in with my second disagreement. Mahrer always presents the dissolving of the primitive personality field as a positive process – perhaps some sadness goes with it, as in the example just given, but on the whole it feels good. In my view, the emergence of the self can come about (and often does) as a result of trauma, as suggested in the work of Winnicott (1975), Janov (1973), Duval and Wicklund (1972) and the other investigators referred to earlier in this chapter. The split into the real self and the false self would be equivalent to the split between operating potentials and deeper potentials in Mahrer's terminology. The operating potentials would be false selves or subpersonalities, and one of the deeper potentials would be the real self. The other deeper potentials would be other false selves, repressed and denied for various other reasons.

My final disagreement is about the lack of any spiritual element in the theory (except for a few references to Zen). It seems to me that since Mahrer does provide for different levels of the deeper potentials – he speaks for example about 'mediating potentials' and 'basic potentials' – it would be an interesting extension of the same idea to say that there are some very deep spiritual potentials which may arise and need to be dealt with. That is precisely the view of Ken Wilber, whose position has also influenced me very much.

WILBER'S TRANSPERSONAL THEORY

Wilber says that we start life with a spiritual nature that has been developed in many previous lives, and which lies within us as a potential which requires to be unfolded during the process of our current life.

> Enfolded and enwrapped in the ground-unconscious of the newborn lie all the higher states of being. They were put there by involution, and they exist there as *undifferentiated potential*. Development or evolution is simply the unfolding of these enfolded structures, beginning with the lowest and proceeding to the highest: body to mind to subtle to causal.

> (Wilber 1980)

The last few words may be unfamiliar or confusing. Wilber has a well-worked-out map which clarifies his meaning. From this map we can see that the early stages are much as they have been laid down by the Jungians, by the object-relations people and the primal integration people. Then comes adolescence, which has been well described by the social-psychology people. Then comes adult life, which is the most researched part of the arc, though much of the research is not at all good, as we have pointed out elsewhere (Reason and Rowan 1981). Then comes the centaur stage, which most of this book is about, and which also forms the centre of my earlier books, particularly of course *Ordinary Ecstasy* (Rowan 1988a). Then comes the subtle stage, which Wilber divides into two – the lower subtle and the higher subtle (see Diagram 9.2).

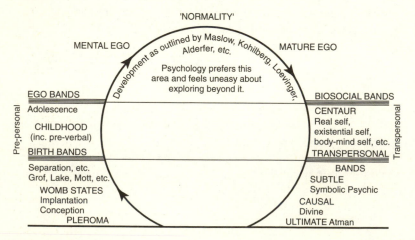

Diagram 9.2

The lower subtle, which he also calls the psychic, is where we are concerned with things like out-of-body experiences, auras, ESP, clairvoyance, dowsing, healing, and so on. By some form of spiritual discipline we acquire skills which are not reducible to the ordinary material categories we have been using up to now. (I would argue, however, that some of these skills can come through quite other means, and that they should therefore be treated with great caution as evidence of spiritual progress.) At this stage we are transpersonally sensitive, and this intuitive power can be developed by practice. We are going beyond the centaur categories of 'meaning in my life'; we are giving up intentionality and self-actualisation; we are letting go of self-autonomy. We are thinking more in terms of obedience and surrender.

In the higher subtle all these things go further, and we really get in touch with higher powers outside of ourselves, which we may see (depending on our cultural surroundings) as higher presences, guides, guardian angels, ishtadevas, higher archetypes, the higher self or the overself. We can have symbolic visions, religious inspiration, literal dictation, experiences of blue, gold and white light, audible illumination, brightness upon brightness, experiences of rapture, bliss and compassion. Bijas and affirmations become particularly powerful tools at this stage, being given to us rather than chosen by us.

The causal realm is the realm of the divine proper, where the archetypes and other entities dissolve into final-God, the source of all archetypes and angels. And in the higher causal, the final-God itself dissolves into the Ground of formlessness which lies behind. At the Nondual stage, this Ground itself disappears. My own opinion is that Wilber is less good a guide at the causal stage and beyond, because he performs the amazing feat of talking about the Divine without ever mentioning Jehovah, Allah or God the Father! Any account of the Divine which is going to be worth listening to must include these somehow, even if only to explain them away.

So that is the map, but the most interesting thing about it is the precise way in which Wilber says we move from one stage to another through the process of development, which is what the map describes.

At each stage, he says, we have to give up one notion of the self and adopt another. We actually have to revise our whole self-image or change our ego. This is very clear and familiar at the earlier stages. We know how difficult it is to leave the womb and become a separate body – Grof and others have described this very well. We know how difficult it is to leave the primitive personality field and be born psychologically – this is Mahrer's great area of expertise. We know how difficult it is to leave the family and become a separate individual – Madison (1969) has given a very fine account of this. At each of these stages we had to give up our safe identity and pick up a new and less certain identity.

> Thus, at each point in psychological growth, we find: 1) a higher-order structure emerges in consciousness (with the help of symbolic forms); 2) the self identifies its being with that higher structure; 3) the next-higher-order structure eventually emerges; 4) the self dis-identifies with the lower structure and shifts its essential identity to the higher structure; 5) consciousness thereby transcends the lower structure; 6) and becomes capable of operating on that lower structure from the higher-order level; 7) such that all preceding levels can then be integrated in consciousness, and ultimately as Consciousness.
>
> (Wilber 1980)

This is a dialectical model of self-actualisation through self-transcendence. There is no smooth evolution – we have to say a loud 'No!' to our previous sense of self. This is exactly what Mahrer (1989) says happens in therapy, when we move from the mental ego to the real self. We have to abandon our existing self-image (what he calls in his terminology our operating potential) and plunge into and identify with that which we fear (what he calls our deeper potential):

> The centre of the person or self or person-as-operating-potential kills itself by hurling itself into the very core of the deeper potential. No longer is the centre of the person lodged within the domain of the operating potentials; no longer is the centre of the person separate from the bowels of the deeper potentials . . . In this adventure, the very core of the person plunges into the metamorphosis of self-transformation. Nothing is held back or withdrawn.
>
> (Mahrer 1989: 480–1)

What Wilber is saying is that this process continues. Having got to the integrated and actualised stages which Mahrer talks about, there are further stages to go through, and they require more of that same process of losing the self to find it again. At each stage, Wilber says, there is incest and castration. The incest is the hanging on to a self which we should have outgrown; the castration is the fear of losing it – of having it taken away before we are ready. But we are never ready – it is always scary.

What we are really about, says Wilber, is Ultimate Unity with whatever is behind everything. This is what we most desire; that is what we have inside us as our deepest and most important potential. And we resist this and fight against it with every means in our power. At each stage in development we say, in effect, 'Let me have some peace now – I've been through such a lot.' But there is no peace to be had. There is only stagnation, unless we go on, and on. Wilber puts this with eloquent concision:

> We have seen that psychological development in humans has the same goal as natural evolution: the production of ever-higher unities. And since the ultimate Unity is Buddha, God or Atman (to use those terms in their broadest sense as 'ultimate reality'), it follows that psychological growth aims at Atman . . . From the outset, the soul intuits this Atman-nature, and seeks, from the outset, to *actualize* it as a reality and not just as an enfolded potential. That drive to actualize Atman is part of the Atman-project. But it is only part, because – even though each stage of psychological growth is a step closer to God – each stage is *still* only a stage. That is, each stage towards God is still not itself God. Each stage is a search for God under conditions which fall short of God. The soul must seek Unity through the constraints of the present stage, which is not yet Unity. And *that* is the other side of the Atman-project: each individual wants only Atman, but wants it under conditions which prevent it . . . And that is why human desire is insatiable, why all joys yearn for infinity – all a person wants is Atman; all he finds are symbolic substitutes for it. This attempt to regain Atman consciousness in ways or under conditions that prevent it and force symbolic substitutes – this is the Atman project.
>
> (Wilber 1980: 100–3)

This seems to me a very powerful statement, and it makes sense of so much of my own experience that I feel I cannot ignore it. And I find it helps very much to clarify what is happening to those of my clients who are getting into transpersonal material. It is a much more persuasive and well-worked-out map than the Assagioli egg or the Jung diagrams of Esther Harding (1965) or Erich Neumann (1963).

CONCLUSION

These, then, are the three theories of development which have helped me at various times. The primal integration story is very flexible, and can deal with the mental ego, the centaur and the subtle stages very well, as I have explained in detail in a recent chapter (Rowan 1997a). The Wilber story is very wide-ranging, and really covers the whole gamut in an extraordinary way. But the Mahrer story is purely humanistic, and deals almost exclusively with the centaur stage, so of the three I think it is the most pertinent to the aims of this book.

But even the Mahrer story, profoundly social though it is, is not sufficient in and of itself to do justice to the political and social considerations which bear on therapy and the counselling situation. It is this which we must now look at.

Chapter 10

Listening with the fourth ear

In 1967 an extraordinary book appeared – *The Politics of Experience*, by R.D. Laing. During the next ten years, all the issues raised in that book were acted on in various ways by different groups. In the Introduction, Laing says:

> We are bemused and crazed creatures, strangers to our true selves, to one another, and to the spiritual and material world – mad, even, from an ideal standpoint we can glimpse but not adopt.
>
> We are born into a world where alienation awaits us. We are potentially persons, but are in an alienated state, and this state is not simply a natural system. Alienation as our present destiny is achieved only by outrageous violence perpetrated by human beings on human beings.

If anything like this is true, the whole task of psychotherapy has to be seen in a new light – not as helping people to adjust to a world which is basically all right, but as freeing people from their internal shackles so that they may effectively go about ridding themselves of their external shackles.

SOCIAL AWARENESS

This means, however, that anyone working in the field of personal growth has to be aware of the way in which mental disturbance is systematically created by the conditions in which we live. Robert Seidenberg (1974a) put this in a memorable way when he said: 'Often the therapist is still listening with the "third" ear when the times call for a fourth.' This was in the context of a case history of a woman who came to him with symptoms of 'fear of losing her mind, episodes of severe apprehension in the street and in stores, and fear that she might harm her three-year-old daughter'. This woman seemed to have no external problems, and so she was referred for psychotherapy on the assumption that the problems must be internal and neurotic. So Seidenberg set out to discover what her blocked impulses were, what traumas she might have had and so forth.

What he found himself impelled more and more towards, however, was the discovery that her problems were current and external, and even about the future, rather than internal and in the past. Her life had been chosen for her by her husband and her father – it was a secure trap. Her life would be the same for the next thirty or forty years as it had been for the last twenty. There would be no challenge, no decision-making, no problem-solving, no choices. And she could see her daughter going the same way. The realisation came to her that her brother had been treated quite differently because he was male. Her destiny was to be a female and therefore to be basically unimportant, pushed around and controlled by men, in a safe, cared-for but featureless world. Seidenberg called this 'the trauma of eventlessness', and said:

> A lack of external events and appropriate internal responses can constitute a trauma no less than the 'dramatic' assaults against the ego. More than that, the anticipation of more and more eventlessness may similarly constitute a danger of severe proportions to one's well-being.

> (Seidenberg 1974a)

Recognition of this made it possible for this woman to take herself seriously and to start to think in terms of what she needed for her own survival. She got a part-time job which involved going into unfamiliar parts of the city, and here she experienced no fear, only exhilaration. She refused to have any more children.

Once this area has been opened up, it is easy to see how it applies in many other areas as well. We start looking for external factors and for anticipatory factors. We look not only at what is inside or what is in the past. We look not only at the emotional, the intellectual or the spiritual, but also at the political. As Jean Baker Miller (1974) put it:

> One permits all so-called symptoms to be seen in a new light – no longer merely as defences, manoeuvres or other such tactics, but as struggles to preserve or express some deeply-needed aspects of personal integrity in a milieu that will not allow for their direct expression.

This does not only apply to oppressed groups, but it is oppressed groups which become most quickly aware of the problems, because for them the whole process is intensified. And so it is the women's movement which has had most to say about the distortions of therapy and counselling caused by lack of attention to the social and political context. Phyllis Chesler (1972) says:

> Women are in a continual state of mourning – for what they never had – or had too briefly, and for what they can't have in the present, be it Prince Charming or direct worldly power. It is not very easy for most women to temper, idle or philosophise away their mourning with sexual, physical or intellectual exercises. When female depression swells to clinical proportions, it unfortunately doesn't function as a role release or respite . . . [Women's] depression may serve as a way of keeping a deadly faith with their 'feminine' role. It is safer for women to become 'depressed' than physically violent. Physically violent women usually lose physical battles with male intimates; are abandoned by them as 'crazy' as well as 'unfeminine'; are frequently psychiatrically or (less frequently) criminally incarcerated. Further, physically strong and/or potentially assaultive women would gain fewer secondary rewards than 'depressed' women; their families would fear, hate and abandon them, rather than pity, sympathise or 'protect' them.

The point is that if the therapist is unaware of these issues, the client may ignore them too. In all counselling and psychotherapy, the unspoken assumptions of the therapist can have a profound effect on the client, in what she says or does not say. It is not necessary for the therapist to do anything wicked to miss all this important material – all that is necessary is that the therapist pays no attention to the fourth ear. As one of the authors says in Ernst and Goodison (1981):

> Yet [my analyst] was obviously a kind man, he never told me what to do, or what I should think, or laid interpretations on me. He was not oppressive in the blatant ways that feminist writers on therapy have documented. He didn't try to seduce me, tell me I should use make-up or dress differently, accuse me of being incapable of real love because I didn't have orgasms. I have no doubt that overt oppression of women does go on in therapy . . . but I think what happened to me is equally common and perhaps more difficult to particularise. The oppression lay in *who he was*, the questions *he didn't ask* and the material *I didn't present*. It lay in the way I felt when I arrived at his house on my bicycle and he drew up in his large car; the sense I had

that he must see his wife and family and home as normal and my household as a sign of my abnormality. To be cured would be to be capable of living like him.

But if we can open up the fourth ear, we can become much more open to noticing this sort of thing.

It is women who have been most vocal in this area, partly no doubt because most therapists find that most of their clients are women, and so there is a wealth of experience to draw on. But listening with the fourth ear does not only apply to women, but to all oppressed groups. Gelb (1973) gives the example of a thirteen-year-old orphaned boy who was referred to him as 'depressed, failing in school and often truant'. He had a 'severe behaviour problem' and was 'unmanageable'. After some attempts at conventional therapy, which were unsuccessful, Gelb began to see that this boy had been the victim of poor teachers and a series of foster homes where he had been cruelly exploited. So he took up the cudgels politically: 'Partly as a resuit of my joining my patient in his angry reaction, the agency reorganized its foster placement programme and provided family counselling.' Through this process of having his anger accepted as legitimate rather than neurotic, the boy began to take an interest in education, and eventually became a photographer. This combination of practical action and therapy is of course much easier to achieve in a group, because the whole group can be involved in some activity.

There are some good examples of this in the book by Jill Freedman and Gene Combs. They speak very thoroughly about the social context in which all therapy takes place. They have a perspective which locates the individual client in a matrix of supporters, antagonists, reference points and social realities. And they are prepared to enter into this social process and get involved with it. They talk about not just having these ideas, but living them.

> When people, through the 'unmasking' process of relating problems to societal discourses, see their local problems as particular instances of political problems in the larger society, they can become motivated to deal with them differently. When people stop living by the dictates of a political problem at a local level, they help deconstruct the problem at a societal level.
>
> (Freedman and Combs 1996: 68)

They talk about 'an insurrection of lost knowledges', and there is a radical flavour about their whole approach. They look on the list of people who have abused the client in the past as the 'abuse team', and encourage the client to look around for a 'nurturing team' to compensate and help in the fight back against such treatment. Instead of relying solely on autonomy and self-reliance, they see the social context as having a part to play in the ultimate mental health of the person. Instead of criticising the person for being too dependent, the aim is to set up good forms of dependence and interdependence which will be genuinely nourishing for the person. For example, the client may be encouraged to join or help to set up an 'Anti-Anorexia and Anti-Bulimia League'. Or a book may be put together by several therapists and several clients (who may be adults or children) such as 'The Temper Tamer's Hand-book' and 'The Fear Facer's Handbook'. There is a good discussion of ethical principles in relation to community and social context. There are some good examples of this in the Ernst and Goodison book already mentioned:

> In a separate therapy group women were able to explore feelings of loneliness, lack of confidence, anger, exhaustion in the struggle to establish any independence; this activity ran parallel to the more outward looking activities of the food co-op and the community issues raised there.

But in a way this enables us to avoid the awkward questions about the one-to-one relationship between therapist and client. If one of the main external reasons why women feel bad is the oppression of a male-dominated society, then there is something very curious about women coming to a male therapist. A therapist is an authority figure (and as we have seen, this is so irrespective of orientation or of subjective wishes) and perhaps the woman's whole problem is with very real and very present male authority figures. In such a case, maybe a male therapist is the last thing she needs. Certainly some women feel this. Nadine Miller (1973) writes a moving piece about a woman saying goodbye to her therapist, in which she says: 'I was lucky enough to realise that my hostility toward men was real, and was not an individual problem. You bet I had reasons to hate men – you not being the least.' But is this fair? Certainly Robert Seidenberg (1974b) thinks it is. In his discussion of power he draws attention to the very unequal gender distribution of power, such that women defer to men, and men expect women to defer in that way, to their expertise and their egos. And Jean Baker Miller (1978) has explained in great detail, from a psychological standpoint, exactly how this works. This is a book which anyone interested in this whole area must read.

Is the answer for women to go to female therapists and counsellors? This might seem to be the obvious solution. But it is not an open-and-shut answer, because many women therapists were trained by men and have internalised the male values and assumptions of their trainers. It is notorious that two of the psychoanalysts who were most anti-woman in their pronouncements were Marie Bonaparte and Helene Deutsch. The recent history of women prime ministers is enough to demonstrate on a much more public stage that merely being a woman is not enough. Any woman who wants to be a good therapist has got to cultivate her fourth ear with just as much care and difficulty as any man. The patriarchal culture surrounds us all. There is a very good discussion of these matters by Betty McLellan (1995).

CO-COUNSELLING

One of the changes which has taken place in the whole field since Laing wrote his disturbing book is the increase in various kinds of peer counselling, starting with re-evaluation counselling (Jackins 1965) and resulting later in four different networks of co-counselling in Britain alone. This movement seems to have diminished in recent years, but its lessons are still worth examining. It is important because it enables us to look afresh at the whole question of authority in the counselling relationship. Although there are several schools of co-counselling, they all have in common the idea of two people meeting and each spending half their time together as counsellor and half as client. There is no mystification, because they have both learned the same techniques, often from the same person at the same time. There is no authority problem, because the relationship is precisely equal in its basic assumptions. And no money changes hands, which eliminates another source of imbalance. The only exception to the money question is for the initial training: this takes two weekends, or some equivalent period of time – about forty hours. It is not expensive, but for those who reject paying even this amount, or who don't even have that much money, one co-counsellor can teach another in a quite informal way. Or there is now a self-teaching manual (Southgate and Randall 1989) which can be used by a dyad or a group without a teacher.

It then becomes clear that all therapy requires a differentiation of roles. I am either the counsellor or the client (the assistant or the worker, in the Barefoot Psychoanalyst version) and the role of the counsellor is quite different from the role of the client. This is an enormous clarification at once, because once we see through the authority and power question, we often tend to go to the opposite extreme, and assume that the good, radical, nonauthoritarian therapist must be just the same as the client – not using techniques, not playing any role, denying all special expertise and so on. This is rubbish, because it just doesn't work, and there is no way of making it work. Therapy and counselling are essentially role-oriented relationships, where the initiating activities are different from the responding activities – both being equally necessary and equally capable of being done well or badly.

And just here there arises a most important paradox. Usually there is a contradiction between playing a role and being authentic. But a therapist or counsellor is playing a role which essentially involves and entails being authentic. It is 'the game of no game' as someone once put it. This belief makes it impossible for humanistic therapists to go along with the idea that everything in the therapeutic relationship must be either transference or countertransference. The authentic relationship is one of the five (Clarkson 1995) which are continuously operating in all therapy.

There is a corresponding paradox on the other side. The client has to try hard to let go. Of course, trying hard is the opposite of letting go. This is the central paradox in all personal growth, and also in activities like meditation and the Zen koan solution. The harder you try, the more the letting go means when it finally does happen. Through the medium of co-counselling, all these things can be seen much more clearly, because it removes all those awkward and confusing questions about authority figures, whether they be therapists or gurus. We can then see the process as it is, and this takes away all our fears about being manipulated by techniques we do not understand.

Another insight which becomes crystal clear through co-counselling is that therapy takes a long time. As long as we were worried about getting into the hands of the therapist, and worried about the money being made by keeping the client dependent, we could not look straight at the question of how long therapy might take. And of course we were further confused by new innovators in therapy, because each one always claims that their new method is really fast and effective, and that the old methods were designed to prolong therapy for the benefit of all the unscrupulous therapists. Co-counselling helps us to see that this is not so, and that any real attempt to change the personality is going to take years of effort. Someone told me once that the CG Jung Institute in Los Angeles had a motif on their letterheads which looked at first like a mandala; but when one looked more closely, it became clear that it was actually a picture of four snails following each other round in a circle. This is a good symbol of therapy, in my own opinion, because it emphasises the slowness of it all. Someone else told me of the slogan – 'Fast as a speeding oak' – which again seems a helpful sketch of the issue at hand.

Once we fully realise and accept this, we can then look much more rationally at the question of which practitioner we are going to see, and how much we are willing to pay. And as therapists, it makes us less worried about our own motives. We can be more relaxed about the whole thing, once we see that our role is a legitimate one. And we can recommend co-counselling to our clients when extra sessions are required, or when the client runs out of money, without feeling that there is anything second-best about this.

Going back now to the question of male and female therapists, we can see more clearly that although some women at some particular times may need a female therapist, there is no reason in principle why a man cannot be sensitive to the issues involved, and be able to do a good job with a woman client. As Lester Gelb (1973) says:

> It took us many years to realize that when a woman described many of the men who wanted to take her out as 'no damn good', she was likely to be right. It became necessary for me to re-examine my theoretical bias which ascribed the difficulties that women presented to their own psychopathology. I gradually began to accept that their painful failure to adapt was often an unsuccessful protest against impersonal social forces deriving from the larger social system in which they were helpless victims.

A male analyst like this gives one hope that therapists can step out of their early conditioning and work on themselves sufficiently to deal with prejudice and general social attitudes – what Bem (1970) calls the 'nonconscious ideology' of patriarchy.

THE PATRIPSYCH

There is, however, an even deeper way in which we can listen with the fourth ear, and that is to listen for the patripsych. This is a word invented by John Southgate to represent the internalised patterns of patriarchal thinking, and is pronounced pay-tri-syke.

> The patripsych is a shorthand term for what we have called the 'internal constellation of patriarchal patterns.' By this we mean all the

attitudes, ideas and feelings, usually compulsive and unconscious, that develop in relation to authority and control. This development is closely related to learning about sex roles – learning about whether you are a little boy or a little girl.

(Southgate and Randall 1989)

It is the patripsych we have to contend with when we are touching on compulsive feelings of dependence on authority figures, so that I assume they know best, I want to get near them, I want to be like them and so forth. It is also the patripsych I have to contend with when I have a compulsive need to fight authority figures, opposing them regardless of what they do, dedicating my life to their destruction and seeing them as symbols of evil. And it is also the patripsych I have to contend with when I am touching on compulsive needs for flight from authority figures, withdrawing into myself, refusing to compete, being uncommunicative, not engaging in any way and avoiding all the issues of control. Southgate and Randall (1989) say:

It is important to remember that we not only develop compulsive ways of relating to people who are in authority over us but also develop compulsive ways of relating when we are in positions of authority ourselves. The general point about this is that it is very difficult for anyone to relate to authority (theirs or others) in a fully creative way. There is frequently little choice in our actions (although we may think there is) and power relations are mystified and confused.

And they make the point that the patriarchal family continues to exist still, even though the outward appearance of many families may be relaxed and equal. This usually becomes more apparent when children come along, and the 'crisis of parenthood' (Neugarten *et al.* 1964) pushes men and women into more onesided roles.

This kind of insight is of course very similar to what Mitchell (1975) has said about the extraordinary way in which patriarchy has entered into our language and our thinking at deep unconscious levels. It seems closely parallel to the kind of thing which Wyckoff (1975) classically said about the Pig Parent:

In women's groups, women can become familiar with what insidiously keeps them down – not only the obvious, overt male supremacy of which many of us are already aware and struggling against, but also oppression which has been internalized, which turns women against themselves, causing them to be their own worst enemies rather than their own loving best friend. This internalized oppression I have called the Pig Parent. It is the expression of all the values which keep women subordinate.

The idea of the Pig Parent is again an internal pattern of responses – the voices within us which tell us that we are no good, that we need good, pure, strong figures to lean on and depend on and admire, that we can never make it on our own, that it is wrong to aim at equality. Another version of this has been described as the *self-hater* by Starhawk in her excellent book *Dreaming the Dark: Magic, Sex and Politics* (1982). The self-hater can be a powerful subpersonality.

And this applies to men just as much as to women. Both men and women have internalised the oppression of a patriarchal society, and both have these internal voices. It is just that society tells men that they have to be leaders, and so they lead, but still with the voices telling them that they are no good, that they are unworthy, that they have no right to be equal or to be loved for themselves. And so they perpetuate the structures which will make it all seem impersonal and objective, and nothing to do with them personally.

Masculine bias, thus, appears in our behaviour whenever we act out the following categories, regardless of which element in each pair we are most drawn to at any given moment: subject/object; dominant/ submissive; master/slave; butch/femme. All of these false dichotomies are inherently sexist, since they express the desire to be masculine or to possess the masculine in someone else (Dansky *et al.* 1977). Under patriarchy, it is the stereotyped masculine qualities which get all the acclaim and all the interest, and this is true both for men and for women. I have discussed these issues in much more detail elsewhere (Rowan 1997b).

This is all very reminiscent of the discussion about penis envy, except that as Firestone (1972) puts it, we should talk rather about power envy. And except that we now see it as applying to men as well as women, and as being much more complex – not only wanting to be close to penis-power, but also wanting to oppose it or withdraw from it – and all these in a compulsive way, driven by unconscious demands.

It is extraordinarily difficult to deal with the patripsych in therapy – all the most successful attempts seem to have been in groups, rather than in one-to-one work. This is simply because as fast as we break down the patterns in our therapy sessions, society puts them back again. If we really want to deal with the patripsych, it seems that we have to set up some kind of living community which will have different values; but then it seems that we lose all power to change the broader society.

Ultimately, then, we are faced with the answer that in order to deal with this aspect of therapy thoroughly, we have to change the whole society. I have dealt with this problem elsewhere (Rowan 1997b) and this is not the place to go into it fully. Enough to say that this is one of the most important areas, and that it is therefore imperative to sort out one's own personal attitude to it. Someone who has been writing about this in recent years is Andrew Samuels.

He draws attention particularly to the question of subjectivity. While it has been downgraded in most of our discourse, in psychotherapy it is respected and taken seriously and disciplined. And now he says that in politics, too, our subjectivity must be reframed and re-evaluated. Our feelings, our sensations, our wild fantasies even, must be taken seriously, disciplined, and used constructively to inform and inspire our politics. Far too much of politics is deadly serious and deadly dull and mind-numbing to most of us. We seem to have forgotten, he says, the late sixties in France and the USA and elsewhere, when politics came alive. But Samuels is not a romantic, and has a very full discussion of the possible dangers of taking our subjectivity seriously.

One of the dangers of therapy, some interested in politics have supposed, is that it may divert the feelings which could be used to change the world into a private examination of private troubles and private solutions. Samuels has a spirited answer to this concern:

> I do not agree that therapy inevitably syphons off rage that might more constructively be deployed in relation to social injustices. In fact, I think that it is the reverse that often happens: Experiences in therapy act to fine down generalized rage into a more specific format, hence rendering emotion more accessible for social action.
>
> (Samuels 1993, p.51)

Samuels has also pointed out with good evidence that psychotherapists are often deeply involved with politics. He actually carried out a postal survey of 600 psychotherapists in seven countries, including Freudians, Jungians and humanistic psychologists. He asked them many questions about politics, including what political issues arise in the course of therapy. Number one on the list was a range of gender issues.

The questionnaire asked how therapists responded to political material. Did they deal with it on a symbolic and intrapsychic level, treating it as fantasy referring to the inner world? Did they deal with it by exploring its meaning for the client, without any concern for its external reality? Or did they explore it with the client as reality, as real concern about the external world? There was much overlap, with a number of therapists adopting more than one of these approaches, but the overall figure for those who did deal with the issues raised as reality was 71 per cent. The overall figure for those who did not deal with reality at all was only 22 per cent. These are quite exciting and unpredictable figures. Therapists of even the most rigid theoretical positions proved to be far more political, far more open to discuss reality, than anyone would have supposed.

IMPLICATIONS

It seems very important for any therapist or counsellor to know how to listen with the fourth ear, particularly when working with women, children, immigrants, working-class people, handicapped people or anyone else defined by society as second-class or third-class. And this will be in two main areas: firstly the environment – what needs changing there; and secondly (but not less importantly) the therapist himself or herself – what am I as a therapist standing for in the client's eyes, and how can I bring that out and use it?

As I have said already, the majority of the most penetrating thinking on this topic has been done by feminists, and there is a huge literature now available to women on the subject, some of which has been referred to in this chapter. Much of this literature is less helpful to men, though men should certainly read it to pick up on the strength of feeling which comes through, and to empathise with that strength of feeling. More directly useful to men are the books written specifically for men, such as those by Osherson (1986), Kupers (1993), Meade (1993), Levant and Pollack (1995) and the masterly book by Bob Connell (1987).

In approaching this area, it is often useful to have some idea as to where we are heading, what our aims and goals are. One useful chart explaining this comes from Riane Eisler (1995). In it she shows the main distinctions between a dominator culture (such as patriarchy) and a partnership culture (see Chart 10.1). I have also given some hints and tips for men wanting to move in this direction in my own recent book already mentioned.

Any decent training in psychotherapy or counselling, it seems to me, must cover these areas. And it means very specific work on uncovering one's feelings about power and authority, about the male and the female, about the masculine and the feminine, about all kinds of gender-related assumptions and expectations. There are some good exercises in the Ernst and Goodison book already referred to. In a way there is an advantage of working this out on a man/woman basis, because on most courses there are men and women, whereas there may not be any children, immigrants, handicapped people, or suchlike. Of course one can invent these other groups by role-playing, and this is also worth-while.

One of the best exercises I ever went through myself was at a conference of the Association for Humanistic Psychology at Princeton University, where we were asked to 'be gay for part of a day'. We started off lying on the floor, while a tape was played giving typical phrases and news items and snatches of conversation which might be particularly relevant to gay people, and might make them feel bad about being gay. This built up until it became clear that to be gay was to live under a considerable burden of prejudice and ill-will. Then we were told to get up and walk around feeling the fear: it is not OK in our culture to be gay – you might get found out. You mustn't look anyone in the eye: they might find out, it might slip out suddenly, it might reveal itself in a glance – so keep your eyes down. Then some more tapes were played, bringing us to the point where we had decided to take a risk and look for a member of the same sex to be with. I chose somebody (can't remember how) and sat opposite him; we had to interact non-verbally. I was hot and embarrassed and sweating, and found it really hard to do. We held hands. I put my hand on his knee (he was wearing shorts). I found that the flesh contact was easier than the eye contact. If I could keep it all below the neck it somehow felt safer than if I engaged with the man above the neck. This was a powerful experience for me.

Then there were some more fantasy suggestions about having now decided to come out, and feeling more confident about our gayness, and now being able to have fun with other gay people. We had to form groups of three or more, and just interact in any way we liked. I found myself in a group of three, with two men I didn't like particularly, but by talking about my feelings I got to the point of feeling a lot of warmth and sympathy for one of the guys, who was gay and married and not sure where to go from there. Then we had to write a letter to a close relative or intimate person, saying that we were gay, and how we wanted the other person to feel about that. I wrote to my father, and half-way through changed it to father and mother. Then we discussed in small groups (single-sex or mixed) about what had happened. And so it ended.

It seems to me that this basic format could be adapted in various ways, and used for initiating people into what it feels like to be in someone else's shoes, over quite a wide range.

Chart 10.1 The dominator and partnership models: Seven Basic, Interactive and Mutually Supporting Differences

Component	Dominator model	Partnership model
1 *Gender relations*	The male is ranked over the female, and the traits and social values stereotypically associated with 'masculinity' are valued more highly than those of 'femininity'.	Females and males are equally valued in the governing ideology, and stereotypically 'feminine' values such as nurturance and nonviolence can be given operational primacy.
2 *Violence*	A high degree of social violence and abuse is institutionalised, ranging from wife-and-child beating, rape, and warfare to psychological abuse by 'superiors' in society at large.	Violence and abuse are not structural components of the system, so that both boys and girls can be taught nonviolent conflict resolution. Accordingly, there is a low degree of social violence.
3 *Social structure*	The social structure is predominantly hierarchic and authoritarian, with the degree of authoritarianism and hierarchism roughly corresponding to the degree of male dominance.	The social structure is more generally egalitarian, with difference (be it based on gender, race, religion etc.) not automatically associated with superior or inferior social and/or economic status.
4 *Sexuality*	Coercion is a major element in mate selection, sexual intercourse, and procreation, with the eroticisation of dominance and/or the repression of erotic pleasure through fear.	Mutual respect and freedom of choice for both females and males are characteristic of mate selection, sexual intercourse, and procreation. Primary functions of sex are the

	Primary functions of sex are male procreation and male sexual release.	bonding through the give and take of mutual pleasure, and the reproduction of species.
5 *Spirituality*	Man and spirituality are ranked over woman and nature, justifying their domination and exploitation. The powers that govern the universe are imaged as punitive entities whose orders must be obeyed on pain of terrible punishments, and hence must be placated.	The spiritual dimension of both woman's and nature's life-giving and sustaining powers is recognised and highly valued, as are these powers in men. Spirituality is linked with empathy and equity, and the divine is imaged through myths and symbols of unconditional love.
6 *Pleasure and pain*	The infliction or threat of pain is integral to systems' maintenance. The pleasure of touch in both sexual and parent–child relations are associated with domination and submission, and thus also with pain, be it in the so-called carnal love of sex or in submission to a 'loving' deity.	Human relations are held together more by pleasure bonds than by fear of pain. The pleasures of caring behaviours are socially supported and pleasure is associated with empathy for others. Caretaking, love-making, and other activities that give pleasure are considered sacred.
7 *Power and love*	The highest power is the power to dominate and destroy, symbolised since remote antiquity by the lethal power of the blade. 'Love' and 'passion' are frequently used to justify violent and abusive actions by those who dominate.	The highest power is the power to give, nurture and illuminate life, symbolised since remote antiquity by the holy chalice or grail. Love is recognised as the expression of the evolution of life on our planet, as well as the universal unifying power.

Source: Eisler 1995: 403–5.

But I think it is also important to remember that a therapist is always bound to be a limited person, with a restricted range of sympathies and abilities, and there is no point in trying to be perfect. One should not take oneself too seriously as the only recourse the client has. Society is rich in all manner of resources which may be much more use than a therapist at a given time. So it is good for a therapist to have some contact with available resources, whether it be women's groups, co-counselling networks, Alcoholics Anonymous, local residential facilities, legal aid or whatever. But unless we first cultivate the fourth ear, we shall not know when to call on these other resources; it is this awareness which is so important.

SOME FALSE TRAILS

On the other hand, it is important not to fall for some of the false criticisms which have been made of counselling and psychotherapy. There have been a number of critics in recent years who have been far too keen to denounce the therapeutic endeavour in all its forms. We do not have to lie down in front of every passing steamroller.

One of the prime examples is David Smail, who has written a number of articles and a book saying that people's problems are largely external, and can only be cured by external means, which the therapist cannot control or even influence. He also says that therapy cannot change character – if a person has character flaws or defects, that is something permanent and fixed. Here is an actual quote from one of his articles:

> The best hope of rescuing a life from tragedy – certainly of the 'flawed character' variety – may well be the exact opposite of attending to and working on its origins within the private individual. Once character has been fatefully impressed upon [us] as relatively powerless infants by the overwhelmingly much greater powers around us, there is not a great deal to be achieved by our trying to turn ourselves inside-out in a desperate attempt to reconstitute ourselves as other than we are, by trying to replace the forces that created us by optimistic but impotent myths, or by rejecting the truths we have learned about life for falsehoods we would prefer to believe.
>
> (Smail 1996: 9–10)

This is a crazy account of psychotherapy. No therapy known to me, or mentioned in this book, has this attitude to events. The paradoxical theory of change, which we have often referred to in these pages, does not even try to work in the way suggested by Smail, and nor does any reputable form of therapy known to me. He is destroying his own straw man.

A striking book by Alan Howard does much the same thing. He attacks therapy for being irrelevant to the real concerns of people, and specifically attacks client-centred approaches (such as some of those mentioned with approval in this book), psychodynamic approaches and psychological approaches in the clinical field. Here is a sample:

> In his failure to observe such broader contexts to the counselling relationship, Carl Rogers in particular was, I think, extremely naive and therefore considerably overrated. He seemed to entertain an almost Pollyanna-like belief in the ultimate potential goodness of mankind . . . The Rogerian claim is that, with enough unconditional positive regard, the vicious personality will soften into a loving, caring human being.
>
> (Howard 1996: 80–1)

This abstract denunciation ignores what Rogers was most famous for. He was one of the pioneers of direct audio recordings of therapy sessions, in the days when that endeavour involved large and unwieldy equipment. His case histories are remarkable, and all the more convincing for being published in the form of actual verbatim accounts of what really goes on in therapy sessions. He does not ask us to believe in theory. He practises, and then says what seems to him to emerge pretty directly from that practice, in his own experience. We who come later do not have to take his word for it – we can examine the practice directly. There is no evidence in Howard's book that he has ever read any case histories: certainly he does not quote any. He also says that Rogers ignores the question of power, when in fact Rogers (1978) is one of the few therapists to have written a whole book on the question of power in all its aspects.

Another attack on therapy comes from Jeffrey Masson (1989), which again contains some telling points about how much abuse there can be within the therapeutic relationship, but is so overheated and imprecise that it refutes itself. Masson is clearly not going to find any good in any kind of therapy, no matter how sophisticated or politically defensible. It is really not worth arguing with in detail.

Similar remarks apply to the wonderfully titled *We've Had a Hundred Years of Psychotherapy and the World is Getting Worse* by James Hillman and Michael Ventura (1992). It is a freewheeling extravaganza of a book which in my opinion gets nowhere in spite of a wonderful display of fireworks.

It seems then that the best critics of therapy, those with the most to say which can actually be used and acted upon, are those from inside therapy itself. We shall see more on this when we come to Chapter 13 and the subject of ethics.

Chapter 11

Research

The question everyone asks is 'How do you know that counselling or psychotherapy works?' And there are basically three possible answers to this:

'I don't care if it works or not – I just get so much satisfaction from doing it.' This is the 'faith' answer.

'I see such good results in my work with clients.' This is the 'anecdotal' answer.

'Well-designed research studies say so.' This is the 'research' answer.

Most counsellors and psychotherapists are quite happy with faith or anecdotes, but hardy souls like me are eager to have research answers.

Unfortunately, good and relevant research is hard to find. Most researchers in this field seem to be more interested in what is measurable than in what is important. For example, in the 1,024-page handbook of Garfield and Bergin (1978) there are no entries in the index for bioenergetics, birth, conception, foetus, Gestalt, implantation, memory, potentials, primal, psychodrama, regression (one reference to mathematical regression to the mean!), resistance, transpersonal, trauma, umbilical or womb.

This means that most of the specific things which we have been interested in as practitioners do not figure in the research reports. So in this chapter we need to do two things: firstly to see what the existing research does say, and secondly to see what new research needs to be done, and how.

A PIECE OF HISTORY

Anyone interested in this area must read the paper which appeared in the first issue of *Psychotherapy Research* (the journal of the Society for Psychotherapy Research) in 1991. The abstract reads as follows:

> In 1952, Hans Eysenck published 'The effects of psychotherapy: An evaluation' in which he concluded that the effect of psychotherapy is no greater than that of spontaneous remission. In the present paper, we tested this conclusion using Eysenck's original panel of 'untreated' patients. A probit analysis of rates of improvement by time of assessed improvement was conducted on these data, and results were compared to a probit analysis conducted on a panel of patients who had received psychotherapy. Treatment was associated with significantly higher rates of improvement when compared to the effects of spontaneous remission. In fact, 50% of psychotherapy patients were estimated to improve after 8 weeks, whereas only 2% of untreated patients were estimated to improve in this time. Probit analysis showed that the 50% improvement rate for Eysenck's spontaneous remission group occurred at a much later time than the 50% improvement rate for psychotherapy. According to his % improvement estimates, psychotherapy accomplishes in about 15 sessions what spontaneous remission takes two years to do. Thus, Eysenck's data reveal that psychotherapy is very effective.
>
> (McNeilly and Howard 1991, p. 74)

This is quite delicious, because it uses Eysenck's own data and finally lays to rest his assertion that psychotherapy is ineffectual. It is seldom that so neat a come-uppance is available. It is interesting to note that in Eysenck's pronouncements since that date, no reference has been made to this paper.

EXISTING RESEARCH

Luckily for us, the major work has been done for us by Roberta Russell (1981) in going through the literature and spelling out the main results. She gives extensive references for all these statements, and the interested reader is referred to her report for checking all the many sources. Although her report is now quite old, nothing published since seems to contradict it. A useful summary of some of the more recent work is to be found in Bartram (1990). Her six conclusions are as follows:

1 Comparative studies show that the outcome of psychotherapy does not depend on the school to which the therapist adheres.

2 Experienced therapists are generally more effective than inexperienced therapists. Experienced therapists resemble each other to a greater extent than they resemble less experienced therapists trained in their respective disciplines.

3 Paraprofessionals consistently achieve outcomes equal to or better than professional outcomes.

4 A professional training analysis does not appear to increase the effectiveness of the therapist.

5 Therapists who have undergone traditional training are no more effective than those who have not. Microcounselling and skills training appear to be useful procedures in the training of therapists.

6 Congruent matching of therapist and patient increases the effectiveness of therapy.

Now in view of our criticisms of the body of existing research, how should we regard these conclusions?

Item 1 probably needs to be checked out much more thoroughly before we accept it. If hardly any of the existing research deals in any way with Gestalt therapy, psychodrama, bioenergetics, transpersonal therapy and so forth, how can we say how they compare with psychoanalysis or behaviourism or cognitive therapy? And also we need to be very critical of the use of the word 'outcome'. If the outcome is that someone stops washing her hands thirty times a day, that is easy to check on and easy to keep track of; if the outcome is that someone gets in touch with her real self, that is much harder to pin down and measure . If we look at the more than sixty case histories in Corsini (1981) we see that each of the cases is rated as successful, but the criteria of success in each case are different. Some of the shifts are very small, others are very large.

So the whole question of values comes in here. When we accept a client for therapy, what are we trying to achieve? And does that client know that this is what the aim is? Unless there is some agreement worked out, therapist and client may be at cross-purposes. If there is agreement, it may still be hard to compare one client with another. The whole idea of adding up outcomes like apples may be a nonsense.

Item 2 is in two parts. The first sentence is contentious for the reasons already advanced – the concept of 'more effective' entails and takes for granted the concept of 'outcomes' which we have seen some reason to doubt. But the second sentence may well make sense. It would certainly be much more amenable to test, and a variety of dimensions might be used; this would be a much more possible area for research efforts of one kind or another.

Item 3 again uses the concept of 'outcome' and has to be questioned on that basis. So does item 4, 5 and 6. The second sentence of item 5 is more testable and more interesting for that reason.

It seems that not much is left, if we don't believe in measuring outcomes; so let us have one more look at that concept. In the masterly paper by David and Diana Shapiro (1982) we find the outcome study to end all outcome studies, putting together the results of no less than 143 carefully evaluated pieces of work. The first thing we find is that:

> The source studies were primarily of behavioural methods, with systematic desensitization the most widely represented method, followed by relaxation and rehearsal/self-control monitoring. Cognitive and minimal therapies were less widely represented, and verbal methods figured very little in the data.

So once again there is very little information about what we are interested in as humanistic practitioners. It is clear that this kind of outcome research much prefers very specific outcomes, preferably small and easily measured.

> The predominant mode of therapy was group, and the average therapist had some 3 years of experience, the level of an advanced post-graduate student. Therapy typically lasted for around 7 hours, and most procedures were at least moderately reproducible.

How much change can take place in seven hours? It seems to be getting more and more obvious that research in this area is subject to the besetting sin of all academic research, a trap which it falls into again and again in every psychological field – do studies which will represent another notch on your academic belt, rather than studies which are useful to anybody (cf. Rowan 1974).

> The most common target problems were performance anxieties, followed by physical and habit problems, social and sexual problems and phobias. (In fact, the biggest single group suffered from test anxiety.)

Again it becomes obvious that the clients in these studies were students – the usual subjects in university laboratory work. The university causes test anxiety by setting test after test and making academic progress dependent on the results, and then kindly provides a group to get rid of the anxiety so produced, thus providing material for another academic paper.

If this is what outcome research leads to – which of course it does – it seems not only worthless but actively harmful. The search for outcomes is the search for numbers; the search for numbers is the search for things to count; human beings are not things. It is all right to count human beings if all you want to know is where they are or what they have done; but the moment you want to count what is going on inside them you run into trouble. Human beings are freedoms and choosers.

A NEW APPROACH

One of the most important new approaches comes from our old friend Alvin Mahrer, in a book called *Psychotherapeutic Change*. This talks about a type of research called 'in-session outcome research', which Mahrer has pioneered and written about a good deal now.

Mahrer (1985) was very struck by the early work of Carl Rogers (1961) in the research field. He quotes Rogers as saying that he was particularly impressed by the presence of 'moments of movement' – moments in therapy where it appears that change actually occurs. These are often moments of strong emotion. What Mahrer has done is to specify in some detail what these moments actually consist of. He found thirteen indices of psychotherapeutic movement, and gives examples of each of them. Here they are:

1　Providing meaningful material about personal self and/or relationships;
2　Describing/exploring the personal nature and meaning of feelings;
3　Emerging of previously warded-off material;
4　Showing insight or understanding;
5　Communicating expressively;
6　Manifesting a meaningfully significant working relationship with the therapist;
7　Expressing strong feelings towards the therapist;
8　Expressing strong feelings in personally meaningful life contexts;
9　Radical shifting into deeper personality states;
10　Risking new ways of being and acting within the real world of the imminent future;
11　Expressing or reporting positive target actions;
12　Expressing or reporting reduced negative target actions and ideas; and
13　Expressing or reporting a state of well-being.

In the piece of research I am now going to talk about (Mahrer *et al.* 1987), categories 1, 5, 8 and 9 were the most often used. Would this be the case with other clients, other therapists, other approaches?

For each of these categories, it was true that the good moments came in bursts or series rather than as isolated events. From 5 to 10, statements tended to follow one another. And it also seemed that one could detect stages within each session.

It was also found that certain categories clustered together. Categories 1, 5 and 8 tended to go together, and also whenever category 9 was found, category 8 was also found. Mahrer says:

> These findings suggest that for a therapy which values very good instances of the client's expression of strong feelings in extratherapy contexts (category 8), it may be useful for the client's voice quality to be alive, vibrantly energetic, with vivid and rich language (category 5), and for the client to be providing meaningful material about personal self- and/or interpersonal relations (category 1). For a therapy which values very good moments in which the client undergoes a radical shift into a qualitatively altered personality state (category 9), the findings suggest that this is facilitated when the client expresses strong feelings in extratherapy contexts (category 8).

I think it is worth while looking at these findings simply to see what sort of results can come out of this type of approach. The methodology does not really come alive unless we can see something of how it can be used.

Mahrer and his colleagues also looked at the question as to which actions of the therapist were associated with these good moments and clusters of good moments. In this way we can investigate the associations of therapist actions with client responses. They would of course be different for other types of therapy. This sort of research seems to me much more useful than most, because it actually refers to recognisable things which we can work on and take account of in the actual session with a client.

NEW PARADIGM RESEARCH

So we need a new approach to research if we are to do any kind of justice to the way human beings work, and what goes on inside them during the process of therapy. And it so happens that over the past twenty years or so, another kind of research has been slowly growing up – and in the recent past it has accelerated its progress considerably.

It will help us to see the similarities and the differences between new paradigm research and old paradigm research (such as that quoted so far in this chapter) if we construct a diagram of the general research cycle (see Diagram 11.1). This is the cycle that is common to all forms of research without exception. We start at the point of BEING. This is where I am working in my own field – in this case as a student of the process of therapy. All goes as normal, until some problem or insight comes along, something which seems to be a matter of fact, such as 'Does a depressed person respond better to being pushed deeper into the depression (in the Rogerian or existentialist manner) or to being pulled in the opposite direction (in the co-counselling or transpersonal manner)?'

We then move into the THINKING mode, where we get information which is already available, and combine it in our own minds. Maybe the answer is there already, in some book or paper, or maybe one of our friends knows the answer; we keep on searching until we have tracked down all the hints we can find.

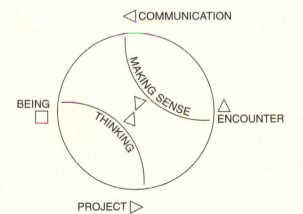

Diagram 11.1 The cycle model

Assuming that we cannot find the answer, we move on to the point of PROJECT. Here we start to ask the question 'What kind of investigation would *in principle* give me the answer I need?' And here immediately at this point the difference between the two paradigms starts to appear. Because in the old paradigm I was alone in this search for a plan or design, apart from the help given by colleagues perhaps. In the new paradigm I search for a plan together with a number of people who have the same problem *from the inside*. In other words, they are people who have suffered from depression or who do at present suffer from depression. And together with them I work out what form of questioning would be possible and acceptable; what form of observation or self-observation would be all right; what forms of recording would be suitable and so forth. And when we have agreed, these are the people who will carry out the research, on themselves, not on others.

At this point we move on to the ENCOUNTER, where we actually try something out for real. There is some action, some engagement, such that reality can come through and be registered in some way. At this stage I must lay myself open to the possibility of improvisation and spontaneity, based on the very specific plan which has been agreed. Real involvement is needed in this phase, so that we are genuinely open to what may happen. This is the crux of the whole process.

But at a certain point we have done enough of this very intense work, and the time comes to make sense of it all. So we go on to the MAKING SENSE section of the diagram, where we stand back from what we have done and what we have all been through, and ask ourselves 'What did it all mean?' And we may answer this question in very crude terms, or in terms of a rough model, or in terms of a very elaborate theory; this is the stage at which we see what kind of a story can be extracted from the activities in which we have been engaged, and what happened as a result.

And when we have done this to our satisfaction, we move on to the point of COMMUNICATION, where we communicate amongst ourselves, or to others, about what we have discovered. This may go on for a brief moment, or for several years, it all depends on how deep or elaborate the information is. But at the end of this process we are ready to come back into our field with this new knowledge at our fingertips. Perhaps one cycle is enough, but more likely we shall still be dissatisfied, and start out on another cycle, only this time we shall be able to be more specific and more differentiated because of what we have found out from the first cycle. The idea of multiple cycles is very important in this approach, forming a spiral in this case, or perhaps running parallel to each other in other cases, and knitting together in some pattern.

Now we said that all research styles used this cycle, but they use it in different ways. The two main dimensions on which they differ are *alienation* and *involvement round the cycle*. Here is a list of twenty-three research traditions, each of which has produced a substantial body of highly-regarded research. They are listed in order of alienation, the most alienated at the beginning of the list, and the least at the end:

Tradition	*Example*
1 Pure basic research	*These are the four*
2 Basic objective research	*orthodox forms of*
3 Evaluation research	*research found in most*
4 Applied research	*textbooks.*
5 Participant observation	Polsky (1969)
6 Language and class research	Labov (1972)
7 Personality and politics research	Knutson (1973)
8 Ethogenic research	Harre (1979)
9 Phenomenological research	Giorgi (1975)
10 Ethnomethodology	Turner (1974)
11 LSD research	Grof (1980)
12 Dialectical research	Esterson (1972)
13 Action research	Sanford (1981)
14 Intervention research	Argyris (1971)
15 Personal construct research	Fransella (1972)
16 Existential research	Hampden-Turner (1977)
17 Experiential research	Heron (1981b)
18 Endogenous research	Maruyama (1978)
19 Participatory research	Hall (1975)
20 Co-operative inquiry	Heron (1996)
21 Interactive holistic research	Cunningham (1988)
22 Collaborative inquiry	Treleaven (1994)
23 Transformational research	Rowan (1997c)

Now we can introduce one or two simple conventions for diagramming different research styles. If we use a dotted line to represent alienation, we can show pure basic research as shown in Diagram 11.2. The circle represents the researcher going round the whole cycle. The line

Diagram 11.2 Pure basic research

represents the subject meeting the researcher at one point only – the point of ENCOUNTER. What results is an alienated encounter, where there is a meeting of role to role, rather than of person to person.

The next diagram represents existential research, such as that which is reported in my T-Poems (Rowan 1976) (see Diagram 11.3).

Diagram 11.3 Existential research

Here again the researcher meets the subjects only at the point of ENCOUNTER, but this time both researcher and subjects are non-alienated, or authentic. There is a genuine meeting in which there is mutual disclosure; researcher and others are open to each other, not hiding behind roles. So this diagram and the previous one show how the dimension of alienation makes a difference.

If we then use a dashed line to represent a situation where the researcher or the others may or may not be alienated, depending upon circumstances, we can represent action research, intervention research and personal construct research as in Diagram 11.4.

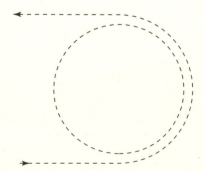

Diagram 11.4 Action research

This is a quite different level of involvement, which makes a huge difference to the way in which people can participate in the research. It makes it almost inevitable that the research project will affect the lives of all those involved in some way. This social effect is very important.

And finally, Diagram 11.5 shows how we can represent experiential research, endogenous research, participatory research, co-operative inquiry, interactive holistic research, collaborative inquiry and trans-formational research. All seven of these have in common a commitment to full engagement on the part of the researcher, and a refusal to let the others hide behind a role. These are the most change-oriented of all the methods, because they set up a context of mutual trust, within which support and confrontation can take place. One of the most striking things about research done in this way is the amount of energy released. That is why it seems fitting to call it a high-energy type of research. What is more, energy seems to be released as each point on the cycle is left behind. It seems that the point is not just left behind, it is *contradicted* in a more or less negative way. This seems to be to do with the much higher degree of involvement and commitment required of the investigator. The researcher is in touch at several levels, not just the one level favoured by old paradigm research.

Diagram 11.5 Participatory research

We can in fact say that there are three kinds of knowledge involved here. As John Heron (1981b) says:

Propositional knowledge is knowledge of facts or truths as stated in propositions: it is entirely language-dependent. Practical knowledge is knowing how to do something, as exemplified in the exercise of some special skill or proficiency. Experiential knowledge is knowing some entity by direct face-to-face encounter with her/him/it; it is direct discrimination of what is present in relation with the knower.

Old paradigm research is for the most part content with propositional knowledge, though some studies in the field provide some practical knowledge. But new paradigm research essentially and necessarily provides propositional, practical and experiential knowledge – the knowing which comes out of it is 'thicker' and more substantial than that coming out of old paradigm research.

In the book by Reason and Rowan (1981) there are given fourteen full examples of this kind of research in action, and further studies are given in Reason (1988) and Reason (1994). It is important to realise that with this kind of research the propositional knowledge of 'what the research says' is only a part of the story.

One interesting piece of research is that carried out by Ninoska Marina (1982) on the process of psychotherapy. She enlisted the help of five people who had been in therapy for at least a year, using humanistic approaches, and went into great depth with them on the question of what changes exactly had happened, using their own statements and their own way of seeing the question and covering five periods of time: Pre-Therapy; Therapy; Post-Therapy; Now; and Future.

What she found is that people always have certain major dimensions along which they seem to move, or want to move. And these tend quite independently and spontaneously to be very similar as between people (see Table 11.1). It seems obvious that much of this could be summed up by saying that therapy is about self and others. But one of her findings goes rather deeper than this. She says that what comes out very strongly is 'A sense of self different to what it had been at the pre-therapy period'. This is extraordinarily important, in view of what we have been saying in this book about the aims of therapy.

She also draws attention to the way in which language is important in enabling people to understand themselves:

> Synergy has been defined within this context as a state brought about by the simultaneous availability for access of all parts of the cognitive-affective system taken as the person. It is possible through the availability to access appropriately both the cognitive-affective level and the alignment level. This availability can be achieved if a person has been able to develop a double language; that is, to create a language of interpreting what is accessed. Given this development a person is able to reach a state where s/he acts, thinks and feels in an integrated way.

This point about a double language is very important, and ties in with the work of Luria (1969) who talks about the way in which inner plans can be formed for getting access to one's own system. It seems clear that research can be useful in finding out what goes on in therapy, but only on condition that it follows the direction pointed out by new paradigm thinking. And we now know how to do this.

Table 11.1 Categories used by people in describing their changes

Person	Categories
Person No. 1	Relating to people Relating to women Getting to know myself better
Person No. 2	Self-knowledge Relating to people
Person No. 3	Having more energy Liking myself more Enjoying sexuality
Person No. 4	Self-image My view of and relationship with the outside world
Person No. 5	Accepting and liking myself better Relating to people

Source: N. Marina (1982), Table 5.1.1.

Chapter 12

Supervision

In previous chapters we have already touched on several issues which have to do with supervision, but it is now time to look at it in more detail. The basic humanistic position is that all therapists need supervision all the time.

What, then, is the function of the supervisor? It is to enable the therapist or counsellor to become aware of blind spots and prejudices and mistakes and inadequacies, and to work on them in such a way that professional development takes place. Because these issues are very emotive, and go to the very heart of the therapist's professional self-image, supervision is always a delicate and difficult business. This is all the more so because of the other pressures which bear on the supervisor–therapist relationship. As Ekstein and Wallerstein (1972) have pointed out, there is a rhombus of supervision in most cases (see Diagram 12.1). In the diagram S is the supervisor, A is the administrator, T is the therapist, and P is the patient. So the supervisor's role is to hold the balance between the perhaps conflicting demands of the administration, the therapist and the client.

Diagram 12.1

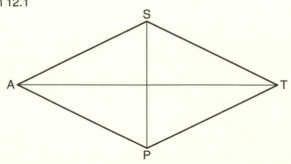

And in this setting the therapist experiences the three other corners in a very personal way. The patient can represent 'the archaic, unorganized aspects of his professional self', but can also 'be a model of increasing mastery, external evidence of inner growth and maturation'. The administrator can represent 'the task of having to live by regulations and of having to live up to professional ideals'. And the supervisor can represent 'skills, areas of technical and human competence' (all quotes from Ekstein and Wallerstein 1972).

Ekstein (1969) has a nice statement about the difficulties which the therapist may be struggling with in supervision. He speaks about the student's dumb spots, blind spots and deaf spots. Dumb spots are those areas where the student lacks the required knowledge and skill in dealing with the client. This is most likely to happen when the therapist is faced with clients who are very different, whether they be poor and disadvantaged, or whether they be the other oppressed groups we mentioned in the last chapter. The therapist just does not know enough about what it is to be like the client. Blind spots are those places where the therapist's own psychodynamic gets in the way of appreciating what is going on in the client. All the phenomena of countertransference which we looked at earlier can come in here. Gardner (1971) has a very good discussion of how particular problems are likely to arise between the white therapist and the black client. The patripsych comes in here as a particularly difficult part of the psychodynamics involved. Deaf spots are those where the therapist not only cannot hear the client, but cannot hear the supervisor either. These are likely to involve particularly defensive reactions based on guilt, anxiety or otherwise unpleasant and disruptive feelings. Hostility to authority figures may come into the picture.

So we may sum up the aims of the supervision session by saying that it is about getting in touch with the covert processes which are going on between therapist and client no matter what the theoretical orientations may be. It may be done on a one-to-one basis, but nowadays in training it is more often done in a group, so it is mainly group supervision which will be dealt with in this chapter. By far the best book on the actual live process as it takes place is Margaret Rioch et al. (1976) and anyone concerned with supervision should read this book.

SUPERVISOR STYLES

Increasingly in recent years we have been moving away from opinion-led practice to evidence-based practice, and many research studies have shown that this is indeed possible and desirable. And as this process has gone on, it has become evident that there is much in common between humanistic education (Rogers and Freiberg 1994) and humanistic supervision. There is also a connection between the balance of confrontation and support which is valuable in humanistic group work (Smith 1973) and the balance of confrontation and support which is valuable in supervision in order to avoid both the Scylla of cosy collusion and the Charybdis of over-criticalness and distance.

There are several different ways in which a supervisor might operate, and five basic styles have been found to operate in practice. Firstly there is the *laissez-faire* style, where the supervisor largely leaves the therapist alone to get on with it, only making consultations where necessary. This is quite suitable for very mature therapists, but even here some lack of support may be felt at times. It is quite unsuitable for immature therapists, who need much more in the way of leadership.

Secondly there is the *authoritative* style, where the supervisor monitors and regulates the therapist's work very closely. This may be welcomed at first by the beginning student of therapy or counselling, but it becomes oppressive quite quickly, and students do not respond well to it after a time (Cherniss and Egnatios 1978).

Thirdly there is the *didactic-consultative* style, where the supervisor offers advice, suggestions and interpretations. This can easily become a 'brilliant performance' which takes away the case from the student, as in the following example taken from Cherniss:

> The other day I had an emergency, a client, a couple of clients, and I was feeling upset about things. But supervision means we get into stuff about clients very objectively and analyze it. And in a way, it feels like my supervisor's show, like she's doing a performance. The main thing that happens is she analyzes the client. And that's great for her. She really gets off on it. It can be exciting momentarily for me. And you know, she can help me see a little more clearly what's happening. But for me, that takes a lot of the fun out of it. My attitude is, 'So you take that client, then!' I don't want my supervisor to take it away from me, the joy of discovering how to work with this person.
>
> (Cherniss 1980: 118)

All supervisors do a little of this at times – the temptation is too hard to resist – but as a main style of supervision students do not like it and do not respond to it too well.

Fourthly, there is *insight-oriented* supervision, where the supervisor asks questions designed to encourage the therapist to think through and solve problems. This works well and is liked by students (Cherniss and Egnatios 1978). The term 'empowerment' is often used in this connection, though it has unfortunately become something of a cliché in recent times.

And fifthly, we have the *feelings-oriented* style, where the therapist is encouraged to ask questions and think about his or her own feelings and responses to the client. Supervision helps the therapist to come to terms with emotions and perceptions (Aponte and Lyons 1980). It is these last two styles which seem most suited to the needs of both students in training and experienced therapists. As Rioch puts it:

> My view is that the work of this seminar is like walking a tightrope between a therapy group and an objective, intellectual course of study. It is more personal than the latter and less personal than the former.
>
> (1976: 13)

In the Ekstein and Wallerstein (1972) book, there are some extended examples of exactly how individual therapists work out their problems with their clients, and this delicate balance between the personal and the professional comes out all the time. As Rioch puts it again:

> If the seminar is to study the interaction between each therapist and his client, then each therapist is part of the study. This involves attitudes, feelings and sensitivities. It requires an extraordinary degree of honesty, which can be quite painful.
>
> (*ibid*.: 14)

I don't think it is a good idea to call a supervision session a 'seminar', but that is a minor point. The main issue is that supervision has to maintain this position of doing justice both to the theoretical and to the personal matters which are thrown up in the process of discussion.

And one of the theoretical points which comes up here is the difference between psychoanalytic and humanistic supervision. Up to now we have been able to quote analysts just as often as anyone else, but now it is time to be a bit more specific. Let us look at an example taken from Rice:

> One apprentice therapist complained that her client often got panicked in the early morning, and called her up at home. These early morning calls became mini-therapy sessions, and afterwards the therapist could not get back to sleep before it was time to get up and start the day. The crowning annoyance was that the client then sometimes cancelled a regular appointment later in the day. The therapist

wondered if she should confront the client with her 'manipulative and exploitative behaviour'. My suggestion to the therapist was to tell the client in the next session about her own limits, that she didn't like to be awakened in the early morning, and that it disrupted her night's sleep . . . The client became angry, and accused her of putting her own comfort first. But this led to a number of explicit discussions of the relationship, and a fuller awareness of the rights and feelings of each of the two participants, which in itself seemed to be therapeutic.

(1980: 139)

What comes out in this example is that the supervisor refused to go along with the label of 'manipulative', and encouraged the therapist to treat the matter on a reality level which assumed the basic health of the client. Words like 'manipulative', which can never be used other than in a negative and disparaging way, are best avoided in supervision.

It may be objected at this point that Fritz Perls was never loath to accuse clients of being all kinds of things; but we have to distinguish between those things that Perls did which were therapeutic and those which were merely self-indulgent. There is no evidence that labelling a client is ever therapeutic, unless the label is clearly temporary and a kind of joke, like the labels of 'zombie', 'marshmallow' or 'peanut brittle' which Eileen Walkenstein (1975) used (once only) in her work. The humanistic practitioner would do well to steer clear of labels altogether, for the reasons already outlined in our discussion of assessment.

Where Perls does seem to be right, however, is in his opposition to gossip. Gossip is talking about people when they are not there. Many case conferences organised and run by people who are not humanistic practitioners consist almost entirely of gossip. They can be opportunities, as we have already seen, for experienced people to show off in front of their colleagues, displaying insights and knowledge of psychodynamics and jargon. In humanistic supervision, all the emphasis is on the person who is in the room – the therapist – not from the point of view of 'therapising' the therapist, but from the point of view of helping the therapist face problems arising out of actual practice. As Cohen and DeBetz put it: The trainee's problems in doing therapy with the patient are fair game for supervisory intervention while personal problems (provided they do not interfere) are not (1977: 59).

So much for the general question of what the supervisor is up to, and the style in which supervision is carried out. Now let us go on to the more specific question of how the supervisee is actually to present the client.

THE MEDIA OF SUPERVISION

There are five main ways in which the supervisor can obtain knowledge of the therapist–client interactions. They are: direct observation through one-way mirrors; direct observation through joint interviews (the apprenticeship model); mechanical recording devices, such as audio-tapes or videotape; process notes taken during or after the session; written reports which are given to the supervisor and later discussed.

The one-way mirror is used in settings with a high degree of organisation and technical expertise. The interview room in such settings tends to be rather bare and impersonal, and not the usual room in which therapy is conducted. It is therefore more suitable for one-off meetings, where for example a whole family is brought in for a session, or for a brief series of meetings, all of which can be followed up in the same way. It is normally easy to record such sessions for later playback. It is even possible to provide the therapist with an earpiece so that suggestions can be given at the time, instead of later.

Joint interviews where the supervisor is present in the same room are more rare except in certain forms of social work. We shall not consider them here.

Recording devices are much more common. Obviously audio record-ing is easier than video recording, because video is more expensive and also needs a technician to handle it in most cases, particularly in humanistic therapy, where both therapist and client move about a good deal. Audio recording is much more easy to arrange, because modern microphones of the omnidirectional type can pick up what is said all over the room, even in a fair-sized room. The effect is particularly good in a soundproofed room, such as many humanistic therapists need for regression work.

The strange thing is that many therapists and supervisors resist the obvious advantages of tape recordings. The reasons for this may be phrased in high-flown ways, such as 'It interferes with the existential flow between therapist and client', 'the emotional matrix is disturbed', 'a third party has intruded into a two-person event', 'we must be human and not mechanistic . . . ' But in reality the reasons may be more simple, as Korchin (1976) suggests:

> Seeing the microphone itself seems not to have any direct effect on patients. Indeed, it is the interviewer rather than the patient who is more likely to be disturbed by the matter of recording. The patient usually accepts it matter-of-factly as part of a generally strange

procedure. By contrast, the interviewer is threatened by having his work presérved and open to later criticism by himself and colleagues.

So let us suppose that we want to use tape recordings in supervision – how do we do it? It is best to use short segments of interviews, about seven minutes at a time works quite well. It is best to have the therapist start the tape at a point where some specific bit of action is starting, and to tell the supervisor and the group what they want listened for and what they want special help with. Wessler and Ellis (1980) make the point:

> We also encourage therapists . . . to present tape recordings of good and bad sessions with their clients. Many therapists, in our experience, seek help only for problems and situations that they think they handle badly, and fail to recognise errors they make with their 'good' cases. Other therapists present only the 'good' sessions, in order to impress their supervisors and supervision groups.

When we listen to tape recordings, what are we looking for? Obviously we are looking for obvious mistakes, things that were missed, points not followed through sufficiently, not listening, over-use of one kind of intervention, and so forth. But many more subtle things can be looked for, as Rice says:

> There is a kind of voice quality that seems to indicate an inner focus on something that is being seen or felt freshly. Sometimes in the midst of a long client discussion expressed in a highly external voice quality one hears just a small blip of focussed voice. The voice slows, softens without losing energy, pauses, and loses the 'premonitored' quality of the externalizing voice. This should be an indicator to the therapist that this part *must* be heard and responded to. There is a liveliness here that might flower into a whole new moment of experiencing . . .
>   Another indicator of liveliness is the presence of highly sensory or idiosyncratic words, or combinations of words. For instance, the client is talking about approaching situations with trepidation, and reports feeling 'cringy', or talks about a 'stretched' smile on his face.
>   (1980: 143)

These are the sort of things which come out on a tape which are very hard to pin down in any other way. Voice tones are very hard to describe, but they affect us emotionally below the level of conscious awareness.

Tape recordings, so easy in theory, are not so easy to achieve in practice. Windy Dryden has a list of possible errors, which I think is both funny and revealing:

Plug faults
- The plug did not contain a fuse.
- The plug contained a defective or incorrect fuse.
- The plug wires were not properly attached.

Mains faults
- The mains lead was not attached to the recorder.
- The mains lead was not inserted into the wall socket.
- The socket switch was not turned on.

Microphone faults
- The external microphone was not attached (or not properly attached) to the recorder.
- Batteries were not inserted into the battery-operated microphone.
- The microphone was placed incorrectly.
- The external microphone was not powerful enough.

Battery faults
- Batteries were not inserted into the battery-operated recorder.
- Dead or fading batteries were used (batteries not checked).
- Batteries were incorrectly inserted.
- Too few batteries were inserted.
- Batteries were left in the recorder causing corrosion.
- The battery pack had not been recharged.
- The battery pack had been incorrectly inserted.

Recording faults
- Incorrect controls were depressed.
- No controls were depressed.
- A radio programme was recorded instead of the session.
- The internal microphone was not sensitive enough.
- Recording heads were not clean.

Recorder faults
- The recorder was faulty in 'recording' mode.
- Interference was present on the recording.
- The recorder picked up local police or taxi broadcasts.

Tape faults
- – No tape was inserted.
- – The tape was incorrectly inserted.
- – The tape was inappropriate for the purpose.

(Extracted from *Dryden on Counselling: Vol. 3. Training and Supervision* (Chapter 6) Whurr Publishers, London 1991)

My experience is that students often approach the idea of tape recordings with some fear, as adding yet one more difficulty to their relationship with a client, which is difficult enough already; but that when they see how useful they can be, they come round to using them regularly. As Marshall and Confer put it:

> Some of the most profitable (for us) interventions by our supervisors were those which permitted us to experience the pitfalls of our efforts. An example of this strategy is 'therapeutic alter ego' whereby the supervisor wears out his fingertips on the 'stop' button of the tape recorder to inquire 'why did you say this?', 'what are you leading to?' and 'how do you think the patient received that?'
>
> (1980: 99)

It is important, of course, to avoid any suggestion of punitiveness in the supervision session. Some therapists seem to be punitive towards themselves, blaming themselves for their clients' failure to progress or change. But the constructive use of tape recordings can help to establish an impunitive focus. The therapist and the supervisor can join in listening for clues to process, letting the tape speak for itself. As Rice says: 'The optimal climate for the therapist's growth is a great deal of moment-to-moment feedback based on listening to tapes, and a minimum of evaluation as a person.'

Much the same considerations apply to videotape. Console (1978) has a good discussion of the value of videotape as a teaching medium. As an experienced practitioner, he found it valuable to make tapes of his initial interviews with clients, and to play these over for teaching purposes, stopping the tape often to make comments and allow the group to comment in turn. And he found that it was the little things – apparent mistakes, hesitations, slips of the tongue – which were the most revealing and helpful: just the things which would tend to get eliminated in any presentation based upon notes. After one such incident, he said:

> I mention this episode in some detail because if it were not for the videotape technique, it would be extremely unlikely, in my trying to reproduce the session verbally and present it to the residents, that I

would have included this interchange in my account, because it was so simple and natural a thing for me to have said . . . And I would therefore have missed the opportunity of making clear to the residents in the most vivid fashion, that the psychotherapeutic stance which we encourage – that of relative anonymity, of avoiding a social relationship and so on – does not preclude being human.

(1978: 29–30)

From all this we can see that recordings can be a very useful adjunct to the supervisory process. For a full discussion, bringing in much research evidence, see Gill *et al.* (1954).

Process notes are the most common method of bringing in material to the therapy session. These should always be as full as possible, using actual quotations whenever this is practicable. But they should neither be attempts to label the client, nor attempts to theorise the interaction; they should simply be a record of the interaction itself. What went on between therapist and client, and what stages did this go through? Therapy sessions quite often divide themselves up quite naturally into sections, and to treat each section separately is usually a helpful move.

Process notes are normally written up after the session, not during it. (Verbatim notes taken during the session tend to get in the way of the personal interaction, and in any case do not lend themselves to the more active type of intervention used by the humanistic practitioner.) They tend to be rather bare and scrappy (or overloaded with unnecessary detail) in the early days of supervision, but gradually improve, so that in the end they are in the personal style of the individual therapist, while containing all the relevant information.

What information is relevant? This is partly a matter of what the therapist needs, and partly a matter of the institution within which the work is taking place. Some places require a certain sort of record to be kept, and of course these rules have to be adhered to. But it is always wise for a therapist to keep a record of what is going on; this becomes particularly important if the client suddenly does something unexpected, and the therapist wants to go over the previous sessions which led up to it, looking for explanations and insights. Much the same considerations apply to written reports. Normally the supervisor will make it quite clear as to what form these reports should take.

Of course, supervision can and should be creative. Other methods which may be used are well described by Steve Page and Val Wosket:

Approaches such as sculpting, where small objects such as coins, pebbles or Russian dolls are assembled to represent aspects of, or individuals involved in, an issue, or the drawing of an image or metaphor relating to a client may prove particularly useful where the supervisee is uncertain about the specific issue.

(1994: 80–1)

Role-playing can also be used in various ways, one of the most powerful being where the supervisee role-plays the client. This very often gives new insights into how the client's mind works. If there is a group, a more elaborate role-play can be used, where other people in the group take up the roles of the others who may be involved in the problem.

Summing up, then, on the media of supervision, we have seen that those media which offer direct feedback and self-confrontation are the most suitable for humanistic psychotherapy, counselling or personal growth.

HUMANISTIC EDUCATION

This fits with the whole approach of humanistic education, with its emphasis on experiential work and personal feedback, and the production of self-actualising people. I have written about this elsewhere (Rowan 1988a) and this is not the place to go into it in detail, but there is a good recent account of what is going on at present in Rogers and Freiberg (1994).

The essence of it is that in humanistic education we have a tradition of treating the student as a complete human being, with total responsibility for what he or she does. To apply this to supervision is to say that the supervisor must at no time take that responsibility away from the student.

One of the ways of applying that approach in practice is to introduce a system of self- and peer-assessment. This means that it is the student who decides what he or she is ready to work on at a given time, and lays down the criteria according to which this is to be assessed. John Heron (1979) has argued powerfully and persuasively that this is the only way of translating humanistic values into educational practice. So the supervisor, on this model, would be a facilitator for the student's own self-assessment process.

What humanistic educators tend to find when they carry out this sort of approach (Rogers 1969) is that students initially resist. They want to be told what to do and how to do it. But if this initial resistance is worked with and negotiated about and generally worked through, it is usually possible to work out some way of achieving a relationship which is genuinely democratic and participatory.

Table 12.1 Orientation to learning test: sixteen humanistic values

1 *Process-oriented* 'How' is more important than 'what' or 'why'. This orientation emphasises 'processing', talking over how an activity is being conducted and how it is being experienced.

2 *Self-determination* Includes autonomy, self-direction and self-evaluation. In this approach, students assume initiative, responsibility and accountability whenever feasible and possible.

3 *Connectedness* Encourages empathy, pluralism and good relationships. This approach is sometimes contrasted to individualism. Involves mutual caring and understanding.

4 *Relevance* Stresses the students' personal meanings and readiness to learn. Instruction is related to underlying concerns and needs of the students as well as to society's interests.

5 *Integration* Affect is combined with cognition and living is combined with learning. Stresses educating the whole person including the values, feelings and attitudes, body, mind and spirit.

6 *Context* This includes awareness of the environment, culture, history, political and economic climate in which the learning takes place. Awareness of oppression and prejudice.

7 *Affective bias* Preference for the use of feelings and concrete experience in learning. Also includes sensory awareness and the expression of emotions as a central part of learning.

8 *Innovation* An anti-authoritarian, social and educational orientation toward change. Concern with something new intended to benefit those involved, both teachers and students.

9 *Democratic participation* Emphasises social equity, consensus and collaboration in learning. Co-creation with students, teachers, administrators and the community.

10 *Personal growth* Stresses both methods and outcomes of learning as self-actualisation through self-awareness. Persons take precedence over hardware and software in education.

11 *People-oriented* People have intrinsic or ultimate value, not merely instrumental value. The educational process has to trust in the learner's capacity to work hard and care for others.

12 *Individualism* The person who is the learner is unique, self-determining and self-aware. There must be freedom of expression and room for authentic selfhood in education.

13 *Reality* We can only know true reality by direct, primary feelings and experiences, not by fantasy or mental constructions. It is in the present, not in the past or the future.

Table 12.1 continued

14 *Evaluation* Formative evaluation is favoured over summative evaluation. The process is emphasised and quality is preferred to measures of quantity.

15 *Variety and creativity* Valuing of spontaneity, originality and diversity. Not conformity, standardisation and preset goals. Flexibility is encouraged in the instructional approach.

16 *Transpersonal* The development of the whole human being includes spiritual, potential, and mystical, intuitive and receptive modes as well as rational and active modes of consciousness.

Extracted from Stewart B. Shapiro (1997) 'The UCSB confluent education program: Its essence and demise' *Journal of Humanistic Psychology* 37/3 80–105 (slightly abbreviated).

One of the best simple summaries of what humanistic education is all about is to be found in a recent paper by Stewart Shapiro. He has devised a test of orientations to learning, which can be given to students, teachers and others. It can be seen how well it summarises the values we have been emphasising all the way through this book. If taken seriously, it could be a very helpful instrument for training courses of all kinds (see Table 12.1).

But what we are also saying is that if this is good for the beginning student, it is also good for the experienced supervisor. Every humanistic practitioner, no matter how experienced, needs some continuing system of self-education, possibly along the lines of self- and peer-assessment, or possibly along the lines of the peer supervision group as described by Aponte and Lyons (1980). There is no point where a good therapist has finally 'got there' and needs to do no more self-development. As even Ekstein and Wallerstein (1972) say:

> Supervision is not only an integral part of the training in social work school but remains a permanent pattern in most agencies. It is often maintained even for those who supervise, who then in turn become dependent on case-work consultants employed by the agency, or on outside psychiatric and psychoanalytic consultants.

For Ekstein and Wallerstein this is a peculiarity of social work, which is of dubious value, but for me it is of very central value. The point is that anyone who works with people is either keeping up and keeping on with self-knowledge and self-development and self-education, or is stagnating in some mould which was laid down long ago, perhaps in the worst cases by someone else entirely.

As far as we in this book are concerned, humanistic education means that the therapist goes on learning throughout life. This is because the process of self-actualisation, which we start on in therapy, never ends. Eventually it goes beyond therapy, if we let it continue, into spiritual territory. But if we carry on being therapists, so long as we do so, some process of supervision is necessary. There is no spiritual being who can be so useful as a good human supervisor.

Chapter 13

Ethics

In recent years much more attention has been paid to the ethics of therapy. One of the strongest influences in making this happen was the revelation of Alice Miller (1985) that not only was there such a thing as child abuse, but that the therapist in the session could often be abusing the client all over again. This created an enormous impression, not only on the psychoanalysts who were Miller's main targets, but also on therapists of all persuasions who suddenly saw many of their interventions in quite a different light.

In the 1970s it was quite common for group leaders to fly in, run a weekend group and fly out again. On the Saturday night they would often sleep with one of the more attractive women in the group. In fact, in some cases the women would jostle for position as to whom was going to be favoured in this way. Nowadays this does not happen, and it would be seen as abusive, because the power of the leader was used in an unaware way. More books have come along after Alice Miller's, making it clear that sexual abuse in the therapy hour is all too common, and that many therapists have still not taken on board the message.

PRIVATE PRACTICE

One of the issues which is sometimes raised as an ethical issue is the question of private practice. Is it ethical to make money out of someone else's misery? People like David Pilgrim (1990) have certainly raised this as a serious question, saying 'To say the least, the edge is taken off the humanitarian advantages of psychotherapy if these are selectively awarded to richer and lesser disturbed members of society.' Let us look, then, at the case for private practice.

Counselling grew up in institutions, often educational institutions, and later other institutions such as churches, hospitals, prisons and commercial organisations. It also flourished in social work settings of one kind and another. It was only later that it became something offered on the market on an individual basis, and later still that it became something obtainable through insurance. Today it is widespread and daily growing more so. There is no way of containing it between narrow boundaries and insisting that it only be offered within institutions, even if one wanted to do so.

The trouble with institutions is that they impose their own values upon what is done in them. It is hard for them to realise that they do not have the right to control something which goes on within them. Social workers are sometimes called the 'soft cops' by working-class people because they serve the system rather than the person. This is why there has been a persistent confusion between counselling in the British Association of Counselling (BAC) sense of the word (which is really about personal growth), and counselling in the older sense of guidance and advice-giving. It is even true that the major journal in this country in this area is called the *British Journal of Guidance and Counselling*: the confusion is perpetuated in that very title.

In private practice it is easier for therapy to be therapy, because we do not have the institution looking over our shoulders. Confidentiality, which I believe to be crucially important, can really be confidentiality. In an institution there is always the suspicion that juicy information will somehow leak out. There is often a whole list of people who are entitled to look at case notes and hear case reports. In private practice this is not so. A supervisor may hear the information, but in the best practice the supervisor never hears the client's real name (more about this later on).

In private practice there is no ambiguity as to whom the therapist is working for. The therapist is working exclusively for the client: hence it is a secure relationship. And most of us believe that a secure relationship is very important, particularly when it turns out that a long-term stint is needed. In an institution, it is quite common for a client to find that suddenly he or she is faced with a new counsellor or therapist, because the old one has left, or been transferred, or it is just more administratively convenient.

The question of choice seems extremely important to me. The relationship between a client and a practitioner is a personal one. It is not a service which can be done just as well by one person as another. There is a delicate matching which needs to take place, which ideally works out by the client choosing the therapist. Unless there is genuine choice, the relationship can be dogged by mismatch, and a mismatch which cannot be questioned or changed. It is often hard enough to change therapists in private practice, because of feelings of inferiority and self-blame, but it can be made doubly and trebly hard by institutional rigidities and resistances.

If we value the autonomy and empowerment of the client, and aim at increasing these things through the therapy process, we have to be consistent about it. We must not take away the client's power of choice by allocating a therapist arbitrarily. All the research seems to indicate that it is the genuine two-person relationship which is most effective and valuable in therapy. But it is only the choice which can make it genuine. Take that away and you have a constrained relationship in which other values dominate. Therapy is not a medical matter. If I have a broken leg, it is a matter of complete indifference to me which surgeon operates on it: I assume that one surgeon is as good as another for this purpose. But if I have a personal problem to talk about and explore more deeply, it matters a lot to me that I trust the person I am talking to, and have a choice as to who that is. If I get the wrong person, I may not be able to do it at all.

Therapy can become a form of social control. It can be a way of keeping tabs on people for the benefit of the institution and its smooth running. I am not saying this always happens or is bound to happen: for all I know it is rare. But if it is rare this is due only to the decency of the people operating the system. The system itself allows it. But in private practice the safety of the client from social control is built in and assured.

There is, of course, the question of cost. In an institutional setting, the costs tend to be hidden, but of course they are still there. Somebody somewhere pays for the service. In private therapy this is out in the open. But there are several stages of removal from the most expensive services which are offered. Therapists charge different amounts, and a little searching can often find people with reasonable charges. Even the most expensive therapists may operate a sliding scale: many of them are conscientious about seeing a certain proportion of clients at a reduced rate, so that people without much money do not have to be turned away. So there is no ethical problem about cost – Carl Rogers never avoided private practice, and helped to train many people for private practice.

Then there is the network of trainees: most training centres have a system by which people in training – most of whom are mature, and all of whom are working under professional supervision – see people on a low-cost basis.

In a slightly different way, there is also the system of co-counselling, by which people go on a brief course to learn how to engage in reciprocal therapy with another person. Some of these courses are quite expensive, but others are put on by local authorities with the customary concessions, and in the final analysis there is the book *The Barefoot Psychoanalyst* (Southgate and Randall 1989) where you can learn the system from a book of cartoons, which can be borrowed from the public library. I used this method for several years, and taught it too, and got a great deal of benefit from it. All these methods honour the basic requirement of a relationship which is chosen and secure and personal.

To me there is something sacred about the therapy relationship. It sets up a space within which true openness is permissible and often possible. And this entails the setting-up of a framework which is reliable and genuinely agreed to by both parties. Within this safe frame the process can continue as long as it needs to. To interfere with this, or to make it impossible, destroys therapy as I understand it.

ACCREDITATION

Another question which has been raised as an ethical issue is as to whether accreditation is an ethical activity. The argument in the book by Richard Mowbray (1995) is that all forms of accreditation or registration are opposed to the public interest in that they favour the professional against the general public.

In 1980 I helped to found the Association for Humanistic Psychology Practitioners, because I wanted to grasp the nettle of accreditation. A couple of years earlier I had resigned from the Psychology and Psycho-therapy Association because it had (after several inconclusive meetings) failed to do this.

The point of accreditation, as we spelled it out at that time, was to put some structure into a disorganised field which had become quite messy. We felt we wanted to put our own house in order, so that we could say to all and sundry that there were some decent standards of practice, and that some of us cared enough about that to make sure that they were upheld, at least within the bounds of the organisation we were setting up. And so we set out some guidelines for how people could assess themselves and their practice, and submit themselves to the judgement of their peers. We also set out some ethical standards, and a complaints procedure so that clients or others who felt offended against by one of our members could find redress.

INWARD AND OUTWARD

We were clear that there were two sides to the issue of accreditation: an inward side, where we became clearer about what we were doing ourselves and the kind of values we wanted to uphold for ourselves; and an outward side, where we said to the world 'We take collective responsibility for our practice, and are prepared to have it examined for its adequacy by anyone who wants or needs to do so.' We were also clear that there were many different kinds of humanistic practitioners, and that we wanted to cater for all of them – therapists of various persuasions, group facilitators, counsellors, organisation consultants, educators, researchers and so on.

Then came, gradually and bit by bit, the United Kingdom Standing Conference for Psychotherapy, which later became the UK Council for Psychotherapy. This consists of some eighty organisations representing all the main schools of psychotherapy in Britain. I'd like some acknowledgement that the people involved with it have done a tremendous job under enormously difficult conditions. To hold together in one regular meeting all the various tendencies within psychotherapy, to enable dialogue and mutual understanding to take place, and to find a growing mutual respect emerging, is no mean achievement. The reason why this has been possible is that it is not agreement on theory which is being attempted, but agreement on staying together so that the UKCP can be recognised as the only competent authority in the UK which can speak for psychotherapists of all schools – hopefully thus preventing the atrocious oppression which has taken place in most countries of Europe, where only such psychotherapy as is approved and controlled by the psychiatric establishment is allowed to take place. Those countries where strict control is also exercised by the psychological establishment are regarded on the Continent as liberal. The UKCP stands for a system by which free organisations freely combine into groupings with explicit criteria of membership, which can be scrutinised and modified by mutual criticism. It is unfortunate that some of the narrower schools of psychoanalysis eventually split off and formed their own exclusive organisation, the British Confederation of Psychotherapists.

Now because of the UKCP's existence, and the pressure from Europe to produce some kind of rationale for what we were doing in this country, the Association of Humanistic Psychology Practitioners had to devote special attention to psychotherapy. Our work on accreditation in this particular area was not only under scrutiny from our peers in the Humanistic and Integrative Psychotherapy Section (HIPS) of the UKCP, but also under scrutiny from other sections, and from the Board of that organisation. In the event, AHPP members took a leading role in drawing up criteria for membership of the Section which took into account many of the lessons we had learned in the AHPP.

But what this meant was that the *outward* aspect of the accreditation process now became much more important. We had to satisfy not only our own consciences, but also the critical gaze of outsiders. So our requirements, and our procedures, had to be tight enough to stand up to this. One of the things we took on board was the necessity to have an External Moderator – someone senior and sympathetic, but not connected with the organisation, who could scrutinise what we were doing, and tell us whether we were living up to our own self-description, or if we were kidding ourselves in some way. We also took to heart the formal assessment by two other organisations in the same Section, which could reveal any weaknesses and holes in our procedures. So now the accreditors were getting, so to speak, accredited by peers. Just the same as what they were doing for others, and just as valuable.

CRITICISMS

In the light of all this history, consider the articles in *Self & Society* by Shohet *et al.* (1991), House and Hall (1991), Postle and Anderson (1990), Brown and Mowbray (1990), Kalisch (1990a and b) and Heron (1990).

In the Shohet *et al.* article, five people got together to experiment with accrediting each other, and discovered many interesting things. But it seems to me that they concentrated on the *inward* aspects of accreditation, and ignored all of the *outward* aspects.

Similarly with the House and Hall article – here thirteen people got together, and again discovered a great deal of value for themselves. Again it seems to me that they ignored the outward aspects of the matter.

Postle and Anderson quarrel with many of the details of AHPP accreditation, and eventually suggest their own substitute for that, which in my view really amounts to much the same thing as the proposals just mentioned – and like them refers much more to the inward than to the outward requirements of any viable accreditation process.

Brown and Mowbray want to argue that psychotherapy should not adopt a medical model. Here they are pushing at an open door, because all of us in the HIPS group agree on that, and will argue it to the door of hell if necessary. We don't want to abandon psychotherapy to the psychiatrists, or even the psychologists: we want it to be recognised as a diverse activity with many different expressions, all legitimate. It is the strength of the UKCP (and its weakness in the eyes of those who want narrower definitions favouring their own approach) that it has insisted on the legitimacy of this diversity.

The Kalisch articles both say that bureaucratisation is a bad thing, and that instead we should adopt the myth of rebellion, in which endeavour the figure of Hermes might help us. This seems to me a kind of either–or which is not helpful. To argue against bureaucracy is like arguing against traffic lights: at a certain stage in the development of an organisation it has to become more bureaucratic, just as at a certain stage in the development of traffic it becomes appropriate and helpful to introduce traffic lights. This doesn't mean that we have to abandon Hermes, whom I find personally a very helpful figure, particularly in relation to psychotherapy, with his ability to go back and forth between the underworld and the overworld carrying messages. The whole essence of the Greek pantheon is that we need many gods and goddesses, not just one. Not the either–or, but the both–and.

The Heron piece is marred by a determination to use the word 'transference' as often as possible, but seems basically to be trying to say that psychotherapy creates its own clients, or at any rate 'exacerbates and reinforces the very processes' which create them. I don't think this can be seriously maintained: of all the forces creating the kind of distress which brings clients into therapy, I would have thought the existence of psychotherapy itself was one of the weakest. He also seems to be saying – though I find it hard to see how he can – that the fact that we are involved in psychotherapy and the UKCP makes it impossible, or less likely, that we will be involved in personal growth through workshops, therapy, group work, education of various kinds, organisational work, community work and so forth. These are activities which are very central and important to the whole humanistic approach, and will in my view continue to be so. This kind of work in the area of what Heron calls 'emotional competence' is something which humanistic practitioners have always done and will presumably continue to do. Again there is the appearance of this either–or which I find so hurtful and damaging.

The thoughtful articles of Hawkins (1990a and b) and of Young (1990) seem very useful to me in correcting some of the misinformation still being carried around, but even they do not mention some things which are well known to those of us who have been involved in all this stuff since the beginning. For example, the way the UKCP is often referred to makes me think that many people have an idea of it as a very formal and hierarchical setup, such that it would surprise them to find out that informal clothes are worn even in formal sessions of the conference. One of the best articles I have seen on accreditation is the one by Alan Frankland (1996), and this should be seen by anyone involved in these issues.

To me it seems obvious that accreditation is here to stay, and that it has to take a form which does justice both to the outward face and to the inward face of our work as practitioners. I am sure we can do this better as time goes on, but not if the criticism comes out in the virulent form which it sometimes seems to.

BOUNDARIES

One of the most important ethical issues which arises in all forms of therapy is the question of boundaries. It is the job of the therapist to hold the ring, to maintain the frame, to secure the *temenos* (the sacred space), to keep the *vas* (the alchemical vessel) closed. We need to keep the energy in, on the one hand, and to keep distractions out, on the other.

It is within the boundary that the relationship takes place. As Petruska Clarkson (1995) has told us so brilliantly, there are at least five relationships all going on at the same time in therapy.

The *therapeutic alliance* is where we make a contract with the client, make sure that time, place and money are taken care of, that the client is motivated and responsible – all the practical things which have to be secured if the process is to be protected.

The *transferential relationship* is where we pay attention to the unconscious part of the transaction, where both the client and the therapist may be subject to influences from the past which provoke reactions not under conscious control.

The *reparative relationship* is where the therapist has to be willing to be what the client's fantasy needs. The therapist may turn into a mother, a father, a sibling, a teacher or other authority figure, and the client may regress into a much earlier age state.

The *real relationship* is where the therapist is authentic, relating to the client in an I–You way, not in an I–It fashion. This is particularly important in humanistic work, where authenticity is a prime value, and must be actually available in the session.

The *transpersonal relationship* is where the therapist is paying attention to the spiritual dimension of the work, and where the client's spiritual aspirations and spiritual problems are taken seriously for what they are, and not reduced to something else.

More details about all of these are of course to be found in the book mentioned: here we are simply admitting that they exist and can only be ignored at our peril. In all of them the question of boundaries is important.

As mentioned earlier, we have become more aware since about 1985 of the boundaries of sex and anger. It has become crystal clear that sexual relations between therapist and client are always harmful, because they are always based on a difference in power, such that the therapist is the abuser even when they feel like the seduced. There is a good discussion of this issue in Russell (1993).

This does not mean that the therapist has to be cold – indeed, Rogers has told us that nonpossessive warmth is an essential quality for any therapist. But it does mean taking care of the difference between acceptance and approval. Acceptance is fine – taking clients as they are, not as they should be. But approval is a kind of warmth that goes too far. We do not tell clients that they are OK, that they are good-looking, that they are well-dressed, that they are intelligent – none of these things or others of the same kind. That is reassurance, that is our judgement, that is manifesting our superiority. And we take care not to let our private opinions about the client become a part of the therapy, unless there is clearly some therapeutic gain to be achieved by doing so. There is a good discussion of this point in Chapter Two of Windy Dryden's book (1985).

This leads to the whole question of dual relationships. In a 1997 issue of *Self & Society* the dilemma is raised by Moira, someone who runs a small psychotherapy training. Among the applicants for training this year is someone who is currently a client of Moira. Should this person be accepted for training, and should this person change therapists? In other words, can the same person be a therapist and a trainer to the same individual at the same time? The general rule for this is that such a dual relationship is to be avoided. One of the main reasons for this is that people often find therapy training very stressful, one of the sources of stress being the relationship with the trainers. If a student is having problems with a trainer, such as thinking the trainer is no good, and the trainer is also the therapist, this is not going to work. Another problem which can arise in such situations is that other members of a seminar group may get jealous or rivalrous when it becomes known that one individual has the seminar leader for a therapist. Also the individual may come to feel that their therapy is continuing in the seminar, and is becoming inescapable, particularly if the degree of transference is high. It used to be quite common in psychoanalysis and in Jungian circles for the training analyst also to be one of the trainers, and even one of the people responsible for passing the candidate as accredited, but this has now changed a great deal.

Other dual relationships are therapist and supervisor. Can the same person be my therapist and my supervisor? Again the answer is no, for the same sort of reason. If my relationship with my supervisor got into difficulties, such as feeling dissatisfied with the service I am getting, I would normally go to my therapist in the first instance, to explore my feelings about this and trying to decide whether the problem is in me or out there – but if it is the same person how can I? This can be a very difficult problem in rural areas, where there is a shortage both of therapists and of supervisors. I even came across the case, in one such area, where the therapist, and the supervisor, and the wife were all the same person!

On the other hand, humanistic training centres see no problem in the trainee having several therapists one after the other. It is quite common for people to move from a male to a female, or from a female to a male, in order to get the benefit of a different gender perspective. The ideal of one central relationship which continues indefinitely, is not held by the humanistic schools. What has to be watched, however, is the question of why the client is transferring *now* at this precise moment. Is it out of health – a readiness to end with one and begin with another – or is it out of sickness – to avoid resolving problems with the first therapist? The boundary question is this: am I really ready to end with this therapist, or not?

Probably the most important boundary issue is confidentiality. This is something which few people outside the world of therapy understand. Social workers don't understand it, nurses don't understand it, teachers don't understand it. It means that the words of the client are sacred. They are not to be repeated or quoted to anyone else. The obvious exception to this is the supervisor, but in the best practice even the supervisor does not know the client's name or address. In supervision it is best to give the client a pseudonym or a letter or a number. So the therapist does not gossip about the client, the supervisor does not gossip about either the client or the supervisee. I use the word gossip to describe any conversation about someone when that person is not present.

Still further, the therapist attempts to ensure that the client does not talk about what happens in their therapy to a third party. This is particularly important when that third party is involved in the therapy, often being mentioned or referred to – partners and parents are the obvious examples. It is all too easy for someone to refer to their therapy in terms which bring forth a defensive reaction from the hearer. Also there are times in therapy when strong negative feelings are expressed towards someone, and if the client then meets that someone and reveals that, the hearer may take the message much too strongly and finally, as if it were the last word on the subject. If the client, later in the therapy, discovers that some of those negative feelings were exaggerated or unwarranted, it is hard, and may be impossible, to undo the damage. People go through phases in therapy, and even the most definite conclusions may turn out to be not the final conclusions after all. So confidentiality is important in this way too.

Finally there is the issue of competence. It is wrong to take on a client if there are clear indications that such a client is beyond the expertise of the therapist. The most obvious example is that of a therapist who takes on a child in therapy when they have had no training in child psychotherapy. This kind of training is very rigorous, particularly in the area of ethics, and it deals with the vexed question of who the client is, which may otherwise be very confusing. Another example would be the case of someone who wanted to work through material pertaining to their birth and the perinatal period, if the therapist had no training in or experience of this kind of work. Another would be to take on a client experiencing a spiritual emergency, when the therapist had not worked through their own material in this area. There are plenty of examples of where an overoptimistic therapist has taken on the wrong client, and both of them have ultimately had a bad experience.

TELLING THE CLIENT

The question sometimes arises about the therapist leaving town or moving house, or going in for major redecorations. When to tell the clients about this? In my opinion the best time is as soon as the date is known and the full story can be given. If the therapist tries to anticipate trouble by telling the clients too far in advance, it merely gives them anxiety unconnected with any other real benefit. This also applies to the question as to whether the therapist should take on new clients during the period of uncertainty, and what to tell them. Again I think the therapist had better carry on as normal, and as if nothing were happening, until the actual date is known. Then is the time to break it to all concerned. In these days of much greater mobility, this is quite likely to arise at some time or another.

Ethics is an area which has come under more scrutiny lately, and it may be confidently predicted that it will become more and more complex and hard to handle.

List of criteria for doing good therapy

These were developed out of a number of meetings of the AHPP Self and Peer Assessment Group. They are all things which can actually be monitored in training.

1 *Awareness of client*
Listening and hearing, seeing and sensing, responding at various levels:

- Body level
- Sexual level
- Emotional levels
- Conscious level
- Imaginative level
- Spiritual level
- Political level

Openness, empathy, resonance, phenomenal experiencing, telepathic leaps, intuition. Ability to pick up cues which client is offering. Ability to at least see the obvious.

2 *Awareness of self*
Congruence, genuineness, authenticity. Openness to own responses at various levels, and ability to make use of own countertransference, restimulation, reintegration and so on. Appropriately self-disclosing.

3 *Encouragement of client's autonomy*
Non-judgmental attention and acceptance. Appreciation of client's uniqueness. Concern for client's self-direction. Giving space to client to move in own direction. Respect for client's energy. Hence at the very least:

- Not putting client down

- Not competing with client
- Not knowing better than the client
- Not taking out one's own shit on the client
- Not keeping distance – hostile or scared – from client
- Not seducing client
- Not smothering client with warmth

All these things can be used awarely at times, but appropriateness is all.

4 *Keeping track of the client*
Not ignoring signs or marks of success. Building upon good rapport. Keeping movement going, keeping interaction alive. Not changing direction before the vein has been exhausted. Not taking client away from important material. Not taking client to less appropriate level of working. Staying with the client, and encouraging the client to stay with the client.

5 *Making good interventions*
Appropriate to client and situation, and timed well. Having a sufficient repertoire of skills. Ability to take risks when appropriate. Balance between important opposites, such as:

- Circling round and homing in
- Active and passive (doing and not doing)
- Hard and soft
- Support and confrontation
- Raising anxiety and inducing calm
- Warmth and coolness
- Facilitation and teaching
- Present time and past distress

6 *Long-term considerations*
Regularity of practitioner's own personal growth work. Regularity of practitioner's own supervision, whether traditional or by peer review. Awareness of when the practitioner needs extra help, nourishment, deeper work and so on, and ability to get it. Ability to handle transference, resistance, etc. Ability to grit one's teeth and hang on where necessary. Having a coherent theoretical rationale, and being able to modify this when appropriate.

Note

It is important that these are all means rather than ends. It is tempting to put in things like:

- Produce a breakthrough in client
- Cure client
- Enlighten client
- Get client to go from adjustment to ecstasy
- Ability to facilitate client change of self-direction
- Ability to get client catharsis/insight/body change/pivotal attitude change.

But these are all, ultimately, things the client does, rather than things the therapist or counsellor does. What I think works on a list like this is to stick to things which the therapist does.

Appendix B

Useful addresses

COURSES FOR PROFESSIONAL TRAINING AND EDUCATION

A good list of humanistic and integrative courses can be obtained from the Administrative Office, UK Council for Psychotherapy, 167–9 Great Portland Street, London W1N 5FB. Ask for the list of members of the Humanistic and Integrative Section, which changes from time to time.

Some well-qualified non-UKCP practitioners are organised as the Independent Practitioners Network. The London contact in 1998 was Alan Hancock, the AMAP Organisation, 91 Fortress Road, London NW5 1AG, 0171 284 4143. There are other contacts in Leeds, Norwich, Nottingham, Hereford and Ottery St Mary.

PERSONAL GROWTH CENTRES IN LONDON

The Open Centre, 188 Old Street, London EC1V 9FR. 0171 251 1504.
Spectrum, 7 Endymion Road, London N4 1EE. 0181 341 2277.

HUMANISTIC ORGANISATIONS

Association for Humanistic Psychology in Britain, BM Box 3582, London WC1N 3XX.
Association for Humanistic Psychology Practitioners, BCM AHPP, London WC1N 3XX.
Association for Humanistic Psychology, 45 Franklin St, San Francisco, California 94102, USA.

HUMANISTIC JOURNALS

Self & Society, 39 Blenkarne Road, London SW11 6HZ.
Journal of Humanistic Psychology, 1314 Westwood Boulevard, Los Angeles, Ca 90024, USA.
The Humanistic Psychologist, Psychology Dept, University of West Georgia, Carrollton, Ga 30118, USA.

Bibliography

Alderfer, C. P. (1972) *Existence, Relatedness, Growth*, New York: Collier-Macmillan.

Alexander, F. M. (1969) *The Resurrection of the Body*, New York: Delta Books.

Allen, M. H. (1982) 'Transilience – A new name for a reality experience', *Association for Transpersonal Psychology Newsletter*, Spring Issue.

American Psychiatric Association (1994) *Diagnostic and Statistical Manual of Mental Disorders*, 4th edn, Washington: APA.

Anthony, Dick, Ecker, Bruce & Wilber, Ken (1987) *Spiritual Choices*, New York: Paragon House.

Aponte, J. F. and Lyons, M. J. (1980) 'Supervision in community settings: Concepts, methods and issues', in A. K. Hess (ed.) *Psychotherapy Supervision*, New York: John Wiley & Sons.

Argyle, M. (1967) *The Psychology of Interpersonal Behaviour*, Harmondsworth: Penguin.

Argyris, Chris (1971) *Intervention Theory and Method*, Reading: Addison-Wesley.

Assagioli, R. (1975) *Psychosynthesis: A Manual of Principles and Techniques*, London: Turnstone Books.

Baldwin, Peter A. (1997) *Four and Twenty Blackbirds*, Las Vegas: Bramble Books.

Balint, M. (1968) *The Basic Fault*, London: Tavistock Publications.

Bandler, R. and Grinder, J. (1975) *The Structure of Magic, Vol. 1*, Palo Alto: Science and Behaviour Books.

Bandler, R. and Grinder, J. (1979) *Frogs into Princes: Neuro Linguistic Programming*, Moab: Real People Press.

Banet, A. G. (1976) 'The goals of psychotherapy', in A. G. Banet (ed.) *Creative Psychotherapy: A Source Book*, La Jolla, CA: University Associates.

Barkham, Michael (1990) 'Research in individual therapy' in W. Dryden (ed.) *Individual Therapy: A Handbook*, Buckingham: Open University Press.

Beck, A. T. (1979) *Cognitive Therapy and the Emotional Disorders*, New York: Meridian.

Beckwith, L. (1972) 'Relationship between infants' social behaviour and their mothers' behaviour', *Child Development*, 43.

Beisser, A. (1972) 'The paradoxical theory of change' in J. Fagan and I. L. Shepherd (eds) *Gestalt Therapy Now*, New York: Harper.

Belson, W. (1975) *Juvenile Theft: The Causal Factors*, New York: Harper & Row.

Bem, Daryl J. (1970) *Beliefs, Attitudes and Human Affairs*, Belmont, CA: Brooks/Cole.

Benson, L. (1974) *Images, Heroes and Self-perception: The Struggle for Identity – from Mask-wearing to Authenticity*, Englewood Cliffs, N. J.: Prentice-Hall.

Berke, J. H. (1979) *I Haven't Had to Go Mad Here*, Harmondsworth: Penguin.

Berman, Jeffrey S. and Norton, Nicholas C. (1985) 'Does professional training make a therapist more effective?', *Psychological Bulletin*, 94/2.

Berne, E. (1973) *What Do You Say After You Say Hello?*, New York: Bantam.

Berry, Scott (1996) 'Learning to live with life-threatening illness' in S. Palmer, S. Dainow and P. Milner (eds) *Counselling: The BAC Counselling Reader*, London: Sage.

Boadella, David (1988) *Biosynthesis*, Milton Keynes: Open University Press.

Bond, Tim (1996) 'Counselling-supervision – Ethical issues' in S. Palmer, S. Dainow and P. Milner (eds) *Counselling: The BAC Counselling Reader*, London: Sage.

Boorstein, Seymour (ed.) (1996) *Transpersonal Psychotherapy*, 2nd edn, Albany: State University of New York Press.

Boyesen, G. (1970) 'Experiences with dynamic relaxation', *Energy & Character*, 1/1.

Boyle, Mary (1990) *Schizophrenia: A Scientific Delusion?*, London: Fontana.

Boyle, Mary (1996) 'Schizophrenia: The Fallacy of Diagnosis', *Changes*, 14/1 pp. 5–13.

Brammer, Lawrence M., Shostrom, Everett L. and Abrego, Philip J. (1989) *Therapeutic Psychology: Fundamentals of Counseling and Psychotherapy*, 5th edn, Englewood Cliffs, N. J.: Prentice-Hall.

Brazier, David (1991) *A Guide to Psychodrama*, London: Association for Humanistic Psychology in Britain.

Brenner, C. (1979) 'Working alliance, therapeutic alliance and transference', *Journal of the American Psychoanalytic Association*, (supplement), 27.

Broughton, J. (1975) 'The development of natural epistemology in adolescence and early adulthood', Harvard, MA: unpublished doctoral dissertation.

Brown, Juliana and Mowbray, Richard (1990) 'Whither the human potential movement', *Self & Society*, 18/4 pp. 32–5.

Brown, Juliana and Mowbray, Richard (1994) 'Primal Integration' in D. Jones (ed.) *Innovative Therapy: A Handbook*, Buckingham: Open University Press.

Brown, P. (1974) *Toward a Marxist Psychology*, New York: Harper Colophon.

Buber, M. (1961) *Tales of the Hasidim: The Early Masters*, New York: Schocken.

Buber, M. (1965) 'Dialogue between Martin Buber and Carl Rogers', in M. Friedman (ed.) *Man and the Knowledge of Man*, New York: Harper & Row.

Bugental, J. F. T. (1976) *The Search for Existential Identity*, San Francisco: Jossey-Bass.

Bugental, J. F. T. (1978) *Psychotherapy and Process: The Fundamentals of an Existential-humanistic Approach*, Reading: Addison-Wesley.

Bugental, J. F. T. (1981) *The Search for Authenticity*, enlarged edn, New York: Irvington.

Bugental, J. F. T. (1987) *The Art of the Psychotherapist*, New York: W. W. Norton & Co.

Carroll, Michael (1996) *Counselling Supervision: Theory, Skills and Practice*, London: Cassells.

Chamberlain, David (1988) *Babies Remember Birth*, New York: Ballantine Books.

Cherniss, Cary (1980) *Staff Burnout: Job Stress in the Human Services*, Beverley Hills, CA: Sage.

Cherniss, C. and Egnatios, E. (1978) 'Clinical supervision in community mental health', *Social Work*, 23 pp. 219–23.

Chesler, Phyllis (1972) *Women and Madness*, New York: Avon.

Clarkson, Petruska (1989) *Gestalt Counselling in Action*, London: Sage.

Clarkson, Petruska (1992) *Transactional Analysis Psychotherapy: An Integrated Approach*, London: Routledge.

Clarkson, Petruska (1995) *The Therapeutic Relationship*, London: Whurr.

Clarkson, Petruska (1996) *The Bystander*, London: Whurr.

Cohen, J. M. and Phipps, J-F. (1979) *The Common Experience*, London: Rider & Co.

Cohen, R. J. and DeBetz, B. (1977) 'Responsive supervision of the psychiatric resident and clinical psychology intern', *American Journal of Psychoanalysis*, 37/1.

Connell, Robert W. (1987) *Gender and Power*, Cambridge: Polity Press.

Console, William A., Simons, Richard C. and Rubinstein, Mark (1978) *The First Encounter: The Beginnings in Psychotherapy*, New York: Jason Aronson.

Corrière, R. and Hart, J. (1978) *The Dream Makers*, New York: Bantam.

Corsini, Raymond (ed.) (1981) *Handbook of Innovative Psychotherapies*, Chichester: John Wiley & Sons.

Costello, Timothy W., Costello, Joseph T. and Holmes, David A. (1995) *Abnormal Psychology*, London: HarperCollins.

Cranmer, David (1994) 'Core Energetics' in D. Jones (ed.) *Innovative Therapy: A Handbook*, Buckingham: Open University Press.

Cunningham, Ian (1988) 'Interactive holistic research: Researching self-managed learning' in P. Reason (ed.) *Human Inquiry in Action: Developments in New Paradigm Research*, London: Sage.

Daniels, A. K. (1970) 'The social construction of military psychiatric diagnoses' in H. P. Dreitzel (ed.) *Recent Sociology No. 2*, London: Collier-Macmillan.

Dansky, Steven, Knoebel, John and Pitchford, Kenneth (1977) 'The effeminist manifesto', in Jon Snodgrass (ed.) *A Book of Readings for Men Against Sexism*, New York: Times Change Press.

DeCarvalho, Roy José (1991) *The Founders of Humanistic Psychology*, New York: Praeger.

Doblin, R. (1991) 'Pahnke's "Good Friday Experiment": A long-term follow-up and methological critique', *The Journal of Transpersonal Psychology*, 23/1 pp. 1–28.

Dreyfuss, A. and Feinstein, A. D. (1977) 'My body is me: Body-based approaches to personal enrichment', in B. McWaters (ed.) *Humanistic Perspectives: Current Trends in Psychology*, Monterey: Brooks/Cole.

Dryden, Windy (ed.) (1985) *Therapists' Dilemmas*, London: Harper & Row.

Dryden, Windy (1991) 'Using rational-emotive counselling in the supervision of counsellors' in W Dryden (ed.) *Dryden on Counselling. Vol. 3: Training and Supervision*, London: Whurr.

Dryden, Windy (ed.) (1992) *Integrative and Eclectic Therapy: A Handbook*, Buckingham: Open University Press.

Dryden, Windy and Golden, William (eds) (1986) *Cognitive-Behavioural Approaches to Psychotherapy*, London: Harper & Row.

du Plock, Simon (1996) 'The existential-phenomenological movement 1834–1995' in Windy Dryden (ed.) *Developments in Psychotherapy: Historical Perspectives*, London: Sage.

Durlack, J. A. (1979) 'Comparative effectiveness of paraprofessional and professional helpers', *Psychological Bulletin*, 86/1 pp. 80–92.

Duval, S. and Wicklund, R. A. (1972) *A Theory of Objective Self-awareness*, New York: Academic Press.

Edinger, E. (1960) 'The ego-self paradox', *The Journal of Analytic Psychology*, 5/1.

Egan, G. (1994) *The Skilled Helper*, 5th edn, Monterey, CA: Brooks/Cole.

Eisler, Riane (1995) *Sacred Pleasure: Sex, Myth and the Politics of the Body*, Shaftesbury: Element.

Ekstein, R. (1969) 'Concerning the teaching and learning of psychoanalysis', *Journal of the American Psychoanalytic Association*, 17/3.

Ekstein, Rudolf and Wallerstein, Robert S. (1972) *The Teaching and Learning of Psychotherapy*, 2nd edn, New York: International Universities Press.

Ellis, A. (1970) *The Essence of Rational Psychotherapy*, New York: Institute for Rational Living.

Ellis, A. (1995) 'Fundamentals of rational-emotive behaviour therapy for the 1990s' in Windy Dryden (ed.) *Rational-Emotive Behaviour Therapy: A Reader*, London: Sage.

Ellis, A. and Harper, R. (1975) *A New Guide to Rational Living*, Hollywood, CA: Wilshire Books.

Enright, J. (1972) 'Awareness training in the mental health professions', in Joen Fagan and Irma Lee Shepherd (eds) *Gestalt Therapy Now*, Harmondsworth: Penguin.

Enright, J. (1980) *Enlightening Gestalt*, Palo Alto, CA: Pro Telos Press.

Erickson, Beth (1993) *Helping Men Change: The Role of the Female Therapist*, Newbury Park, CA: Sage.

Erikson, E. (1965) *Childhood and Society*, Harmondsworth: Penguin.

Ernst, Sheila and Goodison, Lucy (1981) *In Our Own Hands*, London: The Womens Press.

Esterson, Aaron (1972) *The Leaves of Spring: A Study in the Dialectics of Madness*, Harmondsworth: Penguin.

Eysenck, Hans (1969) *Behaviour Therapy and the Neuroses*, London: Pergamon Press.

Fadiman, James and Frager, Robert (eds) (1994) *Personality and Personal Growth*, New York: HarperCollins.

Faris, R. E. L. and Dunham, H. W. (1939) *Mental Disorders in Urban Areas*, Chicago: University of Chicago Press.

Federn, P. (1952) *Ego Psychology and the Psychoses*, New York: Basic Books.

Feher, L. (1980) *The Psychology of Birth*, London: Souvenir Press.

Feldenkrais, M. (1972) *Awareness Through Movement: Health Exercises for Personal Growth*, New York: Harper & Row.

Fenichel, O. (1945) *The Psychoanalytic Theory of Neurosis*, New York: W. W. Norton & Co.

Ferrucci, P. (1982) *What We May Be: The Visions and Techniques of Psychosynthesis*, Wellingborough: Turnstone Press.

Firestone, Shulamith (1972) *The Dialectic of Sex*, New York: Bantam.

Firman, John and Gila, Ann (1997) *The Primal Wound: A Transpersonal View of Trauma, Addiction and Growth*, Albany, NY: State University of New York Press.

Fisch, R., Weakland, J. and Segal, L. (1982) *The Tactics of Change*, San Francisco: Jossey-Bass.

Fiske, D. W. and Maddi, S. R. (eds) (1961) *Functions of Varied Experience*, Homewood: The Dorsey Press.

Fizdale, R. (1958) 'Peer-group supervision', *Social Casework*, 39.

Flescher, J. (1973) 'On different types of countertransference', *International Journal of Group Psychotherapy*, 3.

Frankland, A. (1981) 'Mistaken seduction', *New Forum*, 7/4.

Frankland, A. (1996) 'Exploring accreditation' in S. Palmer, S. Dainow and P. Milner (eds) *Counselling: The BAC Counselling Reader*, London: Sage.

Fransella, F. (1972) *Personal Change and Reconstruction*, London: Academic Press.

Freedman, Jill and Combs, Gene (1996) *Narrative Therapy: The Social Construction of Preferred Realities*, New York: W. W. Norton & Co.

Freeman, H. E. and Giovannoni, J. M. (1969) 'Social psychology of mental health', in G. Lindzey and E. Aronson (eds) *The Handbook of Social Psychology*, 2nd edn, vol. 5, Reading: Addison-Wesley.

Freundlich, D. (1974) 'Countertransference in individual and group therapy', *Primal Experience Monograph*, New York: Centre for the Whole Person.

Friedenberg, E. Z. (1973) *Laing*, London: Fontana/Collins.

Fromm, E. (1941) *Escape from Freedom*, New York: Farrar, Strauss & Giroux.

Fromm-Reichmann, Frieda (1950) *Principles of Intensive Psychotherapy*, Chicago: University of Chicago Press.

Gallagher, Shaun (1997) 'Mutual enlightenment: Recent phenomenology in cognitive science', *Journal of Consciousness Studies*, 4/3 pp. 195–214.

Gardner, L. H. (1971) 'The therapeutic relationship under varying conditions of race', *Psychotherapy: Theory, Research and Practice*, 8/1.

Garfield, P. L. (1976) *Creative dreaming*, London: Futura Publications.

Garfield, Sol L. (1978) 'Research on client variables in psychotherapy' in S. L. Garfield and A. E. Bergin (eds) *Handbook of Psychotherapy and Behaviour Change*, 2nd edn, New York: John Wiley & Sons.

Garfield, Sol L. (1979) *Training and Outcome in Psychotherapy*, New York: BMA Audio Cassettes.

Garfield, S. L. and Bergin, A. A. (eds) (1978) *Handbook of Psychotherapy and Behaviour Change: An Empirical Analysis*, 2nd edn, New York: John Wiley & Sons.

Gelb, Lester (1973) 'Masculinity–femininity : A study in imposed inequality', in Jean Baker Miller (ed.) *Psychoanalysis and Women*, Harmondsworth: Penguin.

Gendlin, E. (1969) 'Focussing', *Psychotherapy: Theory, Research and Practice*, 6.

Gill, M. M. *et al.* (1954) *The Initial Interview in Private Practice*, New York: International Universities Press.

Giorgi, A. (ed.) (1975) *Duquesne studies in phenomenological psychology*, vol. 2, Pittsburgh, PA: Duquesne University Press.

Glasser, W. (1965) *Reality Therapy*, New York: Harper & Row.

Glauber, I. P. (1953) 'The nature of stuttering and the treatment of stuttering', *Social Casework*, 34.

Goldberg, Carl (1995) 'The daimonic development of the malevolent personality', *Journal of Humanistic Psychology*, 35/3 pp. 7–36.

Goleman, D. (1978) *The Varieties of the Meditative Experience*, London: Rider & Co.

Gordon-Brown, I. and Somers, B. (1988) 'Transpersonal Psychotherapy' in J. Rowan and W. Dryden (eds) *Innovative Therapy in Britain*, Milton Keynes: Open University Press.

Gove, W. R. (1975) *The Labelling of Deviance*, Beverley Hills, CA: Sage.

Greenley, J. R. (1975) 'Alternate views of the psychiatrist's role', in T. J. Scheff (ed.) *Labelling Madness*, Englewood Cliffs, NJ: Prentice-Hall.

Greenwald, H. (1974) *Direct Decision Therapy*, San Diego: Edits.

Grinder, J. and Bandler, R. (1981) *Trance-formations*, Moab, UT: Real People Press.

Grof, S. (1975) *Realms of the Human Unconscious*, New York: The Viking Press.

Grof, S. (1980) *LSD Psychotherapy*, Pomona: Hunter House.

Grof, S. (1988) The Adventure of Self-Discovery, Albany, NY: State University of New York Press.

Grof, S. (1992) *The Holotropic Mind: The Three Levels of Human Consciousness and How They Shape Our Lives*, San Francisco: Harper-San Francisco.

Grove, David J. and Panzer, B. I. (1989) *Resolving Traumatic Memories: Metaphors and Symbols in Psychotherapy*, New York: Irvington.

Hall, Bud L. (1975) 'Participatory research: An approach for change', *Convergence: An International Journal of Adult Education*, 8/2.

Hall, J. (1977) *Clinical Uses of Dreams: Jungian Interpretations and Enactments*, New York: Grune & Stratton.

Hampden-Turner, C. (1977) *Sane Asylum*, New York: William Morrow & Co.

Harding, E. (1965) *The I and the Not-I*, Princeton, N. J.: Princeton University Press.

Harre, R. (1979) *Social Being*, Oxford: Blackwell.

Harris, T. (1969) *I'm OK, You're OK*, New York: Avon.

Hattie, J. A., Sharpley, C. F. and Rogers, H. J. (1984) 'Comparative effectiveness of professional and paraprofessional helpers', *Psychological Bulletin*, 95 pp. 534–41.

Hawkins, Peter (1990a) 'Registration of psychotherapists – whither, why and how', *Self & Society*, 18/1 pp. 10–12.

Hawkins, Peter (1990b) 'A response to John Heron, David Kalisch and Roger Horrocks', *Self & Society*, 18/4 pp. 30–1.

Hawkins, Peter and Shohet, Robin (1989) *Supervision in the Helping Professions*, Milton Keynes: Open University Press.

Heron, John (1979) *Assessment Revisited*, Guildford: HPRP, University of Surrey.

Heron, John (1981a) 'Self and peer assessment', in T. Boydell and M. Pedler (eds) *Management Self-development*, Westmead: Gower Publishing Co.

Heron, John (1981b) 'Experiential research methodology', in Peter Reason and John Rowan (eds) *Human inquiry: A sourcebook of new paradigm research*, Chichester: John Wiley & Sons.

Heron, John (1990) 'The politics of transference', *Self & Society*, 18/1 pp. 17–23.

Heron, John (1996) *Co-operative Inquiry*, London: Sage.

Hess, Allen K. (1980) 'Training models and the nature of psychotherapy supervision' in A. K. Hess (ed.) *Psychotherapy Supervision: Theory, Research and Practice*, New York: John Wiley & Sons.

Hill, Clara E. (1989) *Therapist Techniques and Client Outcomes*, Newbury Park, CA: Sage.

Hillman, J. (1979) *The Dream and the Under-world*, New York: Harper Colophon.

Hillman, J. (1989) *The Essential James Hillman: A Blue Fire*, London: Routledge.

Hillman, J. and Ventura, M. (1992) *We've Had a Hundred Years of Psychotherapy – and the World's Getting Worse*, San Francisco: HarperSanFrancisco.

Hinshelwood, R. D. (1989) *A Dictionary of Kleinian Thought*, London: Free Association.

Hobson, Bob (1985) *Forms of Feeling: The Heart of Psychotherapy*, London: Tavistock.

Hogan, D. (1979) *The Regulation of Psychotherapists*, 4 vols, Cambridge, MA: Ballinger.

Hollingshead, A. B. and Redlich, F. C. (1958) *Social Class and Mental Illness*, New York: John Wiley & Sons.

Holloway, Elizabeth (1995) *Clinical supervision: A systems approach*, Thousand Oaks, CA: Sage.

Holmes, Paul, Karp, Marcia and Watson, Michael (1994) *Psychodrama since Moreno: Innovations in Theory and Practice*, London: Routledge.

Horney, Karen (1950) *Neurosis and Human Growth*, New York: W. W. Norton & Co.

House, Richard and Hall, Jill (1991) 'Peer accreditation . . . within a humanistic framework?', *Self & Society*, 19/2 pp. 33–6.

Houston, Gaie (1995) *Supervision and Counselling*, revised edn, London: The Rochester Foundation.

Howard, Alex (1996) *Challenges to counselling and psychotherapy*, Basingstoke: Macmillan.

Jackins, H. (1965) *The Human Side of Human Beings*, Seattle: Rational Island.

Jacoby, Mario (1984) *The Analytic Encounter: Transference and Human Relationship*, Toronto: Inner City.

Janov, A . (1973) *The Primal Scream*, London: Abacus.

Janov, A. and Holden, M. (1977) *Primal Man*, London: Abacus.

Jaspers, K. (1931), quoted in Maurice Friedman (ed.) *The Worlds of Existentialism: A Critical Reader*, Chicago: University of Chicago Press.

Jennings, Jerry L. (1992) 'Husserl revisited: The forgotten distinction between psychology and phenomenology' in R. B. Miller (ed.) *The Restoration of Dialogue: Readings in the Philosophy of Clinical Psychology*, Washington: APA.

Joffe, J. M. (1969) *Prenatal Determinants of Behaviour*, Oxford: Pergamon Press.

Johnsen, Lillemor (1979a, b, c; 1980) 'Developmental steps and centres of growth', parts 1, 2, 3 and 4, *Energy & Character*, 10/1, 10/2, 10/3, 11/2.

Kalisch, David (1990a) 'Professionalisation – a rebel view', *Self & Society*, 18/1 pp. 24–9.

Kalisch, David (1990b) 'The living tradition and the division of the spoils', *Self & Society*, 18/4 pp. 36–7.

Kapelovitz, L. H. (1976) *To Love and to Work: A Demonstration and Discussion of Psychotherapy*, New York: Grune & Stratton.

Keleman, Stanley (1985) *Emotional Anatomy*, Berkeley, CA: Center Press.

Kelly, George (1955) *The Psychology of Personal Constructs*, New York: Norton.

Kendall, Philip C. and Hammen, Constance (1995) *Abnormal Psychology*, Boston: Houghton Mifflin.

Kepner, Elaine and Brien, Lois (1972) 'Gestalt therapy: A behaviouristic phenomenology' in J. Fagan and I. L. Shepherd (eds) *Gestalt Therapy Now*, Harmondsworth: Penguin.

Kirschenbaum, Howard and Henderson, Valerie Land (eds) (1989) *Carl Rogers Dialogues*, London: Constable.

Kirschenbaum, Howard and Henderson, Valerie Land (eds) (1990) *The Carl Rogers Reader*, London: Constable.

Knutson, J. K. (ed.) (1973) *Handbook of Political Psychology*, San Francisco: Jossey-Bass.

Kohlberg, L. (1969) 'Stage and sequence: The cognitive-developmental approach to socialization', in D. Goslin (ed.) *Handbook of Socialization Theory and Research*, Chicago: Rand McNally.

Korchin, S. J. (1976) *Modern Clinical Psychology*, New York: Basic Books.

Krim, S. (1960) 'The insanity bit', in S. Krim (ed.) *The Beats*, New York: Gold Medal.

Kupers, Terry A. (1993) *Revisioning Men's Lives: Gender, Intimacy and Power*, New York: The Guilford Press.

Kurtz, Ron and Prestera, Hector (1977) *The body reveals*, New York: Harper & Row.

Labov, W. (1972) 'The logic of nonstandard English', in P. P. Giglioli (ed.) *Language and Social Context*, Harmondsworth: Penguin.

Laing, R D (1965) *The Divided Self*, Harmondsworth: Penguin.

Laing, R. D. (1967) *The Politics of Experience*, Harmondsworth: Penguin.

Laing, R. D. (1976) *The Facts of Life*, Harmondsworth: Penguin.

Laing, R. D. (1982) *The Voice of Experience*, Harmondsworth: Penguin.

Laing, R. D. and Esterson, A. (1970) *Sanity, Madness and the Family*, Harmondsworth: Penguin.

Lake, Frank (1966) *Clinical Theology*, London: Darton, Longman & Todd.

Lake, Frank (1980) *Studies in Constricted Confusion: Exploration of a Pre- and Peri-Natal Paradigm*, Nottingham: Clinical Theology Association.

Lemma, Alessandra (1996) *Introduction to Psychopathology*, London: Sage.

Levant, Ronald F. and Pollack, William S. (eds) (1995) *A New Psychology of Men*, New York: Basic Books.

Levin, D. M. (1981) 'Approaches to psychotherapy: Freud, Jung and Tibetan Buddhism', in R. S. Valle and R. von Eckartsberg (eds) *The Metaphors of Consciousness*, New York: Plenum Press.

Loeser, L. H. and Bry, T. (1953) 'The position of the group therapist in transference and countertransference: An experimental study', *International Journal of Group Psychotherapy*, 3.

Loevinger, J. (1976) *Ego Development*, San Francisco: Jossey-Kass.

Lowen, A. (1967) *The Betrayal of the Body*, New York: Macmillan.

Lowen, A. (1976) *Bioenergetics*, London: Coventure.

Lowen, A. and Lowen, Leslie (1977) *The Way to Vibrant Health: A Manual of Bioenergetic Exercises*, New York: Harper Colophon.

Lukesch, M. (1975) quoted in Verny (1982).

Luria, A. R. (1969) 'The origin and cerebral organization of man's conscious action', an evening lecture to the XIX International Congress of Psychology.

McCurdy, Alexander (1985) 'Establishing and maintaining the analytical structure' in M. Stein (ed.) *Jungian Analysis*, Boston: Shambhala.

MacLean, Paul (1970) 'The triune brain: Emotion and scientific basis' in F. O. Schmitt (ed.) *The Neurosciences* (second study program), New York: Rockefeller University Press.

MacLean, Paul (1973) *A Triune Concept of the Brain and Behaviour*, Toronto: University of Toronto Press.

McLellan, Betty (1995) *Beyond Psychoppression: A Feminist Alternative Therapy*, North Melbourne: Spinifex Press.

McNeilly, Cheryl L. and Howard, Kenneth I. (1991) 'The effects of psychotherapy: A reevaluation based on dosage', *Psychotherapy Research*, 1/1 pp. 74–8.

Madison, P. (1969) *Personality Development in College*, Reading: Addison-Wesley.

Mahler, M. S., Pine, F. and Bergman, A. (1975) *The Psychological Birth of the Human Infant*, London: Hutchinson.

Mahrer, Alvin R. (1985) *Psychotherapeutic Change: An Alternative Approach to Meaning and Measurement*, New York: W. W. Norton & Co.

Mahrer, Alvin R. (1986) *Therapeutic Experiencing*, New York: W. W. Norton & Co.

Mahrer, Alvin R. (1989) *Experiencing*, Ottawa: University of Ottawa Press.

Mahrer, Alvin R. (1996) *The Complete Guide to Experiential Psychotherapy*, New York: John Wiley & Sons.

Mahrer, Alvin R., Dessaulles, André, Nadler, Wayne P., Gervaize, Patricia A. and Sterner, Irit (1987) 'Good and very good moments in psychotherapy: Content, distribution and facilitation', *Psychotherapy*, 24 pp. 7–14.

Malan, D. H. (1979) *Individual Psychotherapy and the Science of Psychodynamics*, London: Butterworth.

Maltz, M. (1960) *Psychocybernetics*, Hollywood: Wilshire Books.

Marina, Ninoska (1982) 'Restructuring of cognitive-affective structure: A central point of change after psychotherapy', Brunel: Unpublished doctoral dissertation.

Marlan, S. (1981) 'Depth consciousness', in R. S. Valle and R. von Eckartsberg (eds) *The Metaphors of Consciousness*, New York: Plenum Press.

Marshall, W. R. and Confer, W. N. (1980) 'Psychotherapy supervision: Supervisees' perspective', in Allen K. Hess (ed.) *Psychotherapy Supervision*, New York: John Wiley & Sons.

Maruyama, Magoroh (1978) 'Endogenous research and polyocular anthropology', in R. E. Holloman and S. Arutionov (eds) *Perspectives on Ethnicity*, The Hague: Mouton.

Maslow, A. H. (1968) *Toward a Psychology of Being*, New York: Van Nostrand Reinhold.

Maslow, A. H. (1970) *Religions, Values and Peak Experiences*, New York: The Viking Press.

Maslow, A. H. (1973) *The Farther Reaches of Human Nature*, Harmondsworth: Penguin.

Masson, Jeffrey (1989) *Against Therapy*, London: Collins.

Masters, R. and Houston, Jean (1978) *Listening to the Body*, New York: Delacorte Press.

Matarazzo, R. G. (1978) 'Research on the teaching and learning of psychotherapeutic skills', in S. L. Garfield and A. E. Bergin (eds) *Handbook of Psychotherapy and Behaviour Change*, 2nd edn, New York: John Wiley & Sons.

May, R. (1969) *Love and Will*, New York: W. W. Norton & Co.

May, R. (1983) *The Discovery of Being*, New York: W. W. Norton & Co.

Meade, Michael (1993) *Men and the Water of Life*, San Francisco: HarperSanFrancisco.

Mearns, Dave and Dryden, Windy (1990) *Experiences of Counselling in Action*, London: Sage.

Merry, Tony (1995) *Invitation to Person Centred Psychology*, London: Whurr.

Miller, Alice (1985) *Thou Shalt Not Be Aware*, London: Pluto Press.

Miller, Jean Baker (ed.) (1974) *Psychoanalysis and Women*, Harmondsworth: Penguin.

Miller, Jean Baker (1978) *Toward a New Psychology of Women*, Harmondsworth: Penguin.

Miller, Nadine (1973) 'Letter to her psychiatrist' in P. Brown (ed.) *Radical Psychology*, London: Tavistock.

Mindell, Arnold (1985) *Working with the Dreaming Body*, London: Routledge & Kegan Paul.

Mintz, E. (1972) *Marathon Groups: Reality and Symbol*, New York: Avon.

Mitchell, Juliet (1975) *Psychoanalysis and Feminism*, Harmondsworth: Penguin.

Miyuki, M. (1979) 'A Jungian approach to the pure land practice of Nien-fo', Paper presented to the Sixth Annual Conference of Jungian Analysts, Asilomar.

Montagu, A. (1978) *Touching*, 2nd edn, New York: Harper & Row.

Moreno, Jacob Levi (1974) 'The Viennese origins of the encounter movement, paving the way for existentialism, group psychotherapy and psychodrama' in I. A. Greenberg (ed.) *Psychodrama: Theory and therapy*, London: Souvenir Press.

Moss, L. E. (1981) *A Woman's Way: A Feminist Approach to Body Psychotherapy*, Ann Arbor: University Microfilms International.

Mott, F. J. (1969) *The Nature of the Self*, London: The Integration Publishing Co.

Mowbray, Richard (1995) *The Case against Psychotherapy Registration*, London: Transmarginal Press.

Netherton, M. and Shiffrin, N. (1979) *Past Lives Therapy*, New York: Ace Books.

Neugarten, B. L. *et al.* (1964) *Personality in Middle and Later Life*, New York: Atherton.

Neumann, E. (1963) *The Great Mother: An Analysis of the Archetype*, Princeton, N. J.: Princeton University Press.

Nichols, M. P. and Zax, M. (1977) *Catharsis in Psychotherapy*, New York: Gardner Press.

Noble, Elizabeth (1993) *Primal Connections*, New York: Simon & Schuster.

Osherson, Samuel (1986) *Finding Our Fathers*, New York: Fawcett Columbine.

Page, Steve and Wosket, Val (1994) *Supervising the Counsellor: A Cyclical Model*, London: Routledge.

Painter, Jack W. (1986) *Deep Bodywork and Personal Development*, Mill Valley: Bodymind Books.

Parloff, M. B. *et al.* (1978) 'Research on therapist variables in relation to process and outcome', in S. L. Garfield and A. E. Bergin (eds) *Handbook of Psychotherapy and Behaviour Change*, 2nd edn, New York: John Wiley & Sons.

Peerbolte, L . (1975) *Psychic Energy in Prenatal Dynamics*, Wassenaar: Servire B V.

Perls, F. S. (1969a) *Gestalt Therapy Verbatim*, Moab, UT: Real People Press.

Perls, F. S. (1969b) *In and Out the Garbage Pail*, Moab, UT: Real People Press.

Perls, F. S. (1972) *Four Lectures*, in J. Fagan and I. L. Shepherd (eds) *Gestalt Therapy Now*, Harmondsworth: Penguin.

Perls, F. S. (1975) Collection of papers in J. O. Stevens (ed.) *Gestalt Is*, Moab, UT: Real People Press.

Perls, F. S. (1976) *The Gestalt Approach* and *Eyewitness to Therapy*, New York: Bantam.

Phillips, E. L. (1977) *Counselling and Psychotherapy: A Behavioural Approach*, New York: John Wiley & Sons.

Pilgrim, David (1990) 'British psychotherapy in context' in W. Dryden (ed.) *Individual Therapy: A Handbook*, Buckingham: Open University Press.

Polsky, N. (1969) *Hustlers, Beats and Others*, New York: Doubleday Anchor.

Postle, Denis and Anderson, Jill (1990) 'Stealing the flame', *Self & Society*, 18/1 pp. 13–15.

Progoff, I. (1975) *At a Journal Workshop*, New York: Dialogue House.

Proskauer, M. (1977) 'The therapeutic value of certain breathing exercises', in Charles A. Garfield (ed.) *Rediscovery of the Body*, New York: Dell/Laurel.

Putney, S. and G. J. (1964) *The Adjusted American*, New York: Harper & Row.

Rachman, S. J. and Philips, C. (1978) *Psychology and Medicine*, Harmondsworth: Penguin.

Racker, H. (1957) 'The meaning and uses of countertransference', *Psychoanalytic Quarterly*, 26.

Rawson, P. and Legeza, L. (1973) *Tao: The Chinese Philosophy of Time and Change*, London: Thames & Hudson.

Reason, Peter (ed.) (1988) *Human Inquiry in Action*, London: Sage.

Reason, Peter (ed.) (1994) *Participation in Human Inquiry*, London: Sage.

Reason, Peter and Rowan, John (eds) (1981) *Human Inquiry: A Sourcebook of New Paradigm Research*, Chichester: John Wiley & Sons.

Reich, W. (1950) *Character Analysis*, London: Vision Press.

Reik, T. (1948) *Listening with the Third Ear: The Inner Experience of a Psychoanalyst*, New York: Farrar, Strauss & Giroux.

Rice, Laura N. (1980), 'A client-centred approach to the supervision of psychotherapy', in Allen K. Hess (ed.) *Psychotherapy Supervision*, New York: John Wiley & Sons.

Riesman, D. (1954) *The Lonely Crowd*, New York: Doubleday.

Rioch, Margaret J., Coulter, Winifred R. and Weinberger, David M. (1976) *Dialogues for Therapists*, San Francisco: Josey-Bass.

Rogers, C. R. (1942) *Counselling and Psychotherapy*, Boston: Houghton Mifflin.

Rogers, C. R. (1951) *Client-centred therapy: Its Current Practice, Implications and Theory*, Boston: Houghton Mifflin.

Rogers, C. R. (1961) *On Becoming a Person*, London: Constable.

Rogers, C. R. (1968) 'Some thoughts concerning the presuppositions of the behavioural sciences', in W. R. Coulson and C. R. Rogers (eds) *Man and the Science of Man*, Columbus, OH: Charles E. Merrill.

Rogers, C. R. (1969) *Freedom to Learn*, Columbus, OH: Charles E. Merrill.

Rogers, C. R. (1978) *On Personal Power*, London: Constable.

Rogers, C. R. and Freiberg, H. Jerome (1994) *Freedom to Learn*, 3rd edn, New York: Charles E. Merrill.

Rolf, I. (1978) *Structural Integration*, New York: Viking/Esalen.

Rosenhan, D. L. (1975) 'On being sane in insane places', in T. J. Scheff (ed.) *Labelling Madness*, Englewood Cliffs, N. J.: Prentice-Hall.

Ross, Peter (1996) 'Paperless client records' in S. Palmer, S. Dainow and P. Milner (eds) *Counselling*, London: Sage.

Rottman, G. (1974) Quoted in Verny (1982).

Rowan, John (1974) 'Research as intervention', in Nigel Armistead (ed.) *Reconstructing Social Psychology*, Harmondsworth: Penguin.

Rowan, John (1976) *The Power of the Group*, London: Davis-Poynter.

Rowan, John (1978) *The Structured Crowd*, London: Davis-Poynter.

Rowan, John (1988a) *Ordinary Ecstasy*, 2nd edn, London: Routledge.

Rowan, John (1988b) 'Primal Integration' in J. Rowan and W. Dryden (eds) *Innovative Therapy in Britain*, Milton Keynes: Open University Press.

Rowan, John (1990) *Subpersonalities: The People Inside Us*, London: Routledge.

Rowan, John (1992) 'Integrative encounter' in W. Dryden (ed.) *Integrative and Eclectic Therapy: A Handbook*, Buckingham: Open University Press.

Rowan, John (1993) *The Transpersonal in Psychotherapy and Counselling*, London: Routledge.

Rowan, John (1996) 'The Psychology of Furniture' in S. Palmer, S. Dainow and P. Milner (eds) *Counselling: The BAC Counselling Reader*, London: Sage.

Rowan, John (1997a) 'The future of Primal Integration' in S. Palmer and V. Varma (eds) *The Future of Counselling and Psychotherapy*, London: Sage.

Rowan, John (1997b) *Healing the Male Psyche: Therapy as Initiation*, London: Routledge.

Rowan, John (1997c) 'Transformational research' in P. Clarkson (ed.) *Textbook of Counselling Psychology*, London: Sage.

Rowe, D. (1978) *The Experience of Depression*, Chichester: John Wiley & Sons.

Russell, Janice (1993) *Out of Bounds: Sexual Exploitation in Counselling and Therapy*, London: Sage.

Russell, Roberta (1981) *Report on Effective Psychotherapy: Legislative Testimony*, New York: R. R. Latin Associates.

Ryle, Anthony (1990) *Cognitive-Analytic Therapy: Active Participation in Change – A New Integration in Brief Psychotherapy*, New York: John Wiley & Sons.

Sadger, I. (1941) 'Preliminary study of the psychic life of the foetus and the primary germ', *Psychoanalytic Review*, 28/3.

Samuels, Andrew (1985) *Jung and the Post-Jungians*, London: Routledge & Kegan Paul.

Samuels, Andrew (1993) *The Political Psyche*, London: Routledge.

Sanford, Nevitt (1981) 'A model for action research' in P. Reason and J. Rowan (eds) *Human Inquiry: A Sourcebook of New Paradigm Research*, Chichester: John Wiley & Sons.

Sartre, J-P. (1959) *The Age of Reason*, New York: Bantam.

Sartre, J-P. (1964), in M. Friedman (ed.) *The Worlds of Existentialism*, Chicago: University of Chicago Press.

Scheff, T. J. (1966a) *Being Mentally Ill: A Sociological Theory*, Chicago: Aldine.

Scheff, T. J. (1966b) 'Hospitalization of the mentally ill in Italy, England and the United States', in *Yearbook of the American Philosophical Society*.

Scheff, T. J. (1975) 'The labelling theory of mental illness', in T. J. Scheff (ed.) *Labelling Madness*, Englewood Cliffs, N. J.: Prentice-Hall.

Schuster, R. (1979) 'Empathy and mindfulness', *Journal of Humanistic Psychology*, 19/1.

Schutz, Will C. (1971) *Here Comes Everybody*, New York: Harper & Row.

Schutz, Will C. (1979) *Profound Simplicity*, London: Turnstone Books.

Schutz, Will C. (1983) *Professional Manual for Schutz Measures*, Palo Alto: Consulting Psychologists Press.

Schutz, Will C. (1989) *Joy: Twenty Years Later*, Berkeley, CA: Ten Speed Press.

Segal, H. (1979) *Klein*, London: Fontana.

Seidenberg, R. (1974a) 'The trauma of eventlessness', in Jean Baker Miller (ed.) *Psychoanalysis and Women*, Harmondsworth: Penguin.

Seidenberg, R. (1974b) 'For the future – equity?', in Jean Baker Miller (ed.) *Psychoanalysis and Women*, Harmondsworth: Penguin.

Shaffer, J. and Galinsky, M. D. (1989) *Models of Group Therapy*, 2nd edn, Englewood Cliffs, N. J., Prentice-Hall.

Shapiro, David and Shapiro, Diana (1982) 'Meta-analysis of comparative therapy outcome studies: A replication and refinement', *Psychological Bulletin*, 92/3.

Shapiro, Stewart B. (1997) 'The UCSB confluent education program: Its essence and demise', *Journal of Humanistic Psychology*, 37/3 pp. 80–105.

Shohet, Robin *et al.* (1991) 'Peer group accreditation of psychotherapists', *Self & Society*, 19/2 pp. 31–2.

Shorr, J. E. (1972) *Psycho-imagination Therapy*, New York: Intercontinental Medical Corporation.

Singer, E. (1965) *Key Concepts in Psychotherapy*, New York: Random House.

Singer, Jerome (1974) *Imagery and Daydream Methods in Psychotherapy and Behaviour Modification*, New York: Academic Press.

Slavson, S. R. (1953) 'Sources of countertransference and group-induced anxiety', *International Journal of Group Psychotherapy*, 3.

Smail, David (1996) 'Psychotherapy and tragedy', *BPS Psychotherapy Section Newsletter*, no. 20.

Smith, Peter B. (1973) *Groups Within Organizations*, London: Harper & Row.

Southgate, John and Randall, Rosemary (1989) *The Barefoot Psychoanalyst*, 3rd edn, Loughton: The Gale Centre.

Southwell, Clover (1988) 'The Gerda Boyesen method: Biodynamic therapy' in J. Rowan and W. Dryden (eds) *Innovative Therapy in Britain*, Milton Keynes: Open University Press.

Spinelli, Ernesto (1989) *The Interpreted World*, London: Sage.

Spinelli, Ernesto (1990) 'The phenomenological method and client centred therapy', *Journal of the Society for Existential Analysis*, 1/152.

Spinelli, Ernesto (1994) *Demystifying Therapy*, London: Constable.

Staemmler, Frank-M. (1997) 'Towards a theory of regressive processes in Gestalt therapy', *The Gestalt Journal*, 20/1 pp. 49–120.

Starhawk (1982) *Dreaming the Dark: Magic, Sex and Politics*, Boston: Beacon Press.

Stevens, B. (1975) 'Body work', in J. O. Stevens (ed.) *Gestalt Is*, Moab, UT: Real People Press.

Stevens, B. and Rogers, C. R. (eds) (1967) *Person to Person*, Moab, UT: Real People Press.

Stevens, J. O. (1971) *Awareness: Exploring, Experimenting, Experiencing*, Moab, UT: Real People Press.

Sullivan, C., Grant, M. Q. and Grant, J. D. (1957) 'The development of inter-personal maturity', *Psychiatry*, 20.

Sweigard, Lulu E. (1974) *Human Movement Potential: Its Ideo-kinetic Facilitation*, New York: Dodd, Mead & Co.

Temerlin, M. K. (1975) 'Suggestion effects in psychiatric diagnosis', in T. Scheff (ed.) *Labelling madness*, Englewood Cliffs, N. J.: Prentice-Hall.

Thera, N. (1972) *The Power of Mindfulness*, San Francisco: Unity Press.

Tompkins, Penny and Lawley, James (1997) *Principles of Grovian Metaphor Therapy*, London: The Developing Company.

Torbert, W. (1972) *Learning From Experience: Toward Consciousness*, New York: Columbia University Press.

Treleaven, Lesley (1994) 'Making a space: A collaborative inquiry with women as staff development' in P. Reason (ed.) *Participation in Human Inquity*, London: Sage.

Truax, C. B. and Carkhuff, R. R. (1967) *Toward Effective Counselling and Psychotherapy*, Chicago: Aldine.

Truax, C. B. and Mitchell, K. M. (1971) 'Research in certain therapist interpersonal skills in relation to process and outcome', in S. L. Garfield and A. E. Bergin (eds) *Handbook of Psychotherapy and Behavior Change*, New York: John Wiley & Sons.

Turner, R. (ed.) (1974) *Ethnomethodology: Selected Readings*, Harmondsworth: Penguin.

van Deurzen-Smith, Emmy (1997) *Everyday Mysteries: Existential Dimensions of Psychotherapy*, London: Routledge.

Varela, Francisco (1997) 'The specious present: A neurophenomenology of time consciousness' in J. Petitot, F. J. Varela, J-M. Roy and B. Pachoud (eds) *Naturalizing Phenomenology: Issues in Contemporary Phenomenology and Cognitive Science*, Stanford, CA: Stanford University Press.

Vaughan, F. (1979) *Awakening Intuition*, New York: Anchor.

Verny, Tom (1982) *The Secret Life of the Unborn Child*, London: Sphere.

Walkenstein, E. (1975) *Shrunk to Fit*, London: Coventure.

Warner, R. (1994) *Recovery from Schizophrenia*, London: Routledge.

Watkins, J. (1978) *The Therapeutic Self*, New York: Human Sciences Press.

Watson, K. W. (1973) 'Differential supervision', *Social Work*, 18.

Watts, A. W. (1961) *Psychotherapy East and West*, New York: Pantheon Books.

Werthman, M. (1978) *Self-Psyching*, Los Angeles: Tarcher.

Wessler, R. L. and Ellis, A. (1980) 'Supervision in rational-emotive therapy', in Allen K. Hess (ed.) *Psychotherapy Supervision*, New York: John Wiley & Sons.

West, William (1994) 'Post-Reichian Therapy' in D. Jones (ed.) *Innovative Therapy: A Handbook*, Buckingham: Open University Press.

Wheelis, Allen (1972) 'How people change', in J. F. Glass and J-R. Staude (eds) *Humanistic Society: Today's Challenge to Sociology*, Pacific Palisades: Goodyear Publishing Company.

White, J. (1972) *What is Meditation?*, New York: Anchor.

White, J. (ed.) (1979) *Kundalini, Evolution and Enlightenment*, New York: Anchor.

Wilber, Ken (1980) *The Atman Project: A Transpersonal View of Human Development*, Wheaton: The Theosophical Publishing House.

Wilber, Ken (1981) *No Boundary*, London: Routledge.

Wilber, Ken (1991) *Grace and Grit*, Boston: Shambhala.

Wilberg, Peter (1979) 'Inner Theology', unpublished.

Wilson, Jenifer Elton (1996) *Time-conscious Psychological Therapy*, London: Routledge.

Winnicott, D. W. (1975) *Through Paediatrics to Psychoanalysis*, London: Hogarth Press.

Wolberg, L. R. (1977) *The Technique of Psychotherapy*, vol. 1, 3rd edn, New York: Grune & Stratton.

Woolger, Roger (1990) *Other Lives, Other Selves*, Wellingborough: Crucible.

Wyckoff, Hogie (1975) 'Problem-solving groups for women', in Claude Steiner *et al.* (eds) *Readings in Radical Psychiatry*, New York: Grove Press.

Yalom, Irvin (1980) *Existential Psychotherapy*, New York: Basic Books.

Young, Courtenay (1990) '1992 and all that', *Self & Society*, 18/1 pp. 4–9.

Name Index

Subject Index